# Power, rule and domination

**International Library of Sociology**

Founded by Karl Mannheim

Editor: John Rex, University of Warwick

Arbor Scientiae
Arbor Vitae

A catalogue of the books available in the **International Library of Sociology** and other series of Social Science books published by Routledge & Kegan Paul will be found at the end of this volume.

# Power, rule and domination

A critical and empirical understanding of power in sociological theory and organizational life

**Stewart Clegg**

**Routledge & Kegan Paul**
London and Boston

*First published in 1975*
*by Routledge & Kegan Paul Ltd*
*Broadway House, 68–74 Carter Lane,*
*London EC4V 5EL and*
*9 Park Street,*
*Boston, Mass. 02108, USA*
*Set in Monotype Times by*
*Kelly, Selwyn & Co., Melksham, Wiltshire*
*and printed in Great Britain by*
*Redwood Burn Ltd*
*Trowbridge & Esher*

*ISBN 0 7100 8237 1 (c)*
*ISBN 0 7100 8238 X (p)*

# Contents

CONTENTS

# Preface

I would like to thank Professor David J. Hickson and Dr David Silverman for their thoughtful and considerate comments on this text. I have incorporated many of our dialogues in revisions that I have made to the various drafts that the book has been through. I owe a special debt of gratitude to Michael Hall, for first teaching me to think, and later, for showing me how to write. Peter McHugh, with whom I had a most pleasant discussion in the park, was instrumental in inducing my thought in the direction which it has followed. Among the many people who have been kind enough to offer me constructive advice and criticism along the way, I would like to extend my thanks to the following: Jeff Coulter, Alan Dawe, David Dunkerley, Arthur McCoullough and Ad Teulings. Naturally enough, none of them is in any way responsible for anything that they would not want to acknowledge!

Peter Hopkins and Stephen Davies have both been very helpful. In particular they offered me editorial advice on what material to include in the book, and what to leave out, in terms of my transcripts of tape-recorded conversations. These form the basis for my empirical analysis. Not all of the material that I collected has been used here, and the material not included may be found in Clegg (1974). The material was collected using a Sony cassette-recorder with a built-in microphone. Although I made no pretence of hiding the recorder, and although the members of the organization were aware that I had been granted permission to use it, its inconspicuous nature greatly facilitated the collection of 'natural' conversations.

My wife Lynne, and my parents, have helped me in innumerable and important ways during the writing of this book—I have been fortunate to have them.

I would also like to acknowledge the assistance of the members of the construction site that I researched, and the financial support of the Social Science Research Council, whose studentship supported my endeavours. To all these people—thank you!

My interest in the concept of 'power' developed from an under-graduate course in the sociology of organizations, an area in which its absence was perhaps the most striking feature. It was during this course that I first became acquainted with David Silverman's book *The Theory of Organizations* (1970). This book articulated the dissonance that most of the work on organizations had induced in me. Additionally, it suggested a sociological perspective which might develop the study of organizations in a different direction, one which was formative in shaping my own research.

The work begins with the following threads. First, a desire to contribute to the discussion of 'power', in particular as it applies to organizations. Second, a disposition to do so from a phenomeno-logical perspective, informed in particular by my understanding of Wittgenstein's *Philosophical Investigations*. Third, to do so in a rational way, as one who writes not only about his self and tradition, but also as one who writes about a meaningful world. Although it may appear to some readers that I do so from an 'ethnomethodo-logical' perspective, I feel that a word of caution is in order. This is not the case, thus my book may be interpreted as a critique not only of more conventional ways of conceptualizing 'power', but also as a critique of ethnomethodology. At certain key points I implicitly criticize the view that 'usage-adequacy' is the standard for sociological concepts. For me, that would merely represent another variant on the theme of 'nihilism'. For myself, I should like this to be thought a story about a sociologist attempting a research into the concept of 'power'. For that is what it is.

Like all good stories it begins at the beginning, by asking what we mean when we use the concept of 'power'. From there it is a fairly clear route to the end—but the end is merely another beginning, through which, hopefully, *you* will be drawn *into* the text.

# 1 The problem of definition

## Power and conceptual puzzlement

> Power (pouwr) is ability to do something; strength, force;
> vigour, energy; ability to control or influence others, ability
> to impose one's will. . . . (*The Penguin English Dictionary*,
> Second Edition, 1969.)

Therein, in whatever dictionary which comes to hand, dwells the
first major conceptual puzzle concerning power: its definition. The
dictionary tells us that power is 'an ability to do something . . . to
control or influence others . . . to impose one's will'. The something
that power does, its 'strength, force; vigour, energy', it is suggested,
is an ability which consists in controlling or influencing or willing
others. Is it then the case that power might mean control, and that
both are synonymous with will and influence?

We might say of X that he is powerful, and we can also say that
he is wilful, but would we mean the same thing? One can possess
the power of speech, but can one have the influence of it? One can
have control of it, but could one have will of it—is such a phrase
even ordinarily sensible? One can have indirect influence, perhaps
one might have indirect power, but could one have indirect imposition
of one's will? One certainly cannot share one's will, whereas one
can share power as in 'power-sharing', but could one have 'influence-
sharing' or 'control-sharing'? One can be in a position of power, as
one can be in a position of influence or of control, but one cannot
be in a position of will, nor can one be in influence of something,
as one can be in power or control of something.

That one can *have* power, control, and influence, that one can
*be* in a position of control as one cannot be in a position of will
suggests that these terms do differ among themselves, that they are
not merely synonymous. Whereas will seems to be involved with the

1

'doing' aspect, power and control seem also to embrace a more passive notion of 'being'.

A return to our dictionary cannot help us now, because we have already moved beyond its scope into the world of free usage which lies outside its pages. To re-enter the dictionary's pages is to become involved in a circuitous puzzle in which the same terms, 'power', 'control', 'authority' and 'influence' appear in each others definitions.

Sociologists' attempts at defining power are also embedded in the fibre of our everyday language, so that they merely reflect the seeming circularity of the dictionary, or the unexplicated nuances of our ordinary speech. Dahl, for instance, who will be one of the subjects of this study, wants to use the word 'power' in a general way additionally to cover near synonyms such as 'influence' and 'control' (Dahl, 1968). But as Pitkin (1972, pp. 278–9) points out, Dahl, even in his own interchangeable use of the terms 'power' and 'influence' uses each in phrases or contexts where the other would sound distinctly odd.

Pitkin (1972, p. 279) suggests the possibility that complex concepts such as 'power' may not be subject to a theory of language which stresses that words provide pictures of objects which exist separately in reality. This is because it is not at all clear what object could *correspond* to power. When we come to discuss such theoretically complex terms as power, then perhaps we should abandon any notion of conceptualization as 'referential' work, in the way that we might associate a picture of some thing with some concept of it. Dicta which propose that 'language pictures reality' neglect the fact that many words cannot be constrained within a picture theory. 'Power' is such a word.

Power is not a thing like a cat or a dog which we can point to and correctly identify as 'cat' or 'dog' and be sure we are right. We can not do this because power is not something animal, vegetable or mineral which we can sample, and compare against communally agreed criteria of what a thing is. Unlike dogs or cats there are no breed standards to determine what type of thing it is, and even more difficult, no criteria which even allow us to recognize species.

Power cannot be thought to be a thing, or species of thing, which has a definite being in the world, that comes wagging its tail, recognizably dog-like in a way that a particular dog might correspond to our concept of dogs in general. None the less, the concept of 'power' does have a use in our language, which, following Pitkin's (1972) suggestion, we may investigate as a 'tool' of language, something we actively use in an everyday workmanlike context. One way of getting to know an unfamiliar tool is to know how to use it. We may then find that some of the ways in which we use the language-tool of power are such as to make us think that perhaps it is like a thing that people have, rather as one can have a cat or a dog, and so we talk of the 'unions' or the 'government' having power, as if it were something we could picture them holding as one holds a cat. It would be almost as if when we said that a Prime Minister no longer has power, then a before and after photograph would picture him differently—as if some thing, some visible, tangible, photographic thing was missing from the 'after' picture.

The idea that 'power' may not correspond to some 'thing' in the world is prompted in this instance by the work of the philosopher Ludwig Wittgenstein, and the course that the development of this work took from his first published book, the *Tractatus Logico-Philosophicus* (1961) to his *Philosophical Investigations* (1968).

Wittgenstein is the crucial arbiter of any puzzlement about the correct definition of a concept, if only because in the *Tractatus* he proposed what for a considerable number of sociologists has become a conventional wisdom of definition. This regards ordinary usage as inherently 'spoiled for scientific use' so that 'one is forced to look for something better' (Marshall, 1947, p. 18). Viewing the problem of definition in this way, Science exists to legislate on the 'incorrectness' of our common sense understanding of the world, by translating the vagaries of everyday language into the clear, precise and unambiguous statements attributed to Science. The *Investigations*, as we shall see, goes on to suggest a somewhat different view of the nature of language, which implies quite a different remedy for the conceptual puzzlement of the problem of the problem of definition.

## Wittgenstein and sociological definition

Wittgenstein's *Tractatus Logico-Philosophicus* is based on the crucial assumption that every proposition has a clear and definite sense, and that this sense lies in that proposition's relation to the world. Propositions refer to the world; the language they are phrased in ought to picture that world. Such a picture can be accurate or inaccurate, true or false, depending on how accurately it agrees or corresponds with reality: 'The fact that the elements of a picture are related to one another in a determinate way represents that things are related to one another in the same way' (Wittgenstein, 1961, par. 2.15).

The proposition serves to depict reality much as a blueprint or map should. To arrive at a determinate sense of a proposition, Wittgenstein suggests that we must define by means of a logically proper language, which it is philosophy's task to provide, so that understanding a proposition would depend on knowing what would count as verifying or falsifying it: 'The sense of a proposition

3

is its agreement and disagreement with possibilities of existence and non-existence of states of affairs' (Wittgenstein, 1961, par. 1.2).

Philosophy, defined as the *Tractatus* would have it, becomes an 'under-labourer', in Locke's phrase, rather than a generative source of enquiry. Its labour is to clarify concepts, because 'without philosophy thoughts are, as it were, cloudy and indistinct' (Wittgenstein, 1961, par. 4.112).

The connection between sociological practice and the philosophy of the *Tractatus* is the historical stream of positivism, into which the latter was merged when it became allied to the contemporary philosophical respect for natural science methodology which centred around the chair of inductive science at the University of Vienna. At the turn of the century this was occupied by Ernst Mach, who constitutes a link with sociological positivism as it is properly understood, in his respect for the doctrines of Auguste Comte. Mach had argued that all claims to knowledge had to derive from our observation of sense-data, a sensationalism which the members of the Vienna Circle allied to Wittgenstein's conviction that a proposition was a representation of reality, to be considered meaningful when empirical and rendered in the elementary propositions of more complex statements. Each elementary proposition was to contain terms ostensively defined by association with empirical sense-data. In this way, then, the correctness of, for example, Newtonian dynamics would reside in the statements of the abstract formal axioms being taken to be empirical demonstrations of the natural world as we perceive it (see Janik and Toulmin, 1973; Passmore, 1957).

Given the positivist emphasis in Mach on sense data, an epistemological reliance central to the Circle's position, then it is hardly surprising that in their reading of the *Tractatus* they should have taken his representational model not so much as a plausible and elegant formal ensemble of possibilities, but rather as actually existing bedrock data open to the senses. The latter reading depends on an immediate relationship between the elementary proposition and that which it corresponds to, and this is an isomorphism which is found lacking in use in empirical instances. Where it does occur it may be taken as a practical accomplishment of reasoning rather than the providence of Nature.

It could be the case that those sociologists who do arbitrarily achieve this isomorphism by using operational measurement and definition might be taken as being warranted in this use by Wittgenstein's remark that 'we make models for ourselves' and that a model is 'laid against reality like a measure' (Wittgenstein, 1961, pars 2.1, 2.1512). One could then proceed as do many sociologists who assert operationalism as a creed. That is, they assume that what is modelled is representational, and then treat that assumption as if it were proven. But this proof can never be forthcoming. It is based on the assumption that the correct structure of language is propositional. This assumption is the basis of a further one, which is that the real world is describable in such a way. And about such assumptions one can offer no proof and can only be silent.

What would be the implications of following this assumption in defining terms like 'power'? The term 'power' would be taken to represent some thing in the world, which we would strictly define by a 'logically proper language'. We would then take this model definition and attempt to compare it 'against reality like a measure'. As in Godard's 'Alphaville' those uses of the word which we considered to be illogical would have to be suppressed. Power would then be what our dictionary of 'logically proper language' said it was. Given our present attempts at such definition in the dictionary, this hardly advances us at all. Were this not to be the case, power would have had to have been defined *ex nihilo* as 'X', by some apparently arbitrary stipulation, which may serve to disguise what we might once have considered power to be. The suppression of difference in the dictatorship of science over language presents a chilling spectacle.[1]

Peter McHugh (1971) has interpreted Wittgenstein's later ideas about 'language as an activity', which are contained in the *Philosophical Investigations*, as signifying the 'failure of positivism'. He regards positivism as asserting 'that a proposition is true if there is an object corresponding to the proposition' (McHugh, 1971, p. 323). He rejects this on the grounds that 'no institution can go outside itself to a world of independent objects for criteria of knowledge, since there is no other way except by its own rules to describe what's being done with regard to knowledge' (McHugh, 1971, p. 335).

He argues this through a distinction between the activity of 'sensing' essential to any representational model, and the activity of 'ascribing' truth, which is 'warranted by socially organized criteria' (McHugh, 1971, p. 329). This 'warranting' is a separate and subsequent question to one which asks whether or not we can have knowledge by sense observation. This latter knowledge, of whatever sort it may be, is achieved through an individual's sense perceptions, which are inherently incoherent, as the psychology of perception demonstrates.

Agreement over and above individual differences in sense observation results from collectivity phenomena. Agreement is a social process in a way that sense observation is not. To know that our sense perceptions cohere with, or correspond to, those of some other persons' perceptions, is a feature of linguistic activity which is both public and communal, whereas sense observation is argued to be private and individual.

It is because 'truth', as McHugh proposes it, is what it is collectively conceded to be (in Science, or whatever), that McHugh can submit that

a finding is true (or false or ambiguous) . . . only after applying
to it the analytic formulation of a method by which that
finding could have been understood to have been produced . . .
an event is transformed into the truth only by the application
of a cannon that truth seekers use and analysts must formulate
as providing the possibility of agreement (McHugh, 1971,
p. 332).

The 'problematic' of this and the following chapter has now emerged: if truth-ascription is to be regarded as the activity by which the label of 'truth' becomes attached to any statement, then are there as many truths as ways of conceding it, as for instance, about the topic of 'power'?

Wittgenstein *might* be interpreted as having implied this when he remarked that 'It is what human beings say that is true or false; and they agree in the *language* they use. This is not agreement in opinion but in form of life' (Wittgenstein, 1968, par. 241). This would be the way in which one might expect that ethnomethodology, within whose domain McHugh's (1971) essay was collected, would interpret this somewhat opaque remark of Wittgenstein's. Ethnomethodology similarly focuses on everyday language, particularly the way in which members use it to make everyday activities visibly rational and accountable as a socially organized phenomena (see Garfinkel, 1967, pp. vii–viii).

The location of Garfinkel's (1967) ethnomethodology in a related tradition to that of Schutz's (1967) phenomenology is evident in its insistence that those ordered properties which appear to our common-sense way of thinking to be mundane and non-problematic, only achieve that status through the automaticity associated with the vast amount of reflexive work we do in achieving this seemingly ordered world. This work then becomes the focus of ethnomethodological attempts to uncover the formal properties of this world as a contextual, ongoing accomplishment. The emphasis on context produces as a practical sociological programme something seemingly akin to Wittgenstein's attempts to replace the *Tractatus* with the *Investigations*.

The later Wittgenstein (1968) recommended that the search for objective, trans-situational and de-contextualized meanings was derived from inappropriate premises about the way in which we use words. Essentially, words work. And this work is always contextual. Rather than re-form language, Wittgenstein suggests that we should dwell in it, recover it for an analytic exploration and investigation of its use in, to use a term that both Wittgenstein and Garfinkel frequently cite, 'everyday life'.

Garfinkel similarly recommends that the search for objective, as opposed to 'indexical' expressions is mistaken. Indexical expressions refer to the objects they describe in contextual terms, and are thus bound to their occasioned use, whereas objective expressions are de-contextual and typal. To say that an expression is indexical is to say that it is relative to such contextual matters as who said it, to whom it was said, and in what kind of context, where context indexes such features as the occasion, the social relationships between speaker(s) and hearer(s), the place it occupies in the sequence of conversation and so on. Garfinkel argues that the substitution by sociologists of objective for indexical expressions is both an 'endless' (as necessarily reflexive) and unnecessary practice, in that indexical expressions are rational, accountable and ordered prior to any sociological re-formulation (see Garfinkel, 1967, pp. 4–11; Garfinkel and Sacks, 1970; Wieder, 1974). Instead of this 'endless' activity, ethnomethodology recommends that the process by which accounts are constructed and given, the 'glossing' activity itself, should become the focus of study. And thus in this perspective then, 'truth' also becomes a gloss, be it of science, sociology or everyday life, as it does in McHugh's (1971) account.

McHugh's (1971) remarks, in common with those of writers such as Phillips (1973), Kuhn (1962; 1970a; 1970b) and Winch (1958) assume that the problem involved in ascertaining the fact of some matter, say who has power in a particular collectivity, is one which is organized around a concern with the user's rules of procedure, of which he, as a member of a community of practitioners (of science, jurisprudence or whatever) is a warranted purveyor. Such an account essentially proposes that whether or not something is warranted to be 'true' or a 'fact' is a *conventional* arrangement, with no necessity residing in the world; it is simply the case that we should study how the 'truth' of a statement about some thing is granted, and this will be a study of conventions for using language in a particular way. So truth would be warranted through correct linguistic usage. Such views of language as an activity are an upshot of Wittgenstein's *Philosophical Investigations*, whether or not the writers involved explicitly reference this work as such, or whether it is merely implicit in the writers' tradition.

In so far as we accept his stress on meaning as the language in use, and his rejection of the representational model, it appears that Wittgenstein does offer a 'conventionalist' account of the

7

correctness of a concept or a situation. Thus we would argue that to accept a definition of power as correct is to note that this comes not from a question of correspondence with a thing in the world, but through noting the grammar of its use in speech and in language. This in turn would be to recognize that the 'reality' of power may be no more than our ways of speech, part of a language 'like any other (that) is founded on convention' (Wittgenstein, 1968, par. 335; also see 116; 119; 492; p. 185).

Within any language, or 'region' of a language, we may discover certain criss-crossing similarities of detail, and coincidence of activity, as in a comparison of games, but little or nothing that is common to all. As Wittgenstein (1968, pars 66, 67) puts it, such a 'complicated network of similarities' is characterized by the notion of 'family resemblances', so that the different sorts of games, the different types of power, have no essential being other than that 'expressed by grammar' (Wittgenstein, 1968, par. 371).

The conceptual puzzlement of power, one might be tempted to argue, is in order as it is, and only seemingly a problem. It may be naive and distorting to search the grammar of power and its family for a clear, concise and complete definition of the term suitable for a multiplicity of purposes. One may as well search for a patent elixir to cure all ills when it might be wiser to treat each illness as a special case.

Part of our problem with a concept such as power is that we forget our origins. We fail to identify the 'language-game' in which the terms of our enquiry originate. Consequently, conceptual puzzles 'arise when language goes on holiday' (Wittgenstein, 1968, par. 38). Hence, says Wittgenstein, restore language to its home, the language game, and study its 'grammar' in the uses of this game.

Grammar shows what kind of object something is, for instance, power, by relating it to concepts like 'doing', 'exercising', 'having'. This is to say that for something to be power it must be such as to be exercised, done and had. Grammar thus involves a concern with the applications of concepts in the world, and the other kinds of concepts that connect with it, and the general rules that guide these connections.

## The problem of nihilism

Wittgenstein's two remedies for the conceptual puzzle of concepts like 'power' may seem somewhat less satisfactory when considered in tandem, if only in as much as the rather general points made in the *Investigations* seem so appealingly to supercede the *Tractatus*, with the latter's arbitrary assertion of 'representation' as the ground of serious speech. This arbitrary assertion renders the *Tractatus* liable to the charge of 'nihilism':

Nietzsche defines nihilism as the situation which obtains when 'everything is permitted'. If everything is permitted, then it makes no difference what we do, and so nothing is worth anything. We can of course, attribute value by an act of arbitrary resolution, but such an act proceeds ex nihilo or defines its significance by a spontaneous assertion which can be equated with equal justification. More specifically, there is in such a case no justification for choosing either the value originally posited or its negation, and the speech of 'justification' is indistinguishable from silence (Rosen, 1969, p. xiii).

The mainstream of the *Tractatus* provides a rationale for the nihilism of most sociological practice in which whatever phenomenon is being defined or explained is 'granted' existence, through an operational definition. This done, the scientific task is then decreed to be the appropriation of these phenomena. Its method is to combine linguistically willed categories with the objects to which they correspond in the world, having ruled that language ought to be 'logically proper', and reality its arbiter. Knowledge is proposed as being synonymous with the proven; the proven is what science grants. The grant of science thus ordains the field of knowledge.

The *Investigations* similarly resigns itself to nihilism, *if* we read it as recommending the investigation of the grammar of a concept such as power, because as we find from the opening pages, where such an exploration was begun, the grammar is confused, its clarification opaque. That distinctions exist is apparent, but can they be made as apparent as we would require to be able to say what power is? Furthermore, where should the search be conducted, in everyday language or the language of social theory? Or both? And how will it overcome the charge that it elucidates nothing other than convention, such that

The facts of nature have sense only because people talk about them in a customary way; hence one cannot verify the sense of the way we are accustomed to talk by pointing to the facts of nature. Linguistic convention not the facts, are normative (Rosen, 1969, p. 12).

The implications of this for power are apparent. It would not be the case that power is something people possess, as one might possess a commodity. If it seems the case that power *is* a kind of possession then this is because of the way in which we ordinarily use the term. 'Power' may also be defined by the other ways in which we ordinarily use the term, but whatever these may be shows only our conventional forms of speech, not our facts of life.

9

## The grammar of theorizing

Under the influence of an account of language as an activity in which 'To understand a language means to be master of a technique' (Wittgenstein, 1968, par. 159), writers such as Phillips (1972; 1973) have coupled this account with Kuhn's (1962; 1970a; 1970b) work on paradigms in science. They have done so in order to argue that a concern with the production of what passes for 'true' knowledge should focus not on the 'reality' of these objects, but on the ways of seeing which provide for such a reality. Kuhn (1962) has stressed that consensual ways of seeing are maintained through shared paradigms of rules and standards for correct scientific practice. Collectively, in a Wittgensteinian sense, we would call these rules the 'grammar' of theorizing, because they underlie and are constitutive of whatever passes for adequate theorizing. Adequate here means 'to be a master of a technique', implying that one has proceeded in a way which can be seen to be in accord with consensually shared rules. These consensually shared rules thus exercise a 'theorizing power' over the theorist, in that he has first to submit to the collectively recognized grammar before whatever he produces can be 'warranted' in the ordinary course of affairs. The idea of the grammar of a concept is extended to the notion of the grammar of an activity—a usage which Wittgenstein points to when he remarks that 'Grammar tells us what kind of object anything is' (Wittgenstein, 1968, par. 373).

McHugh (1971, p. 332) takes this up by using grammar to mean 'the way in which a statement can be understood to have been made', a meaning which he suggests is rather like Chomsky's (1968) notion of 'the rules of transformation'—how it is that a competence might be said to be possible. In this way McHugh (1971, p. 332) can talk of the collectively developed and enforced 'grammars of agreement and method' as a 'determining and not merely tangential characteristic of science'. These determining features we might term the 'theorizing power' of the tradition(s) of work that the practitioner engages in dialogue.

## Theorizing power and tradition

In attending to the various ways in which theorists have approached and used the concept of power, then, we are attending not only to their definitions and the critiques of these, but to the 'theorizing power' which makes of such definitions and critiques orderly, recognizable and sociological phenomena. The air of authenticity which they wear as plausible scholarship is a manifestation of their mode of production. The actual writing merely re-presents and preserves the deeper possibility of how it is that they are at all possible. Their possibility as features of the sociological enterprise to be discussed, argued, debated and criticized is rooted in their methodical character. They result from the theorists' engagement with method, and are only possible given the theorists' engagement with a tradition of theorizing.

In this version of theorizing then, whatever matter is theorized recedes in importance to the way in which it signifies the power over the theorist of his tradition of thought, so that the matter serves as 'expressing self, or doing a display of mind' (Blum, 1971, p. 304). So, faced with a concept of power to investigate, rather than to analyse the concept of power as corresponding to something, one investigates it as a display of the theorists' commitment, of his Self, as a manifestation of the activity of theorizing within a tradition. To theorize is to reformulate one's self methodically in another form. As Blum (1971) puts it, it is a theorist's method for reforming society, for showing it in one of its many possible ways. Seen this way the method is a procedure for showing the world in the form in which it has its meaning for the theorist. Theory is then methodic, and method theoretic, rather than technique or technology. The method analytically locates the meaning of the world for the theorist, and shows the theorist as he is, where he stands. In the strongest sense, then, theory thus becomes a moral and political stance, for in a discipline which takes its relativity seriously, science or the data no longer compose speech, and thus speech and writing become questions of authorship, of responsibility:

> What can it really mean to speak of the author as the source
> of a discourse? Far from being the unique creation of the
> author as originating source, every text is always (an)other
> text(s) that it remakes, comments, displaces, prolongs, reassumes.
> A text opens in and from that complex formation of modes of
> articulation that gives, as it were, the theatre of its activity, a
> series of settings always already there as its very possibility;
> as the setting of language is always there, without origin and
> elsewhere to any individual moment of discourse, always
> received 'such as it is' (Heath, 1972, pp. 24–5).

Stephen Heath (1972), in the above quotation, is writing of 'the practice of writing' in literature, with respect to the 'nouveau roman'. By the practice of writing he points towards a notion of author as 'authored' in the author-ity of tradition. Dawe's (1973) idea of 'representative experience' would appear to be a similar notion:

> When we are discussing the role of value in sociology, we are
> not talking about the individual sociologist or his personal
> biography and psychology. We are talking about the general

11

traditions of value in which he participates, and which are decisive for the sociological perspective he embraces. One does not just articulate personal values; one participates in the articulation of representative values. And inevitably, these are declared, not in a coy confessional, almost apologetic preface to one's work, but by the kind of sociology one does (Dawe, 1973, p. 17).

Tradition means more than just the conscious citation of like-minded authors. One engages a tradition in dialogue when one writes because one writes as a moment in an ever-changing stream of consciousness greater than one's self, so that whatever matter one writes about is in one sense less important than the veil of silence one must inevitably preserve about the tradition, a silence which enables one to write *that* in the first place. Hence, when we look at sociologists' attempts at defining power then we find that their writing tells us less about the topic than about the tradition. So perhaps we should investigate the tradition, rather than take it for granted in yet another attempt at inductive reasoning on a corpus of definition and work severed from their original source?

This is not to invoke a duality between the content as that which is written about, and the tradition of writing as that for, and by, the sake of which one speaks. Nor is it simply a question of style and content. Style is usually seen as adornment, as decorative, as something outside of, and external to, content. Reverse this and we are nearer the notion of tradition. The matter, the content, or subject is on the outside, the style of the tradition is on the inside. The tradition is the site of the author. What the author writes is what the tradition 'speaks'. The tradition shows through the concrete formulation of what is said.

What is meritable in a work, what could not have been otherwise, is its form. Content as the specific something said could always have been otherwise: think of the exigencies of fieldwork, the role of access, chance, fatigue and distraction. What is invariant is the showing of the saying, rather than anything spoken about.

Tradition always has a specific historical meaning. The visibility of tradition(s) is always a product of the historical consciousness of our writing. Were it not for departures from, or experimentations with a tradition as a way of being in one's work, then we could never recognize the possibilities of a different mode of being as it is exemplified in an emergent tradition (also see Sontag, 1967).

The author's tradition is nothing other than the idiom in which he displays his theoretic form of life as that which has point, purpose and regularity for him. Thus, for instance, we may collect many seemingly diverse traditions of work under the form of life of 'positivism'. This form of life provides the deep similarity of such diversity, by formulating the possibility of the something that is the work.

This is not to deny that a work is a statement about something but to draw into question the 'realist illusions' which clothe the something as the impetus of the work. The work is not only about something but is something—a thing in the world rather than merely a commentary on it, and it is as such that Barthes (1970, pp. 413–14) wishes to restore literature to the sociologist,

> not in order to profess or practice 'fine style' but in order to
> rediscover the crucial problems involved in every utterance,
> once it is no longer wrapped in the beneficient cloud of strictly
> *realist* illusions, which see language simply as the medium of
> thought.

Barthes (1967), like the later Wittgenstein, seeks to dissolve 'language which is ignorant of itself' as something the theorist can 'use' to 'refer' with, and instead seeks to institute an awareness of it as the medium of tradition (see Janik and Toulmin, 1973, for the similarity to Wittgenstein). He attempts to deflect charges of solipsism through his use of the concept of *écriture*. *Écriture* is correctly conceived as a property of language, rather than of an individual writer. Indeed, one could say that the writer as individual writer is only constitutable through the assumption of *écriture*:

> An écriture is a mode of organization, of utilization of language
> (a form) which is social, beyond the individual in a body of
> texts that may, indeed, very well proffer it as an absence of
> forms, as mirror, immediate representation, or whatever. It
> must be thought in all its implications that an écriture is not
> a simple question of style in our normal understanding of that
> term, but of a mode of articulating the real: it is neither
> natural nor innocent, it brings with it not simply a style, but,
> in its form, a whole series of received meanings. The assumption
> by a writer of an écriture is thus, as Barthes stresses, the
> assumption of a certain way of seeing the world, an act of
> socio-historical solidarity (Heath, 1972, p. 208).

Reading, as writing, is similarly a question of dialogue,

> in its insistence on a work of research and exploration, on
> understanding the foundations of intelligibility (of ourselves,
> of our world) in a presentation to the reader of possibilities
> of reading in the realization of which he may read himself in
> his construction (Heath, 1972, p. 33).

The text thus becomes the impetus for a dialogue – renewed each time one turns to it – between the reader and the author, who are both moments of tradition. The dialogue is one of membership, of the grounds of the author's membership in the tradition(s) of writing as that is displayed in the interpretation favoured by the reader's tradition.

Reading is no longer to be regarded as a passive registering of the one correct possibility of a text, but may be more appropriately seen as an activity. A switch in attention has occurred so that the grounds for membership have now become the analytic topic.

In the dominant mode of contemporary sociology, reading is a problem of bringing into agreement each and every interpretation of a text. Just as the sociologist is concerned to give authoritative and correct accounts of social reality, the questioning of the correctness of which is a matter of questioning either the author's method (his optic) or competence in that method, so he is seen as being able to give correct textual interpretations similarly dependent on optic and competence. Both assume the existence of a social reality in which objects enjoy a privileged epistemological position, to whose arbitrary contingency one must surrender.

The Wittgensteinian perspective would stress that such a view of language is a delusion

> solved . . . by looking into the workings of our language, and
> that in such a way as to make us recognize those workings:
> *in despite of* an urge to misunderstand them. The problems
> are solved, not by giving new information, but by arranging
> what we have always known. Philosophy is a battle against
> the bewitchment of our intelligence by means of language
> (Wittgenstein, 1968, par. 109).

Thus the customary, and favoured 'positivist' in McHugh's (1971) sense is but one possible way of viewing society in one possible method, the dominant sociological method for viewing society in one possible form. The fact that this involves seeing the world as describable through and by sociological practice tells us nothing about the world other than that it can be described in such a way, in, to use Blum's (1971) version of Wittgenstein's 'arranging what we have always known', as a 'possible society'.

## The possible society

The conditions for theorizing thus become conditions of formulating one sense of a society as an intentional object for the theorist. The possible society is what society means for him, and should be understood as a way of creating a 'possible' world available in the theorist's tradition.

As a method Blum's 'possible societies' (1971) describe the reflexive movement of the theorist from his particular horizon of possibilities to his particular possibility as constituted by the tradition. Blum (1971) suggests Wittgenstein's (1969b) view of such an accomplishment as being achieved by creating examples which can be interrogated as to whether or not they are true in all possible worlds. Method would consist in inventing, excluding and collating possibilities, so that certainty would be to conceive of no ground for doubt within one's resources of tradition.

Within any enquiry, when we formulate the parameters for the recognition of a topic, as for instance, power, then we are describing it from within the language of a particular tradition. The topic itself is in a sense irrelevant in that we can never hope to exhaust the possibilities of describing it in each and every definition of its situation. We theorize a display of language provoked by an impetus we may locate in the 'real world'.

It is the status of this 'real world' that will become the source of our problems, when we try to apply such an account of theorizing as an activity to some sociological topic such as that of power. The next chapter will apply this account to the Community Power Debate about the structure of power in society. Although an account of 'theorizing as an activity', that some claim to derive from Wittgenstein (1968), will enable us to see how and why such a dispute should have continued, it becomes difficult to see why it should have begun, or what it can be about. It simply exists. And that is all that can be said, unless we have some notion of 'form of life' which grounds the 'conventionalism' that writers such as Phillips (1973) have seen in Wittgenstein (1968).

This 'conventionalist' interpretation proposes that Wittgenstein 'advanced the thesis that language and life rest entirely on social conventions' (Phillips, 1973, p. 123). These social conventions are seen to premise any agreement about 'states of affairs', because such agreement is only to be regarded as a feature of *seeing* something as such. I will go on to ask what this 'something' might be.

The impetus for pursuing such views of theorizing arose from the initial and seemingly insuperable problems of a definition of power based on notions of 'representation'. Precisely because of these problems an alternative epistemological direction seemed called for. The interpretation of Wittgenstein (1968) by McHugh (1971), Blum (1971) and Phillips (1972; 1973) was explored, as was the interaction of this with the work of Kuhn (1962) as it has been developed by Phillips (1973).

The next chapter applies this view of theorizing to the concept of 'power' as it has been used in the Community Power Debate.

Applying these views like this will uncover a number of 'anomalies', which, after Rosen (1969), may be expressed as 'the problem of nihilism'. These anomalies raise the following issues: (1) What

15

happens when we have competing sets of views about something? (2) Are we only able to recite the procedural basis of these particular communities' 'truths', and keep silent about whatever 'states of affairs' this disagreement may be premised on? (3) Do terms and ideas like 'states of affairs' even have any purchase here? Is it then that power is *nothing* apart from our ways of talking about it?

By formulating these topics with reference to the Community Power Debate the following chapter will attempt to provide grounds for the resolution of the problem.

# 2  Power, theorizing and reason

## The Community Power Debate

When applying a view of theorizing to the concept of 'power' which stresses the 'grammar' of these accounts, as in the latter half of the previous chapter, a number of controversies in the field of power studies appear to be somewhat less puzzling.

One of the issues that has dominated American political science studies of power since the post-war period has been the Community Power Debate between 'pluralist' and 'élitist' scholars. On the one hand, there are those scholars who believe that the 'plural' model of countervailing power groups spread over disparate issues is the one which best characterizes American political life. Opposing this view, however, is a group of scholars who maintain that political life is more correctly described as being governed by a relatively coherent 'élite'.

Walton (1966) has noted how sociologists, typically, have tended to identify power structures as élitist, while political scientists have tended to identify these as pluralist. He relates these different outcomes to the different methods that each uses. Sociologists have favoured a 'reputational' method. This was first used by Hunter (1953). It consists essentially of asking 'well placed people' or people designated as 'well informed', who are then chosen as 'judges', to compile a list of the most 'influential' people in the community. Those most often mentioned are then considered to be the most powerful.

Political scientists have favoured a decision making model which entails the study of 'key' decisions covering a number of pre-selected 'issue areas'. Those who successfully initiate or oppose key decisions are then regarded as the most powerful members of the community.

We might be inclined to say, as does Ehrlich (1961, p. 927) that the reputational method does not give us a picture of the real or

17

actual power structure, but merely people's perceptions of it, so that part of the problem at least is one of definition. The 'élitists', through using the 'reputational' method have only collected data on what people think is the case rather than what it actually is. Further, it may be, as Polsby (1963) argues, that many community power studies assume beforehand that there is an élite of coinciding society, business and political leaders, and that this 'Marxist stereotype' has led investigators to look for élites thus dominated. In an earlier work Polsby (1959) suggested that the very term 'power structure' may be similarly misleading: to assume that there is one implies beforehand a relatively stable network of relationships and events, which may be constituted simply by the concern displayed by the term 'power structure'. According to Polsby (1963) the 'Marxist stereotype' encourages research which generates self-fulfilling prophecies.

A number of problems arises from these considerations. How could one derive a picture of a community power structure untouched by people's perceptions? To do so would demand either that language be the cleansed and neutrally abstract category that Polsby clearly indicates it is not, or it would demand some peculiar 'leap to knowledge' which short circuits language. Any study of what people think is the case, if it is a random selection, will merely re-present in a particular form the source of any problems of definition with which one starts. To have stipulated these for oneself is not to close the door to the contradictions of ordinary language, as one applies one's stipulations to other people. The pre-structure of language will persist in tripping us up.

When authors such as Hunter (1953) state that Regional City is not élite-dominated but is instead ruled by different 'cliques', it must not be taken for granted that other readers of their evidence will draw the same conclusions:

> Hunter describes the power structure of Regional City as a 'pyramid' but also describes his forty top influentials as divided into several 'crowds' or 'cliques'. The latter description suggests a poly-lithic power structure while the pyramidial supports the idea of a monolith (Rossi, quoted in D'Antonio, Ehrlich and Erickson, 1962, p. 850).

At least one follow-up study to that of Hunter's (Banfield, 1966, p. 18) found a power structure different from that of the previous study. How are we to assess these contradictory views?

## The Community Power Debate: the conventional grammar of theorizing about power?

Such contradictory views would usually be regarded as a simple case of the social scientist failing to receive the correct 'social-factual' message from the data, a failing on the part of the researcher. The previous chapter, however, has argued that such controversy may be seen instead as arising from the lack of agreement between political scientists and sociologists as to what counts as 'correct procedure' for producing what counts as 'factual knowledge' as divorced from knowledge which is hearsay, heresy, gossip, ideology or repute, rather than 'reality'.

This begins to make the problem clearer. Such criteria, which in community power studies have been lacking, represent an achieved consensus within the specific tradition(s). What we would appear to have here is such a lack of agreement among power study practitioners of what power is, and how it ought to be studied, and how such studies ought to be interpreted. What this would seem to imply for power studies is that the 'truth' about power is not to be regarded as correspondence with what is the case, but rather conformity with agreed standards held in a particular community. These agreed standards are embodied in a tradition about what are to be regarded as 'truths' about what is regarded as 'real'.

That original puzzle which vexed our understanding of conflicting interpretations of the 'same' thing arose from the idea that reality was being unfaithfully rendered. Truth was to be conceded as a relation between propositions and reality, and must therefore be obscured by either an incorrect proposition, or method. We now suggest that the problem involves the investigator's procedural rules, rather than the 'real' nature of the thing itself. As Phillips (1973, p. 25) suggests, 'with scientific propositions, we do not consult what a proposition proposes, but rather the rules used to decide whether what the proposition proposes is warranted.'

What follows from Phillips's (1973) position is that the social reality that sociologists attend to is not something upon which they light with their theory and method, but rather something which is entirely dependent on this illumination. So what the sociologist regards as factually present may indeed be a feature of his method for seeing it as such. The method may be said to constitute that to which it then attends.

When we do come to apply this perspective to an analysis of the Community Power Debate, then we find that it does seem to clarify the nature of the dispute, but only at considerable cost to reason.

The parameters of the debate have emerged around the works of Robert Dahl, whose important contributions to the study of power

19

have consciously tried to develop a behavioural political science. His model of man is derived from epistemological considerations which seek to limit our knowledge of other men to what we can perceive and measure. What we can measure depends on our instruments, which for Dahl are constructed 'operationally', and, as we can perceive people doing and not doing certain things, then measurement consists of ascertaining the extent to which they do or do not do some things.

Dahl's (1957) epistemology of measurement disposes him to regard power as something that a person, whom he calls A, has over someone else, whom he calls B, 'to the extent that he can get B to do something that B would not otherwise do' (Dahl, 1957, p. 203). Dahl's discussion of power comparability extends the definition to the measurement of differences in the responses of B. These he classifies as: differences in the scope of their power, that is in types of responses evoked; differences in the number of comparable respondents, and differences in the change of probabilities.

Dahl further distinguishes differences in the bases of the actors exercising power, from the differences in the ways in which actors respond to these bases. Dahl does this in order to follow behavioural method by separating the 'stimuli' from the 'response', while noting that analysis of the stimulii does not, 'strictly speaking, provide us with a comparison of the power of two or more actors, except insofar as it permits us to make inferences about the last three items (responses)' (Dahl, 1957, p. 206).

Dahl thus moves from a rigorously premised grounding in 'behaviouralism' to note that estimates of the probability of power are made on the basis of the attributes of A, but 'if we could make these inferences more directly, we should not be particularly interested in the first items – at least not for the purposes of making comparisons about power' (Dahl, 1957, p. 206).

But, if we are to accept Dahl's argument, it is hardly possible that power is comparable anyway, as for example in discussing 'scope' – 'The important thing is that the particular definition one chooses will evidently have to emerge from considerations of the substance and objectives of a specific piece of research, and not from general theoretical considerations' (Dahl, 1957, p. 207).

Dahl denies 'general theoretical considerations' while implicitly acknowledging his allegiance to these in terms of an operational version of a 'representational' concept of power, which is to agree with Bridgman (1927) that 'In general, we mean by any concept nothing more than a set of operations; the concept is synonymous with the corresponding set of operations' (Bridgman, 1927, p. 5).

However, Bridgman's notion of 'operationism' was designed to clear up the kind of confusion that arises when a stick is half submerged in water. It looks bent and feels straight. What its 'real' shape is becomes an empirical question to be settled by the operation of looking and touching. These different operations define different concepts; i.e., visual straightness and tactile straightness. These operations can be repeated on all other sticks in similar circumstances, in order to achieve comparison between sticks in terms of a standard criteria of shape. The measured object is taken to necessarily exist before the measuring instrument. This instrument must not be employed in such a way as to be constitutive of the former, and should be capable of generalization to each and every case of the former.

Dahl appears to want to go further than this, in that he insists that such theoretical terms as 'scope' should be wholly definable in terms of the procedures by which they are to be applied in particular cases. The consequence of this is to reduce 'power' to the conceptual level of 'nihilism'. It does not matter what it is in any one instance, because it need not be the same in any other. The standard of operationism thus conceived allows no standard for any comparisons of power. Where such a concept, such as Dahl's (1957), goes powerless to the world, the world of power need not fear.

Dahl's implicit model of power relations appears to resemble classical mechanics, and is formulated after the manner of behaviourism. Power, in sociological analyses of it which attempt to measure it as an 'effect registered' (in terms such as Dahl, 1957), is regarded as being equivalent to the response of some 'other', conceptualized after the manner of an instrument panel which gives off a reading indicating the strength of the power exercised. This is so because the concept of measurement implied in measuring 'responses', or 'effects' implies movement which is related to the 'stimuli' or 'forces' creating the movement, which are for Dahl the 'bases' of power. The concept of power depends on some manifest display of action – what might be termed a 'manifestation'. Something has to be seen to have happened for us to say that something *has* happened. This sociology of power resembles Galileo's physics of inertia. Bodies persevere in motion, or stay at rest, unless forces act upon them causing them to change. Force was later defined by Newton as the product of the mass of a body multiplied by its acceleration. When two unequal forces meet, a movement occurs, and the movement shows the relative strength of the two forces. Similarly, when two social forces meet the movement that occurs is taken as indicative of the relative strength of the two forces. Power = motion caused by the two forces meeting and is to be explained in terms of a 'stimulus' or

21

'force' concept of differences in the bases and means by which power is exercised. It is indicated in terms of a 'response' or 'motion' on the part of the reacting organism.

These assumptions have important consequences for the type of power that is constituted by definitions and programmes which follow Dahl. Dahl's insistence 'that there exists a time lag, however small, from the actions of the actor who is said to exert power to the responses of the respondent' (Dahl, 1957, p. 204) implies that only past actions can be studied for A to have power; not only must B's behaviour change (or remain constant if B intended a change) but B must be known. Power must be specific and deployed. A prior capacity is no power at all.

Dahl insists that 'There is no "action at a distance". Unless there is some "connection" between A and a then no power relation can be said to exist' (Dahl, 1957, p. 204).

This is the necessary and sufficient grounding of the behavioural analogy. It restricts analysis to specific interactions between identified 'units' and can only manage broader settings through the tortuous explication of a causal chain. Should the relationships change over time the situation has changed. The old 'operational' definition may no longer apply, and thus it may not be possible to compare the two situations. In a situation where the members of an organization may arrive at work one day to find the plant closed, the gates locked and the asset strippers in, as a result of a 'takeover raid', then normal and important instances of power may remain out of grasp of one who would follow Dahl's (1957) prescriptions.

With Dahl, as with a behavioural analysis of meaning, a sign means different things to the same organism at different times, and to different organisms: 'given information about the responses, we may be interested in comparing the efficiency of different bases or means; in this case, evidently, we can make a comparison only by holding one or both of the first two factors constant, so to speak' (Dahl, 1957, p. 206). That is, the meaning of power is not to be sought in the bases or means of power, but in the individual responses which cannot be compared outside of a given substantive piece of work. This implies that changes in resources, or the control of new resources, such as the spiralling developments of the arms race, do not change the balance of power. First we must have their actual deployment for them to be worthwhile. The 'realism' of Dr Strangelove finds echo in Dahl. He attempts to avoid identifying a stimulus by a response, by stipulating that the stimulus should be held constant, so as to not contravene a basic tenet of behaviourism. The result of this (that 'we can make a comparison only by holding one or both of (bases and means) constant') is to make investigation of power of relatively trivial scope. Only stable systems with recurrent routines between immutable members may be studied comparatively.

With Dahl (1957) the nihilism of operational definition is revealed in its full political implications. Only statements of little comparative worth may be made because of the (arbitrary) stipulations of the behavioural method. This entails that no research into the structure of power prior to its actual deployment may be sanctioned. To make such enquiry would be to step outside of method.

In order to reconcile real life with method, Dahl (1967) focuses on 'community power' which provides him with 'systems' in which the 'isolation' of differentiated issues yields the topics he requires to discuss 'power' in such cities as New Haven.

Dahl's (1957) model also restricts analysis to particular issues, both theoretically and substantively. Theoretically, if A is powerful with respect to issue X, then this says nothing about his power with respect to issue Y. Hence Dahl's empirical studies, such as his analysis of power in New Haven leads him to a conclusion which suggests that Americans are living in a society in which there is an extreme diffusion of powers. This conclusion is constituted through the methodological stipulations, and has important substantive and ideological implications.

In Dahl's later work (Dahl 1967; 1971) pluralism as theory and practice achieves an impressive unity: 'Instead of a single centre of sovereign power there must be multiple centres of power none of which is or can be wholly sovereign' (Dahl, 1967). American political reality is seen by Dahl to correspond to the rhetoric of pluralism. Given Dahl's grounds it could not be otherwise, because in communities one can at any time isolate any number of issues, over some of which very many different groups may at some time be powerful. The knack resides in pre-selecting the right issues, rather than letting them 'issue forth' from the research setting. The latter research strategy is essential if one is concerned to show that, even given a plurality of interest groups, what becomes an issue may be a structurally generated phenomenon, so that within the guiding rules of that generative framework the key to the plurality, or not, of power, may be the rationality of issues. Where a theory prescribes a pre-selection of issues, then in a society constituted by such a theory it is possible for everyone to be powerful in some way. The point is not Dahl's 'correctness' or not, but the inescapability of his conclusion given his grounds.

Dahl has quite consciously asserted his particular view of social reality – 'pluralism' – as against the 'ruling élite' model exemplified in C. Wright Mills's (1957) *The Power Élite*.

Mills's (1957) model of the 'ruling élite' depends on a number of crucial considerations. These are, first, that there is a clearly differentiated top level of power, distinct from the vast army of organizational middle-men that one ordinarily meets. Second, Mills argues that this 'ruling élite' shares a common and homogenous overlap on fundamental ways of seeing the world, although they may sometimes clash on particular issues that arise within the framework. The crucial factor is that the framework is never questioned. Third, that although there are plural interest-mobilizing associations, these are not countervailing powers. They are not countervailing powers because of the relative inactivity of most of their members. In addition, this membership is at a considerable disadvantage compared to the 'élite', in securing access to key sources of structural power.

Dahl (1971), employing the methodological stipulations previously noted, criticizes Mills (1957) on the basis of his lack of clarity, and he suggests, inability, to specify on what issues the ruling élite customarily prevails. His grounds for criticism are generated by his methodology. This asserts that:

> The hypothesis of the existence of a ruling élite can be strictly tested only if:
> 1. The hypothetical ruling élite is a well defined group.
> 2. There is a fair sample of cases involving key political decisions in which the preferences of the hypothetical ruling élite run counter to those of any other likely group that might be suggested.
> 3. In such cases, the preferences of the élite regularly prevail (Dahl, 1971, p. 359).

Dahl's stipulations may be seen as rules for seeing power structures as being either plural or élite, so that we might enquire what sort of grounds there are, according to these requirements, which would support the existence of a well defined group, whose preferences regularly prevail on a 'fair sample of cases involving key political decisions' (Dahl, 1971, p. 359). What rules would we use for seeing what a 'fair sample of cases' or a 'key political decision' looked like, on which a preference of a ruling élite might be said to prevail? On what basis would a proposition that 'X has a ruling élite' be assigned factual status?

Members of the community might tell us that they agree with the proposition that a well defined group does exist, and does routinely prevail in getting its preferences adopted. What value do we use for determining what given number of members agreeing with the proposition secures that proposition's factual status? Dahl (1971) offers 'all or nearly all'. How near? Would 99 per cent be high enough? Would 60 per cent be too low? Would 69 per cent be acceptable, but 65 per cent not? For what reason?

Clearly, in such a situation the researcher must have some rule which he uses either to weigh the responses of members or to declare a certain response-rate as significant,

> so that he may say that all those who disagree with the proposition are in some sense atypical of the group or that the opinions of those who were not asked are reflected in the opinions of those who indicated agreement (Phillips, 1973, p. 98).

The inference that some élite does or does not exist derives from observing some members doing some activities which are taken to indicate the existence of a ruling élite, but any assignment of fact must clarify the nature of this membership, and the nature of a 'fair sample' and a 'key political decision' as adequate evidence. The rules that Dahl (1971) proposes for determining the existence or non-existence of a ruling élite fail to provide any calculable criteria (and how could they?) for making assessments of the magnitude of difference which the investigator is willing to tolerate between what the proposition proposes and what it excludes. As Phillips (1973) notes, the grounds for the adequacy of a warranted proposition 'are protocol statements like "observer A observed such-and-such" or "such-and-such was reported by persons one, two and three to observer A" ' (Phillips, 1973, p. 101).

How the observer then uses these observations to accept or reject a proposition is not at all clear, except on the basis of some common-sense notion of what a 'key issue' is, what 'always or nearly always' is, and what a 'well defined group' is. There are no rules for the application of Dahl's methodological rules contained within these rules:

> Whether this is good or bad is not the point; it is just the way things are and should be acknowledged by the sociological community. Failure to appreciate the common sense character of factual decisions results in ignoring the judgemental and theoretic components of such decisions (Phillips, 1973, p. 101).

Consider in this light Dahl's (1971) comments on the evaluation of a 'ruling élite hypothesis': 'the hypothesis cannot be satisfactorily confirmed without something equivalent to the test I have proposed . . . *by an examination of a series of concrete cases where key decisions are made*' (Dahl, 1971, p. 362).

Dahl (1971) suggests that we can determine what is the case by inspecting the world with the use of the test he proposes, without acknowledging that its deployment is socially controlled both by our theoretic tradition, and our ordinary notions of commonsense.

25

The implications of Dahl's methodological considerations have been substantively criticized by Bachrach and Baratz (1971), on the grounds that

> the model takes no account of the fact that power may be, and often is, exercised by confining the scope of decision-making to relatively 'safe' issues. The other is that the model provides no *objective* criteria for distinguishing between 'important' and 'unimportant' issues arising in the political arena . . . can a sound concept of power be predicated on the assumption that power is totally embodied and fully reflected in 'concrete decisions' or in activity bearing upon their making? (Bachrach and Baratz, 1971a, p. 378).

The crux of Bachrach and Baratz's critique lies in the proposition that the study of power be extended to a study of 'non-decisions' as well as decisions, and to a study of the 'mobilization of bias' as it is embodied in dominant values, political myths, rituals, and institutions which customarily rule in some issues, while some others are just as routinely ruled out (1971a, p. 382).

Wolfinger (1971, pp. 1065-6), writing in the Dahlian tradition, has remarked that Bachrach and Baratz's (1971a; 1971b) concept of non-decisions is somewhat opaque, a situation which Wolfinger attempts to clarify by specifying types of non-decisions. The simplest of these is 'renunciation': 'A political actor – already a participant in policy making – refrains from making a proposal or rejects an alternative among the many which he might consider because he thinks that it will be unacceptable to some person or group' (Wolfinger, 1971, p. 1066).

This modifies Dahl's (1957) 'power-connection' from a situation where both A and B are aware of each other and B responds, to one where A is not aware but B responds in the manner in which he thinks would be acceptable. Schematically they may be represented thus:

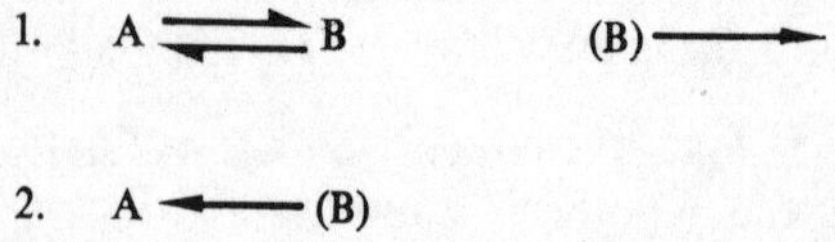

1.  A ⇌ B          (B) ⟶

2.  A ⟵ (B)

FIGURE 1

The first instance would be captured in the following example of Dahl's:

> Suppose I stand on a street corner and say to myself, 'I command all automobile drivers on this street to drive on the right hand side of the road'; suppose further that all drivers

actually do as I 'command' them to do; still most people will regard me as mentally ill if I insist that I have enough power over automobile drivers to compel them to use the right side of the road. On the other hand, suppose a policeman is standing in the middle of an intersection at which most traffic ordinarily moves ahead; he orders all traffic to turn right or left; the traffic moves as he orders it to do. Then it accords with what I conceive to be the bedrock idea of power to say that the policeman acting in this particular role evidently has the power to make automobile drivers turn right or left rather than go ahead (Dahl, 1957, pp. 202–3).

The second instance would be that noted by Nagel (1968) where B anticipates A's intentions, and complies beforehand. A need not be aware, B obviously is. Such a revision would merely serve to re-draw the edges of an unquestioned concept of power as displayed in the outcomes of particular exchanges, by broadening the behavioural grounds to incorporate ideational factors, such as a 'renunciation'. To interpret Bachrach and Baratz thus is to preserve the Dahlian tradition by remaining secure within its conventions.

More imaginative and less conventional interpretations of their work are possible. What would it be like to interpret them not as hints for more methodic research in the Dahlian tradition, but as pointers to a different style of research? Such a research would dwell on the ways in which 'issues' are actually constructed in particular empirical settings, and deal with the distinction between 'important' and 'unimportant' issues not in terms of some *a priori* construct, but in terms of the 'rationality' of the setting under review. But this is to run ahead before we have even found our feet. Before such a study can be proposed we have to know the status of that which we are to study. Dahl, and the tradition which he has fostered and which he represents, have been criticized in terms of the 'nihilism' of their concept of power, a concept under-standable only in the context of its grounds in Dahl's particular method, and its juxtaposition to 'élite' studies in the Community Power Debate.

This chapter has so far been exploring this debate in order to see if recommendations for investigating a concept through its 'conventional grammar' enable us to give a rational (i.e., non-nihilist) account of that concept. As Blum (1971) puts it, in this light, then to theorize is to display a possible version of society which has meaning for the self. What self does Dahl display?

To address the self that Dahl displays is to dwell in the discursive space of behavioural methodology and market ideology. Given his method and perspective you are invited to view power in New

27

Haven, for example, and to regard it as possessing a self-constituted ontological status divorced from that way of seeing. And, given that way of seeing as a premise, then this is how it must be because *that is* the world, out there. The language which addresses it merely lights on what is. The problem, however, is not that 'what you see depends on where you sit', but rather that 'nothing is more difficult than to know exactly just what we do see' (Merleau-Ponty, 1962, p. 78). Under the view of 'theorizing' which stresses its 'grammar' then it might be thought that what we see is brought to life by the complex commitment of our attachments to particular theories, methods, ethics and political beliefs, so that what we say is brought to life by the language in which we speak, by way of which we speak that which lets us be. In the case of pluralism, then critiques of Dahl by writers such as Gitlin (1965) or Druckman (1971), which stress that 'pluralism' is the ideology of a conservative ruling class, charge him with speaking in bad faith. They assert that he speaks alienated speech by assuming the values and voice of the existing social order, while attempting to assert this as amoral, as science. He achieves this by absenting his Self from the methodical world he constructs, by never addressing the grounds of that world, his talk about it, as a topic of enquiry. This world is thus created by behavioural science, constituted by operational definition, and neutered by veiling commitment to the method/life which provides for the sense of this suppression. To do otherwise, and to remain a positivist, would be suicidal, as reflection would liquidate that which was addressed by uncovering the grounds for its speech, revealing them to be as illusory as the emperor's new suit.

What the critics of pluralism assert is the bad faith of pluralism in not being their kind of science, not providing for their kind of commitment, theoretically and politically. What Dahl, and pluralists generally, assert is the bad faith of élitism in not being *their* kind of science, not providing for *their* kind of commitment, theoretically and politically. What makes of each view an overtly political act is the shared belief of each that their vision corresponds to an ontologically self-evident and pre-given reality. Yet, if we take seriously the grammar of theorizing, they themselves are elements in the grammar of their own talk about power, a grammar which is reflexively formulable in these accounts. These accounts are displayed in a state of false consciousness in so far as the commitment itself is glossed over by a concern with the instrumentality of language. Because of this, questions such as whether or not 'X' is really a plural or an élite ruling situation become questions not of the essence of 'X', but of each and any analyst's method for defining it as such. And this is a display of the theorizing power exhibited in each and any analyst doing his (tradition's) ruling on the world. It is not to be taken that if 'X' and 'Y' differ as to the reality of a situation that one or other (or both) of them is incorrect, or using bad method, but that each performed correctly or incorrectly within the grammar of their respective tradition. From this perspective our interest does not focus on one person being more powerful than another (because they possess more 'bases', 'resources', etc.). Instead, we would focus on recognizing how some of the things people do may be stipulated as a doing of power, how they are able to do so, and how it is that we in our tradition(s) are, or are not able to recognize that their doing so is an exhibition of power.

An examination of the Community Power Debate in terms of the conventional grammar of theorizing which constitutes it, has enabled us to uncover that whether a situation is characterized as being either a plural or an élite structure, is not dependent on ascertaining what is the case, if indeed it makes sense even to speak of 'the case' here (what 'sense' would it make not to do?). It is instead dependent on *what* procedures members of *which* scientific community have evolved for agreeing the issue. If distinct communities fail to agree, then we can only decide the correctness or truth of an account within the framework of the procedural rules that produce that account. The question of truth thus becomes an internal matter for the varying communities; hence, we may not expect a 'pluralist' to agree with an 'élitist'. There can be no question of whether or not the system the community embraces is true. And so one can only be committed or non-committed to a particular way of seeing, so that whether one regards a situation as truly pluralist or élitist depends upon one's commitment. The tradition decides what will count as a reason for holding something to be the case, through the theorizing power it exerts over its communicants. Either one is committed to that tradition or one is not, and in a sense that is all that can be said; as Wittgenstein (1968, par. 195) put it:

> All testing, all confirmation and disconfirmation of a
> hypothesis takes place already within a system. And this
> system is not a more or less arbitrary and doubtful point of
> departure for all our arguments: no, it belongs to the essence
> of what we call an argument. The system is not so much the
> point of departure, as the element in which arguments have
> their life.

Thus pluralism or élitism is in effect, the way we think. Are we then unable to say that one is right or wrong? Are notions of correctness between the two thus inappropriate? On this reckoning we can only argue from within that from which we speak, so that

29

for us to refute another's findings through our way of seeing is only to re-affirm our faith in our mode of existence, and to reaffirm our rule by the 'law' of whatever tradition. There can be no neutral and mutually acceptable grounds on which debate can proceed, and rational debate may flourish only within specific communities.

This would be nihilism with a vengeance. Any statements that the social scientist cares to make about the topic of power are consigned to political impotence. Sociology could justly be termed the sophistry of a decadent academy, consigned to the interminable chatter of Babel, until the world about it grows weary of its presence. Sociology would be finally cast as conservatism's eunuch; powerless and impotent as an insubstantial phantasmagoria.

Conceived as a liberal response to the dogma of science, theorizing reveals its illiberal aspect in a final irony: the grammar of sociological theorizing liquidates 'logos' in its own irrational 'socius'.

## Theorizing and reason

The case for theorizing as a 'conventional grammar' is not incorrect, but merely overstated. A comparison with the problems of interpreting Wittgenstein's 'conventionalism' can establish this. Wittgenstein (1968, par. 85) once remarked that rules or conventions can always be variously interpreted. Consider a pupil learning a number series:

Now – judged by the usual criteria – the pupil has mastered the series of natural numbers. Next we teach him to write down other series of cardinal numbers and get him to the point of writing down series of the form

O,N,2N,3N,etc.

as an order of the form '+N'; so at the order '+I' he writes down the series of natural numbers. – Let us suppose we have done exercises and given him tests up to 1000.

Now we get the pupil to continue a series (say +2) beyond 1000 – and he writes 1000, 1004, 1008, 1012.

We say to him: 'Look what you've done!' – He doesn't understand. We say: 'You were meant to add *two*: look how you began the series!' – He answers: 'Yes, isn't it right? I thought that was how I was *meant* to do it' – Or suppose he pointed to the series and said: 'But I went on in the same way' – It would now be no use to say: 'But can't you see . . .?' – and repeat the old examples and explanations. – In such a case we might say, perhaps: It comes natural to this person to understand our order with our explanations as *we* should understand the order: 'Add 2 up to 1000, 4 up to 2000, 6 up to 3000 and so on.'

Such a case would present similarities with one in which a person naturally reacted to the gesture of pointing with the hand by looking in the direction of the line from finger tip to wrist, not from wrist to finger tip (Wittgenstein, 1968, par. 185).

Petrie (1971, p. 146) notes the triad as:

1  A person's understanding some conventional linguistic formula.
2  His performing an action which we would ordinarily say was a mistake in using the rule.
3  His not acknowledging the mistake – believing that he has acted perfectly rationally in accord with what the formula meant.

A conventionalist account would hold this triad to be inconsistent, because part of the rules of use of 'understanding' is to acknowledge that B, or C, or both, fail to hold. Yet Wittgenstein insists that the triad is both comprehensible and consistent, rather than a linguistic oddity. By the conventionalist account it would have to be considered inconsistent because – 'judged by the usual criteria' – the pupil must assent to his mistake, because once the tradition of the convention is established the pupil must be mistaken if the triad is inconsistent: 'the seeming inconsistency arises from a too-narrow conventionalist view of language' (Petrie, 1971, p. 146).

As Wittgenstein (1968, par. 85) insists, it is an 'empirical proposition' that rules leave room for doubt for their application, that they may be variously interpreted, which

means that the sense of '+2' depends not only on the interpretation, but also on the way the interpretation is given . . . the background natural language, which is and must be assumed even to state the notions of calculus and interpretation, is *itself* a set of rules which can be variously interpreted . . . as long as we are assuming that we can assign a canonical role to some language (ideal or ordinary) in the sense that what the rules of that language *say* is 'natural', then the triad will appear inconsistent. But if we see that the canonical nature of any language is relative to what the users of that language find it natural to *do*, we can see that the triad is consistent for the man who finds it natural to go on in that way (Petrie, 1971, pp. 146–7).

In Wittgenstein 'grasping a rule . . . which is exhibited in what we call obeying the rule and going against it in actual cases' (Wittgenstein, 1968, par. 201) is understood in the notion of a 'form of life'. This prepares our path away from nihilism.

## Language games and form of life

The 'conventionalist' interpretation of Wittgenstein's triad which stresses its inconsistency, resonates with views about the 'conventional grammar of theorizing' which in turn stress that this activity is 'intra-paradigmatic' (Phillips, 1973), and not dependent on 'nature's message': 'The absence of nature in any sense other than as linguistic convention or construction reduces Wittgenstein's later teaching to historicism or conventionalism' (Rosen 1969, p. 13).

Not all interpreters of Wittgenstein wish to make him the nihilist that Rosen would have him, particularly Stroud (1971), Pitkin (1972), Cavell (1962; 1969), Petrie (1971), Zabeeh (1971) and Hunter (1971). Their difference is located in the key concepts of 'language game' and 'form of life'.

### The language game

I shall in the future again and again draw your attention to what I shall call language-games. These are ways of using signs simpler than those in which we use the signs of our highly complicated everyday language. Language games are forms of language with which a child begins to make use of words. The study of language games is the study of primitive forms of language or primitive languages (Wittgenstein, 1969b, p. 17).

The term language game is first introduced in the series of drafts and notes published as 'Notes for Lectures on "Private Experience" and "Sense Data"' (Wittgenstein, 1970), as something which 'plays a particular role in our human life' (Wittgenstein, 1970, par. 77). The concept is used to relate speech acts such as 'descriptions of the picture before one's mind's eye' with everyday activity.

To aid this study Wittgenstein introduces what Zabeeh (1971) has termed both 'natural' and 'artificial' language games. Natural language games are introduced by Wittgenstein when he is concerned with 'the correspondence between concepts and very general facts of nature'. But since, as he says, he is not doing 'natural history', then artificial language games may assist as 'aids to a sluggish imagination'. Thus 'we can also invent fictitious natural history for our purposes' (Wittgenstein, 1968, p. 230).

It is with such an artificial language game that Wittgenstein chastises the correspondence theory of language. He elaborates, and then criticizes this theory in the opening pages of the *Investigations*. There he introduces the idea of a simple language game such as one which a builder and his assistant might engage in, in an abbreviated version of the remarks that introduce *The Brown Book* (Wittgenstein, 1969b). It consists of names of building materials to which the builder can point to his assistant and name as 'block', 'slab', 'pillar' and 'beam': 'A calls them out; – B brings the stone which he has learnt to bring at such-and-such a call – Conceive this as a complete primitive language game' (Wittgenstein, 1969b, par. 2).

The language game is made progressively more complex; in *The Brown Book* he introduces the extension of number, and in the *Investigations* the extension of 'this' and 'there' which are employed 'in conjunction with a pointing gesture', and a 'number of colour samples'. The builder calls out 'five slabs' or 'd-slab there'. Wittgenstein makes the assistant understand 'd' by means of something such as a pointing gesture or a colour sample. He carries the correct slab to the correct place. The construction of new language games continues through introducing various additions such as expressions for recalling, comparing, identifying, memorizing, etc. (The sections 7–73 of *The Brown Book* each introduce a variant, and hence a different language game.) After the extensions to the building language game then Wittgenstein reflects

> But how many kinds of sentences are there? Say assertion, question and command? – There are *countless* kinds: countless different kinds of use of what we call 'symbols', 'words', 'sentences'. And this multiplicity is not something fixed, given once for all; but new types of language, new language games, as we may say, come into existence, and others become obsolete and get forgotten. . . . Here the term 'language game' is meant to bring into prominence the fact that the *speaking* of language is part of an activity, or of a form of life (Wittgenstein, 1968, par. 23).

Wittgenstein deliberately stresses the diversity of language games, by remarking that

> It is interesting to compare the multiplicity of the tools in language and of the ways they are used, the multiplicity of kinds of word and sentence, with what logicians have said about the structure of language. (Including the author of the *Tractatus Logico-Philosophicus*.) (Wittgenstein, 1968, par. 23.)

He confronts us with this multiplicity of language uses in order to emphasize that there are no necessary referential grounds for language. Correspondence between words and objects is merely a ground rule of one such language game, rather than a feature of all language use. And of this language use Wittgenstein says 'the speaking of a language is part of an activity or a form of life' (Wittgenstein, 1968, par. 23).

*Form of life*

It is what human beings say that is true and false; and they agree in the *language* they use. This is not agreement in opinions but in forms of life. . . . What has to be accepted, the given, is – so one could say *'forms of life'* (Wittgenstein, 1968, par. 241; p. 226).

The expression 'form of life' appears only five times in the *Investigations* (pars 19; 23; 241; pp. 174; 226), but the idea is clearly implicit in his remark in the 'Lectures and Conversations on Aesthetics, Psychology and Religious Belief' that 'We don't start from certain words, but from certain occasions or activities' (Wittgenstein, 1966, par. 3).

There are numerous textual studies of Wittgenstein which cover in seemingly different ways what Wittgenstein has been taken to have meant by his use of the term 'form of life'. Strawson (1966, p. 62) suggests that the notion implies that in order to understand a concept one has to view it in its linguistic context, which in turn should be framed within its social context. A full description should then follow, bearing in mind that each concept may occur in many contexts.

Hunter (1971) has termed this the 'language-game account', in which

A language game is a prime example of a form of life, and calling it such is saying that it is something formalized or standardized in our life; that it is one of life's forms. It is not necessarily standardized in any permanent way: language games, like any other games, will appear and change and disappear. But at any given time it will be clear enough whether any given utterance counts as 'playing the game or not'.

If asked what would be the point or cash value of saying that a language game is a form of life, one could suggest two things; first, that there can't be any *private* language games, that the game must exist as a standard before it can be 'played'; and second, that unlike most ordinary games, language games are intricately bound up with other aspects of life, with plans and fears and thoughts and activities, and can not be understood in isolation from these (Hunter, 1971, p. 275).

It is a version of form of life that is very like this that I wish to propose, and that I will employ to make sense of the empirical materials that I will introduce in a future chapter. I emphasize the notion of a *standard*, where standard is seen as being the measure of good, sensible and rational speech; so that, given those circumstances, any man could be expected to behave in this rather than that or some other way, and say those sort of things. This is not to propose some degenerate version of 'role theory' whereby automata act out the scenarios interpreted for them by unimaginative analysts, like natural responses jigging helplessly to the rhythm of stimuli. Such responses may be no more than conventionally oriented to features of a scene. For example, pain behaviour and pain language as we know them may be quite different elsewhere. Imagine, or investigate a society of stoics, or fakirs, or instances of individuals who are simply not physiologically equipped to feel pain, or who are narcoticized – in such circumstances our firm grasp of the shared pain of fire, of scorched flesh or broken limb soon recedes. That beds, for instance, are made of foam, or hair, or straw or nails is merely conventional, for they could easily be otherwise.

What kind of convention would it be where everyone in a particular community slept on a bed of nails, much as somewhere foam or hair may be a convention? We might enquire of this community and be told 'Odd? But doesn't everyone do that? How else do you prove yourself?'

There is a sense in which this notion of language as a convention might be seen to relate to form of life, if form of life can be seen as being 'iconic': a material thing whose being is inexplicable apart from the idea(l) projected on to it. The behaviour glossed over by the phrase 'form of life' indicates that it is behaviour which may be seen as the embodiment of actions oriented towards a standard or measure of activity, where activity may be taken to stand for any manifestation of beings in the world who can be constituted as theoretic actors. To be a theoretic actor is to be one who is responsible for one's acts, to be one who could have been held to have done otherwise.

Where the possibility arises that *this* rather than *that* or something else might have occurred then we would be concerned with 'form of life' as I shall be using it. That is as some matrix of human activity considered as having point, purpose and regularity. Under the auspices of such an account of speech activity and behaviour, then ordinarily occurring instances of behaviour could be re-formulated as being *this* rather than *that* by virtue of their producers' orientation towards a standard of such speech activity as an ideal: a form of life as iconically theorizing the possibility of actually occurring behaviour.

In this sense a form of life concerns *what* deed is done, and how far the nature of the 'what' determines how it is done where it might be done otherwise. As Cavell (1962, pp. 97–8) puts it

That *that* should express understanding or boredom or anger . . . is not *necessary*: someone may have to be said 'to understand

35

suddenly' and then always fail to manifest the understanding
five minutes later, just as someone *may* be bored by an earth-
quake, or by the death of his child or the declaration of martial
law, or *may* be angry at a pin, a cloud or a fish, just as someone
may quietly (but comfortably?) sit on a chair of nails. That
human beings on the whole do not respond in these ways is,
therefore, seriously referred to as *conventional*; but now we are
thinking of convention not as the arrangements a particular
culture has found convenient. . . . Here the array of 'conventions'
are not patterns of life which differentiate men from one
another, but those exigencies of conduct which all men share.

The notion of 'conventional' takes on a deeper significance than
the mere surface display of behaviour, the particular possibility of
how some deed is done. Instead it is concerned with what deed is
done, the very possibility of why *that* deed or thing was done and
no other, when some other could have been, in as far as the deed
in question was a 'free' action.

It is through raising the problem of 'why' by relating language to
life, by stressing the interconnection of 'language games' and 'forms
of life' that a way out from the nihilism that has attached to our
investigations of power thus far, will be discovered.

## The everyday and the theoretic form of life

'Form of life' may be distinguished from a 'language game' inasmuch
as the former may be considered as a meta-language in use; a matrix
of human activities with point, purpose and regularity. Any sub-set
of this meta-language considered as an object of study can be formulated as a language game. The form of life is what people do, as they
comment upon, reflect upon and formulate what they perform. These
activities and utterances are exhibited in the language which they use
in their everyday activities, the language which enables us to form
our enquiries. To avoid an infinite regress of rule, interpretation rule
and so on, Wittgenstein appeals to the form of life as a display of
actual performance of human activity contingent upon very general
facts of nature (Wittgenstein, 1968, p. 230). It is not possible to subject this meta-language, the form of life, to further scrutiny (we have
no means of providing a meta-meta-language etc. to do so) but only
to exhibit it and say – 'this is what we do'. Given the 'general facts
of nature' we could perhaps do something else, but this is what we
do at present, for it is where we have evolved to.

Social science, unlike the natural sciences, does not exist in a form
of life where the basic puzzle is one of a correspondence between
theory and nature. Instead it is concerned with the understanding of
particular human forms of life as these have evolved. As Wittgenstein

carefully points out, the limits to our understanding are what we actually do – the whole broad 'form of life' of our entire human purpose and activity, and what we could conceivably do within the parameters of some very 'general facts of nature'. But, not only do we dwell in this life, we also reflect upon it. Our reflections are themselves, in so far as they are organized into meta-languages (science, religion, aesthetics, etc.), a form of life which promotes an ideal for understanding and explanation. In sociology this ideal has typically been taken from the icon of scientific practice. Drawing guidance from the icon, different traditions for reflecting on the various language games of the evolving form of everyday life have evolved.

In a social science that takes the philosophy of Wittgenstein seriously, then everyday life as a display of actual performance of human activity must be the bedrock for any theorizing, functioning as an analogous icon to that of nature in the natural sciences. As Wittgenstein put it: 'If I have exhausted the justifications I have reached bedrock, and my spade is turned. Then I am inclined to say, "This is simply what I do . . ."' (Wittgenstein, 1968, par. 217). This display of actual performance becomes a 'form of life' when viewed reflectively under the auspices of a particular theoretic form of life.

In a social science the performance of everyday activity to which we attend theoretically may involve everyday speech. Theoretically, under our reflective re-constitution of this performance, we may characterize this speech as our object of study, as our 'language games'.

This conception of 'everyday activity' may be seen as the grounding of competing traditions, or conventions of sociological address, such as 'pluralism' or 'élitism'. It is the home, to paraphrase Aristotle (*Metaphysics*, Book II), of the pre-suppositions of our human experience, of that which is most true, because in it are grounded all derivative truths. These must be revealed by the act of looking, a vision which is necessarily acquired through our conventional ways of doing so, because one 'looks' through speech as the means of articulation of our knowledge of things, a knowledge which is revealed by discourse but which is not dependent on this discourse.

Such knowledge is revealed through a twin dialogue, the dialogue with the tradition within which one speaks, and the dialogue with the speech one speaks of – the everyday performance.

Hence theorizing is a twin dialogue, with the tradition and with everyday life. Everyday life is the foundation, as in it we find the source of enquiry, the impulse for understanding. But the dialogue is also with the tradition, the idiom of the author's form of life. Where this dialogue is with the Wittgensteinian tradition, then the speeches of this everyday life-world may themselves be theorized as

37

language games of the 'possible society' of everyday life. Theoretically, we can constitute both our own theoretic endeavours, and those of everyday theorizers, as language games of a possible society which attain their rationality from an organizing, iconic form of life. Both everyday speech, the source of our enquiry that grounds the dialogue with the theoretic, and theoretic speech, may be formulated in terms of their form of life. The everyday is both the impulse, – as the source of our puzzles – and the synthesis, – when it is grasped in the theoretic – of dialectic between the two.

The most rational[1] account would be that which minimized the difference between itself and the subject of its account, which presented what we might call a monadic form of life. In such a possible monadic speech, the dialectic of the dialogue with tradition, and the dialogue with everyday life, would be overcome in a perfect speech which united the disjuncture of grammar. In such a speech there would be no 'grammar', because there would be no competing accounts of anything, if every thing were in harmony with every mind – that is if every thing had a name; the society of perfect operationism.

But to be silent would be to be no longer either a creature of 'logos' or of 'socius', because it is discourse as a social and public phenomenon which grants us our humanity, rather than bequeathing it to rats or monkeys. And so the dialectic between theoretical and everyday speech is what grants us our 'logos'. To overcome it would be both the negation of our humanity and of our reason.

What this implies for an interpretation of Wittgenstein is that we must then distinguish between form of life as *that* way of being-in-the-world, and 'grammar' as opinions about that being. We must do so because opinions could not serve as grounds for rational debate. Where, as in accounts of theorizing which stress its 'grammar', they do serve as grounds, then the 'irrational' debate that evidences in the Community Power Debate serves as a reminder of the folly of the enterprise. It is a folly because by these criteria, the intelligibility of the tradition of theorizing becomes its own standard, its own measure. There then exist as many principles of intelligibility as traditions of thought. If that were so, and if members of different traditions had no access to some overarching and non-conventional standard of rational speech, then what they write would be wholly unintelligible to members of other traditions. In so far as some traditions have almost entirely lost sight of their original grounding in everyday life and speech, then this may almost be the case.

Where we encounter discourse then there we encounter the grounds of reason. If discourse occurs then criteria of intelligibility cannot be merely intra-tradition. Either traditions are unintelligible in each other's terms, with entry visas granted only by a commitment to that way of seeing, or else any tradition's intelligibility can only be formulated in terms of its holistic intelligibility – something that each tradition can partake of, but which is distinct from it. Hence intelligibility must be in terms of some independent and overarching criterion of rationality.

Given that there must be some over all criterion of rationality, then could it be regarded as being achieved in an account that served as the account, the standard, of all other accounts? An instance of such an accounting would be Science, the rational enterprise serving as the measure of any claim to knowledge. Could Science stand as the ratio of both theoretic and everyday speech, as the standard of both that which it seeks to account and as the measure of itself?

Were it not that a reflexive speech about the total monadic body of knowledge thus proposed was possible, one could answer 'Yes' to the previous question. Wittgenstein's *Investigations* stand as a testament to the actuality of such a reflexive speech about one such proposed monad – the *Tractatus*. The possibility of infinite discourse that is opened up by the abyss of reflexive theorizing is an ever present possibility. The point at which we broke off any account would still leave *its* own possibility unformulated. In this manner one could challenge the rationality of Science by enquiring, in a Heideggerian manner (as does Blum, 1974), what the Reason of Science might be.

As the *Investigations* show, rationality has to be located in actual performance (see Wittgenstein, 1968, par. 325) because the 'standard has no grounds' (Wittgenstein, 1968, par. 482). If the idea (and ideal) of rationality were contained in some concrete standard which had grounds then we could point to this, and use it as the criterion. But, any such proposed ground would still leave its own grounding as a topic for questioning. The possibility of such questioning as a performance would be infinite. Each questioning would occasion its own questioning. Each questioning, however, would be a further move in some language game, one which would surely lose its point if its purpose seemed merely to show the impossibility of closure. Where the possibility of the language game resided instead in something with point and purpose oriented towards an understanding of some aspect of our everyday life, then a means of avoiding the infinite regress, and of approaching rationality, would present itself.

This would be the situation where a rational speech would be one in which the form of life of theory would be taken to be an account of both itself (albeit necessarily partial), and of its subject. Where its subject consisted of everyday accounts, then rational theorizing would be that which accounted both for itself, and those accounts it accounted. It could thus intelligibly provide for its agreement or disagreement with other competing traditions' accounts of the 'same phenomena'. The notion of 'phenomenon' invoked here would thus serve as an occasion for theorizing which addressed both the rationality of itself and other accounts of the phenomenon, and the rationality of the phenomenon itself.

## The grounds for a rational analysis of power

There are a number of ways in which the interpretation of Wittgenstein proposed in the preceding pages might offer some points of contact with certain aspects of Marx. In particular one might cite passages such as the following in which Marx appears to be saying something quite similar about the 'bedrock' of 'human activity' as may be found in Wittgenstein:

> The premises from which we start are not arbitrary; they are no dogmas but rather actual premises from which abstraction can be made only in imagination. They are the real individuals, their actions, and their material conditions of life, those which they find existing as well as those which they produce through their actions. . . . By producing food, man indirectly produces his material life himself. . . . The way in which man produces his food depends first of all on the nature of the means of subsistence that he finds and has to reproduce. This mode of reproduction must not be viewed simply as reproduction of the physical existence of individuals. Rather it is a definite form of their activity, a definite way of expressing their life, a definite mode of life. As individuals express their life, so they are. What they are, therefore, coincides with what they produce, and how they produce. The nature of individuals thus depends on the material conditions which determine their production (Marx and Engels, 1965, p. 408).

Although this is hardly newsworthy in the tradition of post-Hegelian German philosophy, it does display some antecedents of the notion of 'form of life', the notion of 'mode of life'. What Wittgenstein contributes to this is a concern with the grounds of explanation as a philosophical problem in which 'What has to be accepted, the given is – so one could say – *forms of life*' (Wittgenstein, 1968, p. 226).

What the stress on form of life suggests is that we can study the realm of language rationally and intelligibly only in its relation to man's wider social being, in particular in the realm of 'practical activity'; which, in a sociology of organizations, is represented by the world of work, the home of Marx's concept of 'labour'. At a certain level in the organization, the level of power and decision making, then empirical observation yields the following: much of what passes for managerial work in organizations such as a construction site, is predominantly composed of 'talk', the spoken aspect of language. If this is then regarded as 'labour', as the focus of an enquiry into 'practical activity', then objections to the 'trivial' aspect of such talk are non-starters. (One would expect this to be the case after the prominence given to the Watergate tapes. It should be only too apparent that the executive branch of organization is very much 'linguistic labour'.)

Given this orientation to the importance of taped materials as a bedrock display of 'practical activity' in an executive context in organizations, then the 'more imaginative' interpretation of Bachrach and Baratz's (1971b) notions of the ways in which issues are constructed may be now proposed. A research into power might wish merely to enumerate 'who won' a number of issues, and in so doing either neglect or define arbitrarily the 'importance' of these, and the way in which they came into being. Alternatively, it might focus on the ways in which power, instead of being displayed in the outcomes of issues, is instead exhibited in the rationality of issues. Before this can be attempted, however, we must first acquire the means to do so.

The conclusion of 'Theorizing and Reason' proposed the dialectical nature of theorizing, as the discourse in the work between the dialogue with tradition, and the dialogue with everyday life, the ground of our daily existence, and the source of our theoretical puzzles. This daily life in its non-trivial, power-full aspect of labour in organizations, can be researched through taped conversational materials. These materials will provide the dialogue with everyday life, the world to which Wittgenstein would have us turn to ease 'conceptual puzzlement'.

By the prescriptions of rational discourse as elaborated in the previous section, this will provide only one half of our re-turn. The turn must be mediated; we have first to acquire bearings for the re-turn, by restoring the concept of power to its traditional 'home', in order to view the topic of power in instances of organizational activity. The topic of power has its home in this everyday world. When we look at it through theoretical discourse, problems arise from the conventions of traditions of reflection and theoretical speculation. These traditions are the home of the concept. However, there can be no point in setting one theory up merely to knock it down with another, for what could be the rationality of that? – And so we must use the grounds of everyday life as the foundations of enquiry.

The re-turn to these grounds will be mediated by exploring the contemporary 'grammar' of the theoretical explanation of power in organizations, which grammar will be restored to the tradition from whence its sociological origins spring: the work of Simmel and Weber. The elucidation gained from this return must then be restored to the form of life that it is reflexive upon, which both provides for it, and of which it effects to be an explanation, in order to show the deep sameness of the world of everyday and sociological theorizing.

Sociological theorizing, restored to the grounds of everyday life, thus enables us to review the tradition of enquiry into power in organizations as deficient in the respect that it charts 'the bumps that understanding has got by running its head up against the limits of language' (Wittgenstein, 1968, par. 119).

The programme is threefold; first, chart the bumps that we may sustain through reviewing contemporary theorizing; second, restore that theorizing to its theoretic origins; third, re-turn those origins to an everyday concern.

# 3 Power in the theory of organizations

## The 'strategic contingencies' theory

If the bibliographies of the majority of standard texts on organizations were to provide the topic of this chapter, then very little justification would be needed to make this an extremely brief section. In part, this stems from a situation where 'within work organizations, power itself has not been explained' (Hickson et al., 1971, p. 216).

That one is in fact able to write at some length is due solely to the work of the authors of the above statement in proposing a 'strategic contingencies theory of intra-organizational power' to redress this situation. This chapter will elaborate this theory and argue that it does not succeed in achieving this redress to any great extent. The dissatisfactions expressed arise because this 'strategic contingencies' theory exemplifies the shortcomings of any theorizing which is conventionally secure within a tradition of work undisturbed by either everyday life, or alternative traditions of theorizing. What ostensibly appears to be a 'synthesis' of several traditions of thought will be seen to be a reformulation of the underlying unity of these seemingly different traditions.

Hickson et al. (1971) offer their explanation of power from within Thompson's (1967) 'newer tradition' which 'enables us to conceive of the organization as an open system, indeterminate and faced with uncertainty, but subject to criteria of rationality and hence needing certainty' (Thompson, 1967, p. 13; cited in Hickson et al., 1971, p. 217).

The elements of this tradition derive from 'the functionalist approach in sociology and the behavioural theory of the firm in economics' (Pennings et al., 1969), and in particular from Thompson's (1967) blend of functionalist theory with the 'behavioural theory of the firm' of Cyert and March (1963), and March and Simon (1958). Hickson et al. add to this elements of Blau's 'exchange theory', Crozier's (1964) stress on 'uncertainty', and Dahl's (1957) behavioural concept of power as used by Kaplan (1964). The approach thus provides a synthesis of the two major recent traditions in the study of power, behavioural and exchange theory.

In the light of the previous chapter, to explore this 'synthesis' is to examine the tradition(s) that enable it, that make it possible. Such an explanation would require analysis of a 'system' framework of exchanges. The outcome of these exchanges decides who has power in the organization. The notion of 'power as outcome' derives from the behavioural terms formulated by Dahl (1957), which Hickson *et al.* apply to an explanation of the power of an organization's 'sub-units'. The theory proposes that the power of such a sub-unit is determined by its relationship to other sub-units in the organization, and by its response to its environment. The division of labour in the organization is seen to provide the functional inter-relationship of an organizational system of inter-departmental sub-units. The theory ascribes power relations to imbalances in this interdependency. In viewing the organization as composed of interdependent parts, then Hickson *et al.* (1971, p. 217) are following Thompson (1967, p. 6). Some parts are more, or less, interdependent than others.

Hickson *et al.* (1971, p. 217) regard the major task element, or work, of these departments, as being 'coping with uncertainty'. The interdependent system of sub-units is an 'open' one, whose work derives from transforming its major input, 'uncertainty', into more certainty than existed in its previous state. The organization is regarded as thus composed of more or less specialized 'sub-units', differentiated by the division of labour, but related by a 'need' for certainty. The organization is 'indeterminate and faced with uncertainty, but subject to criteria of rationality and hence needing certainty' (Thompson, 1967, p. 13; cited in Hickson *et al.*, 1971, p. 217). This 'need' leads to the system's 'essential' behaviour, which is

> Limitation of the autonomy of all its members or parts since all are subject to power from the others; for sub-units, unlike individuals, are not free to make a decision to participate, as March and Simon (1958) put it, nor to decide whether or not to come together in political relationships. They must. They exist to do so. . . . The groups use differential power to function within the system rather than to destroy it (Hickson *et al.*, 1971, p. 217).

A strategically contingent system is thus composed of plural and countervailing powers which constitute the organization, an organization whose 'essence' is limitation of the autonomy of these parts. In short, it is a traditional 'open systems' model of the organization modified by a realization of the points that Gouldner (1967) raised. He pointed out that certain parts of a system may be relatively more autonomous than others. In this particular case their autonomy is not so great that the part may ultimately destroy the whole. The environment of the organization determines the behaviour of the organizational sub-unit, because of boundary exchanges of resources, with the resource inputs to the sub-unit being hypostasized as 'uncertainties'.

The reduction of these uncertainties is the goal of the organization. This reduction work provides the resources for sub-units to 'exchange' with each other, and with the environment external to the organization. Given this, then one would anticipate that changes in sub-unit power might be 'caused' by factors extraneous to the sub-units (in a version of environmental determinism), which is indeed how the 'strategic contingencies' theory does explain change. For example:

> Goal changes mean that the organization confronts fresh uncertainties; so that sub-units which can cope or purport to cope with these experience increased power. Thus if institutions shift in emphasis from custodial to treatment goals, the power of treatment oriented sub-units (e.g. social service workers) increases only if they can cope with the uncertainties of inmate treatment. If they are helpless to do anything even purportedly effective, then they remain weak (Pennings et al., 1969, p. 420).

Such a 'strategic contingencies theory' of power explains changes in power in terms of the adaptation of a system in the face of a changed environment:

> Organizations deal with environmentally derived uncertainties in the sources and composition of inputs, with uncertainties in the processing of throughputs, and again with environmental uncertainties in the disposal of outputs. They must have means to deal with these uncertainties for adequate task performance. Such ability is here called 'coping' (Hickson et al., 1971, p. 219).

Changes in power are caused by a changing capacity to cope with the uncertainty caused by the systemic adaptation of sub-units to changing, or changed, environments.

Qualifications must be made when considering the question of environmental determinism within a sociological perspective. Once we allow that some members of organizations may be in a position to choose the environment in which they operate, then the emphasis on the determining features of the environment diminishes. It might be that the home market is less variable than the export market, and it might be that members who manage exports are more 'strategically contingent', and hence by definition of the theory, more powerful, than these other members. This would tell us little if the crucial and unconsidered question is *who* chose to export, and how and why they chose to. As Child has pointed out,

> the directors of at least large organizations may command sufficient power to influence the conditions prevailing within environments where they are already operating. The debate surrounding Galbraith's thesis (1967) that the large business corporation in modern industrial societies is able very considerably to manipulate and even create the demand for its own products centers on this very point. Some degree of environmental manipulation is open to most organizations. These considerations form an important qualification to suggestions of environmental determinism (Child, 1972, p. 4).

Further qualifications would result from reconsidering the substantive focus on 'sub-units' as the unit of analysis. These are those areas of an organization concerned with a specific function such as sales or production. It is assumed that these will exist as relatively autonomous, contained and identifiable areas. In attempting to argue that these sub-units behave, without at the same time suggesting how they might do so (for example, through the action of some powerful member(s) in formulating sales (or whatever) policy), one implicitly assumes that the entity reified as a 'sub-unit' somehow enacts one definition of the environment to which it then 'reacts'; or that it somehow 'picks-up' the one message that the environment sends it.

If one hypothesizes that a sub-unit is a unitary and harmonious collective, speaking and acting with one voice, then one is on a sticky wicket. The same criticism applies to an apparently more probable and less reified hypothesis. This second hypothesis asserts that a sub-unit is a collective which is spoken for by one voice, and which overrules the chatter of competing interests, attachments, strategies and meanings. The latter hypothesis opens one's theory to charges that it uncritically embraces management ideology, as Fox (1966) has suggested. In such a perspective, the sub-unit is what managers do, which means that the environment would be what managers thought important and problematic. Thus the theoretical concept of 'environment' would be constituted by managerial definition.

This would be to refrain from explaining power in the first place. The theory presupposes a tacit and unexplicated reliance on the very topic that it seeks to explain. This is because the theory implicitly defines both a 'sub-unit' and 'the environment' as being that which managers define them as. This concealment is then used as a resource for circular theorizing which purports to explain its own tacit assumptions. What has been assumed is the power of managers. This assumption enables the theory to talk of 'the environment' and the 'sub-unit' *as if* they were unitary phenomena. Thus a collective of potentially conflicting interests and world-views is regarded as one thing (a 'sub-unit'), which serves only to demonstrate the power of some members of that collective. They are able to 'speak' for it, representing it as one such thing. Any such assumption of identity in the face of difference would have to spell out how that difference was overcome in a way which the 'strategic contingency' theory does not.

The theorists of the 'Managerial Revolution', as for example, Burnham (1941), have argued that, given the 'decomposition of capital' attendant upon the separation of ownership and control, then power no longer resides in ownership, but in management. The theory of 'strategic contingencies' merely takes the managerial thesis one stage further by accepting Galbraith's (1967) argument. This states that the general type of manager has disappeared only to be replaced by different departments (sub-units) of specialists, each of which pursues some key managerial function. Galbraith (1967) and Hickson *et al.* (1971) see these as the locus of power. Galbraith (1967) sees even top management as dependent on these as gatekeepers of information. This information becomes for Hickson *et al.* (1971) a key resource in terms of its degree of uncertainty. Power comes to be in the portals of power.

Power achieves this locus through being attached to the concept of uncertainty. This concept has become current in recent organization theory, largely as a result of its use by Crozier (1964), although similar related concepts have been used by Thompson (1967), and Cyert and March (1963). It is obviously an idea in 'good currency'. Its currency in the use that Hickson *et al.* (1971) put it to is also obscure. Besides the difficulties that Hickson *et al.* (1971) encounter in their use of the concept of 'sub-unit', the opacity that they exhibit in their use of the concept of 'uncertainty' would be sufficient to render suspect any theory based on it. For instance: 'Uncertainty may be defined as a lack of information about future events, so that alternatives and their outcomes are unpredictable' (Hickson *et al.*, 1971, p. 219).

Uncertainty is here defined as something possessed by members of organizations, rather than being something that an 'environment' might have. But, one page later we read that 'Uncertainty might be indicated by the variability of those inputs to the organization which are taken by the sub-unit. For instance, a production sub-unit may face variability in raw materials and engineering may face variability in equipment performance' (Hickson *et al.*, 1971, p. 220). Uncertainty is now located not in members' knowledge, but in the variability of artefacts, this variability being located in the input 'environment' of the sub-unit.

In a sense which is not used in their work, one plausible interpretation of the concept of uncertainty would locate it in member's knowledge for predicting future states of affairs. If this were so, then presumably certainty would be a state of affairs in which all alternatives and all outcomes were equally and absolutely predictable. There would be no possibility of untowardness. Inexplicability, strangeness and surprise would not be possible. Were such a situation imaginable, it would conjure up a state of affairs in which a rule existed for each and every thing that might ever occur. A complete inventory of contingency procedures would exist. So, uncertainty might be seen as a situation in which rules for remedying surprise had yet to be enacted. So, in this world, how would control over uncertainty confer power?

Control over uncertainty might be considered to be achieved when ruling on what causes the uncertainty, the surprise, had been made, and a course of treatment formulated, to bring the occurrence back into line as a routine. Thus, Crozier's (1964) maintenance men (who attended to machine breakdowns referred to them by the production workers) could be said to render an unexpected event into the past tense, by rendering it routine. They did this by providing a reason for it, and implementing a course of treatment. Crozier (1964) suggests that this uncertainty conferred 'power' on these maintenance men, power which they would otherwise not have had.

In the example of uncertainty conferring power, then we could claim that in a structural sense, analogous to the meaning of sovereignty which stresses it as being 'the effective source of or influence upon the exercise of political or legal power' (Marshall, 1964), the source of such power in the organization is a result of structural determinance by strategic contingencies. The inter-relationship of the organization, its structural layout, thus determines the sources of sub-unit power.

Now it may seem odd that structural layout should determine the effective source of power, for one might have wanted to argue the converse. The oddity becomes clearer if one recalls that in this particular formulation, power is seen as the obverse of dependency, so that 'the crucial unanswered question in organizations is: what factors function to vary dependency, and so to vary power?' (Hickson et al., 1971, p. 217).

Dependency in a system can be no more nor less than the degree of functional autonomy and reciprocity that a unit enjoys; that is, the degree to which it is central, or can be substituted for. But if at the same time, power is seen as the obverse of dependency, then power similarly is a function of functional autonomy and reciprocity.

## Power in rules in organization

Power in the organization begins to look rather like an ongoing game of chess in which the pieces gain their power through their current position, rather than gaining their current position through their power to make moves according to the rules of the game. In short, the power which a piece has is defined totally in terms of its relationships. This definition entirely neglects the progress of the game in terms of its history and rules.

Now if power is not something that condenses in a relationship, and evaporates on its termination, what is it? To stay with the example of chess, one might say that it is a function of the relationship of pieces (units) to rules, in that rules invest a certain power in a piece, independently of its position on the board.

Imagine a game more analogous to social reality. In this game the rules are frequently changing and not at all clear. Whoever was able to exploit this uncertainty, and do ruling in his own interest would in this sense have power. This is the essence of Crozier's (1964) formulation. To the extent that all pieces were able to negotiate their positions, more or less, then in a game with a fixed number of pieces, that piece which ended up ruling on the greatest number of pieces, serving its interests in preference to their's, would be the most powerful. But obviously, in an ongoing game, then a piece like the Queen would start in a more privileged position than a pawn, simply because the extant rules, which are now open to interpretation, enable her to begin the sequence with more potential moves to make.

Consider the context of Michel Crozier's (1964) original formulation of the 'control of uncertainty confers power' hypothesis. He did not claim that maintenance men were the most powerful members of the industrial bureaucracy, because of their undoubted success in controlling, in an almost monopolistic manner, discretionary areas of their tasks. What he suggests is that there is an existing context of organization rules. There is, as well, an existing power structure. Within these exist areas of uncertainty which groups or individuals are capable of controlling. Indeed, individuals or groups can, and do, control these areas. So the areas become key resources by means of which individuals and groups procure less dependence for themselves, within the power structure (Crozier, 1964, pp. 150–65).

The concept that transforms 'less dependence' into 'power', (albeit of a local and contextually bound type – as Crozier (1964) himself recognizes, and as Hickson *et al.* (1971) do not), is derived from Dahl's (1957) operational definition of power. This is that the power of a person A over B is the ability of A to ensure that B does something he would not have done otherwise. Dahl (1957) introduces this definition by citing the example of the traffic policeman's power to

49

make motorists obey him (see Chapter 2 above, pp. 26–7, for Dahl's example). This he contrasts with the illusory and vain efforts of an ordinary passer-by to achieve the same results. What would make Dahl's example of a policeman directing traffic an example of the type of power that Crozier (1964) discusses, while the efforts of a bystander would not be so regarded? Presumably it would be the presence of Dahl's three necessary conditions for power. These are, first, that there is a time lag between the actions of the actor said to be exercising power and the responses presumed to signify its exertion. Second, the two actions must be connected. Third, the policeman must be able to get automobile drivers to do something that they would not otherwise have done (Dahl, 1957, pp. 204–5).

I want to extend this discussion of Dahl in order to point to an underlying unity between the seemingly different traditions of Dahl (1957) and Crozier (1964). Crozier (1964) indicates this difference by placing his own work in a context assuredly not that of Dahl's: 'the theory of bureaucracy – that theory in terms of which sociologists since Max Weber have been considering the processes of organization' (Crozier, 1964, p. 175). This 'underlying unity' concerns the way in which power, like uncertainty, depends for its behavioural possibility upon an unexplicated concept of 'rule'. This concept may be found in the very tradition that Crozier (1964) claims to continue, but in fact waives in favour of Dahl's (1957) behaviourism. Having described 'the underlying unity' in more detail, I will argue that the same theme of 'rule' can be seen to underlie 'exchange' based explanations of power. I will argue further that the concrete explanations of exchange theory are as neglectful of the concept of power as are those of the seemingly different behavioural tradition.

All that would appear to mark off the efforts of a passer-by from those of a policeman in conducting the flow of traffic, would be that the passer-by, unlike the policeman, is not able to alter what automobile drivers actually do. The bystander, in willing the traffic to proceed as it was, would be patently not exercising power, although he might be said to be 'connected', and his behaviour might proceed that of some passing motorist.

Retaining the same example, let us alter some of its conditions. Suppose that the bystander, disguised as a policeman, were to attempt to control traffic, and the traffic obeyed. Meanwhile, the policeman, disguised as a·bystander, attempts to exercise his earlier power, but fails. Motorists merely mock his policing pretensions, and are disposed to regard his behaviour as psychotically disturbed.

I think that we would be tempted to explain the traffic control behaviour in terms of motorists' responses to what they presumed, in each case, were a policeman and a psychotic. The 'normal' identity of the two agents is not in question, rather we attend to the way in which their actions were labelled as either responsible or psychotic, according to the typifications that motorists have of police uniformed traffic controllers and madmen. The uniform acts as a symbol which displays a role. The role serves as a shorthand expression for what every motorist knows: motoring is a rule-guided activity, and policemen represent the power of the rules. The rules would be the basis of the policeman's power, and not Dahl's three necessary conditions, which are mere occurrences within the rules. Policemen have a certain power because motorists recognize them as embodying certain rules. Just like pieces in a chess game.

Consider the traffic policeman again. Let him control a traffic light system. We might account for the movement and non-movement of traffic in terms of a correlation between the effects of red and green lights. Although we might say that the traffic policeman 'caused' the traffic to stop and go, we would in effect mean that both the policeman and the motorists know that there are rules which govern traffic movement in such situations. Thus, we could formulate the traffic behaviour in terms of the following rules: red lights mean stop; green lights mean go. Just as with Crozier's maintenance men and production workers, we can similarly say that the behavioural outcome is only possible because of some underlying rule(s) that people use in constituting their actions. The manifestation of power is enabled by an underlying rule.

We can make similar observations about exchange and power. Consider the example of the Mafia. The Mafia control a local commodity market in which all exchanges between the Mafia and its suppliers of materials are conducted on the Mafia's terms. Other markets are available, as are potential competitors of the Mafia in the existing market. None the less, there are no movements in or out of any markets. We might account for the absence of movement into the market in terms of a correlation with monopoly control procedures such as aggressive trade wars, takeovers, and trusts. Although we might in shorthand say that the Mafia thus caused members of some of the other organizations not to sell in that market, while causing members of some of the other organizations not to sell in any other market, we would in effect mean that both the Mafia and those other organizations know that there are rules governing, for example, access to monopoly markets. In this situation what is obvious is that the monopolist constructs the particular substantive instances of them. The exchanges that occur are made possible by people constituting them according to some underlying rule(s). The exchanges that do not occur are made impossible because people similarly constitute them, this time by 'exclusion rules'.

Rules are not simply a property of actors exercising power, but are constitutive of relations between them. And these relations are of differential power and interest. It would be a mistaken assumption to argue from resources as 'things in the world', such as control over uncertainty, to power as something determined by responses to these resources. Doubtless Dahl is correct in that power is sometimes relational, but not in the Newtonian way that he (and implicitly, those who accept his definition) assumes it to be. Its relational aspect is constituted by an assumption on the part of each party that the other knows that there *are* rules, which does not necessarily entail knowing *the* rules.

Crozier's (1964) discussion of rules is almost entirely within the context of the usual interpretation given to Weber (1968) on rules; that is, as the formal codifications of bureaucracy. Had he interpreted Weber on this topic in terms of 'enacted' rules, a legitimate interpretation, then his discussion of power as a concept at both the discretionary level, and at the level of the structure of the organization, could have been made in the same terms. These terms would remain faithful to the meaningful context in which people work.

Crozier (1964) fails to extend the theory of power beyond a technology of manipulation exercised by man as decision maker, with respect to the effectiveness of such decisions. Crozier (1964) thoughtlessly deploys Dahl's (1957) concept of power. He does so in a context which is concerned to develop insights about the different ways in which organization members define their situations, and the limits on their rationality in doing so. His indebtedness to Simon (1957) and March and Simon (1958) provides the concept of 'bounded rationality':

> Such an approach allows us to deal with the problems of power in a more realistic fashion. It enables us to consider, at the same time, the rationality of each agent or group of agents, and the influence of the human relations factors that limit their rationality (Crozier, 1964, p. 150).

His analysis focuses on the ways in which members of an organization can manipulate their situations in such a way as to maintain or enlarge their areas of discretion within the conditions of membership, which are set by a 'controlling group' (Simon, 1957) or an 'organizational coalition' (Cyert and March, 1963). They achieve this manipulation through the use of strategies to protect their interests as they perceive them. Their perceptions are located in the prevailing values of members of the French bureaucracy, which in turn are seen as 'reflecting' French society. Action is seen as situational, resulting from meaningful and bounded rationality, which includes a varying commitment to the ongoing system of interactions, structured as it is by the rules in which they operate.

52

What Hickson *et al.* (1971) do is to take both a similar concept of power (deriving from Kaplan, 1964), and a similar stress on uncertainty. Where they differ from Crozier (1964) is in their neglect of the structural and cultural forms of power to which Crozier (1964) makes reference.

Hickson *et al.* (1971) manage to ignore prior questions of 'rules of the game' which effectively structure the types of issues (and hence outcomes) that arise for power to be manifested. They do this because they dwell in the tradition of an exchange theory allied to a behavioural concept of power, in a functionalist systems framework. The implications of the systems framework and the behavioural concept of power have been considered. What remains is to show how Hickson *et al.* (1971) make Dahl's (1957) implicit notion of an exchange explicit. They do so by making Dahl's (1957) concept of a 'social relationship' one which is determined by the 'division of labour'. This division of labour creates the interdependent relationships which then determine 'power relations' (Hickson *et al.*, 1971, p. 217). The exercise of power is then explicitly related to the author of exchange theory, Blau (1964), in terms of which 'sub-units can be seen to be exchanging control of strategic contingencies one for the other' (Hickson *et al.*, 1971, p. 222), in order to acquire power through the exchange.

## Rules in exchange

The underlying assumption of an exchange theory such as that of Blau's (1964) is that each party to a potential exchange has something which the other(s) also value and want. A typical exchange would be where each party preferred the other(s) to make the greatest contribution, but would himself be willing to do so rather than to discontinue the exchange. Although both actors have shared interests, they diverge on grounds of self-interest. Although both want the exchange to persist, neither wants to make the greatest contribution. While the parties concerned profit from an exchange they have an interest in maintaining it, although self interest leads them to wish to benefit most from any exchange.

Blau's exchange theory stresses the tendency of any participants to try to control the behaviour of others in their own interests. Sometimes only very partial control can be effected, where both have valuable resources to contribute. On some other occasions one party may have nothing immediate to offer. Blau (1964) suggests that such a person in need has several strategies open to him in principle; he can force the other to help him; he can get help from someone else, or he has to do without the valued resource. If he cannot adopt any of these solutions, he has no option other than to submit to power.

53

Power is distinguished from sheer coercion. In the latter, the powerless party would not have a choice. He would be unable to opt for punishment, or withdrawal of facilities, as a sanction for non-compliance. A man thrown into prison would be physically coerced, unless he had voluntarily resigned his freedom in order to save his life. Had he done the latter, then this could be construed as an exchange. Where there is no robbery there must be fair exchange, in however tautologous a sense.

This tradition, although it provides us with a way of seeing exchanges occurring, says nothing about the rules governing exchange processes, or how these operate, or how they have developed.

Exchange-based theories may provide some insight into some aspects of power, but how significant are these in themselves? The insight that they can obtain are on the surface level of appearances, on power as manifested in the outcomes of particular exchanges. Exchange-based theories ignore the 'deep structure' of these appearances as this exists in the particular issues over which power is displayed. Such a deep structure might be uncovered by a research derived from Bachrach and Baratz's (1971b) critique of 'pluralism'.

That critiques such as this may be made of work such as a 'strategic contingency' theory is no surprise. Where thought is constrained within narrowly defined notions of tradition, untouched by conceptualization in dialogue with either everyday life, or other traditions, then one would expect it merely to reiterate the tradition as an affirmation of faith rather than reason.

Where the 'strategic contingency' theory fails, as does the tradition it affirms, is in its neglect of Weber, and to a lesser extent, Simmel. These writers afford us a point of access not only into an account of the concept of 'rule' in its relation to power and domination, but do so in the context of a discussion of the problem of 'rationality'. In returning to their work we are afforded the vital link between discussions of 'rule' and power; and discussions of 'rules' in the more recent phenomenological tradition. At the same time, the twin emphasis in Weber on 'rule' and 'rationality' enables us to conduct a rational enquiry into the topic proposed by Bachrach and Baratz's (1971a; 1971b) critique as being at the centre of a discussion of 'issues' – their rationality. What their critique recommends is research based on a theoretically elaborated model of the relationships between particular issues. In short, it demands an account of the 'rationality' of power in whatever scene is under study, a rationality under whose domination issues become a transparently 'ruled' phenomenon. Such a perspective would not propose that the power displayed in any one exchange was a chance outcome of that exchange alone, but would instead look at its possibility.

The re-turn sketched at the end of Chapter 2 is now mapped in more detail. The itinerary is as follows. In the next chapter, Chapter 4, retrieve the concept of rule from the work of Weber and Simmel. In Chapter 5, compare this with more recent statements in phenomenological sociology, in order to see to what extent we can use these to provide a research perspective which will allow us to research people actually using rules in the structurally significant way that Weber and Simmel recommend. Having done that, then the way is clear for a final re-turn back to the grounds of everyday life, in order to try and uncover the sense of rule provided in the previous chapters.

# 4 Weber and Simmel: power, rule and domination

The crucial turn in the 'strategic contingency' theory of Hickson *et al.* (1971) is that which renders its version of chess such a strange affair. Because 'less dependence' is transformed into 'power', then the power of a piece in the game comes to be seen as a function of the piece's current position on the board, rather than as a result of what the rules of chess are conventionally like.

This interpretation of 'less dependence' as 'power' derives from Crozier's (1964) choice of Dahl (1957) on 'power' rather than Weber (1968).

Max Weber's definitions of *Macht* and *Herrschaft* have typically been taken to translate as 'power' and 'authority', after Parsons and Henderson (1947). Given the difficulties associated with this translation (see Banton, 1972; Gouldner, 1971), one may sympathize with Crozier's (1964) decision to define power in what appears to be Dahl's (1957) clear-cut way, rather than in Weber's formulation of *Macht* as, in Parsons and Henderson's (1947) terms: 'the probability that an actor within a social relationship will be in a position to carry out his own will despite resistance, regardless of the basis on which this probability rests' (Weber, 1947, p. 152).

At a first glance little real difference would appear to separate the two formulations. Both refer to some notion that one party to a social relationship imposes his definition of a situation upon another party, and uses this as an imperative for action. Further Dahl's (1957) text is imbued with notions of probability, which, in Parsons's interpretation of Weber is a constitutive feature of his definition of power.

Dahl (1968) claims to be following a tradition instituted by Weber and continued by seminal political scientists such as Lasswell and Kaplan. What is concealed by Dahl in his reference to Weber is his own location in a tradition which I interpret as virtually opposing Weber at every instance. These are important issues, in that it is because of a neglect of the Weberian context in theorizing about the organization that Hickson *et al.* (1971) are able to interpret Crozier's (1964) remarks on uncertainty as pointing to a theory of power based on control of 'strategic contingency'.

The source of any specifically sociological theorizing on power must be located in Max Weber's work, and as Banton (1972) has pointedly remarked, 'A sociologist's approach to such questions has to begin with Max Weber's analysis. . . . It must start from what Weber wrote, and not from Talcott Parsons's solutions to the difficult problems of rendering the texts into English' (Banton, 1972, p. 86).

That confusion exists as to the meaning in translation of 'power' in Weber's work is not to be taken as a need for definitive remedial work on Weber's texts. What makes Weber's work interesting as a topic is its continuing indexicality, and the various forms of commitment it generates through the provocation that this offers to readers and authors to display their theorizing on it. This theorizing in turn serves to magnify and regenerate the contradictions inherent in Weber. This is then taken as a display of these writers' commitments to Weber's own display of his evolving self. In the final analysis we interpret these, and each and every theorist's work, as a display of a tradition. This tradition brings to light that theoretic activity, rendered in discourse, which, because its language is common with the writing that it addresses, serves both to bind its writer to that writing's authority, while at the same time serving to display that self the theorist formulates.

Consider the context in which Weber developed his concern with questions of power. His definitions of *Macht* and *Herrschaft* are introduced among 'the fundamental concepts of sociology'. As such they are constituted within a particular mode of sociology, that of an 'interpretive sociology'. They occur *after* a discussion of social relationships, which is prefaced by a discussion of social action. Both these concepts are implicit in the definition he gives to *Macht* and *Herrschaft*. *Herrschaft* is the basis for his typology of legitimacy upon which a relationship of domination may rest, expressed in terms of motives (see Weber, 1968).

In addition to Weber's analytical discussion, we can also consider his substantive studies. In an early study of agrarian unrest in German territories east of the river Elbe, Weber described the power of the Prussian Junkers not only in terms of 'economic power', but also in terms of a context of 'domination'. This existed in the strongly defined and traditional superordinate relationship over the populace which was enjoyed by the Junkers.

Weber later argued in his essay on *The Protestant Ethic and the Spirit of Capitalism* (1930), that these relationships of central and dominant authority were sanctified by Lutheranism, the religious ethic of these territories.

Weber's model of sociology which guided these empirical studies defined it as 'A science concerning itself with the interpretive understanding of social action in order to arrive at a causal explanation of its course and consequences' (Weber, 1968, p. 4). In order to facilitate 'explanation' Weber stressed that concepts formulated according to this model should be such as 'to determine that there is a probability, which in the rare ideal case can be numerically stated but is always in some sense calculable, that a given observable event (overt or subjective) will be followed or accompanied by another event' (Weber, 1968, pp. 11–12). This ideal of 'probability' is then applied to the definition of a social relationship: 'Every social relationship thus consists entirely and exclusively in the existence of a probability that there will be a meaningful course of action – irrespective for the time being of the basis of this probability' (Weber, 1968, p. 27). Weber then applies this definition of a social relationship to the two terms *Macht* and *Herrschaft*. These we may translate as 'power' and 'authority':

> Power is the probability that one actor within a social relationship will be in a position to carry out his will despite resistance, regardless of the basis on which this probability rests.
>
> Authority is the probability that a command with a given specific content will be obeyed by a given group of persons (Weber, 1968, p. 53).

Rex (1971, p. 25) has noted how modern positivism has given Weber a 'certain guarded recognition' for his use of notions such as 'probability'. Dahl's (1968) 'recognition' of Weber's work on power, and the seeming similarity of their definitions of power, may be seen simply as a result of his focusing solely on Weber's use of 'probability' in his definition of the German word *Macht*, a term over which some controversy has occurred. Banton (1972), for instance, doubts whether it actually translates as 'power'. Instead he translates it as 'might'. He suggests that *Herrschaft* is better interpreted as 'power'. *Herrschaft* is not even acknowledged to exist by Dahl (1968).

The English word 'power' stems from the French word *pouvoir*. *Pouvoir* means 'to be able'. Both the English word 'power' and the German word *Macht* are used not only to signify the capacity to do something, but also the exercise of that capacity. *Pouvoir* often refers to the exercise of this ability. In French, the notion of 'capacity' is what is meant by *puissance* (also see Emmet, 1953).

The etymology of the term 'power' originally expressed only a part of the meaning that it now has in English. *Macht*, like 'power', has to stand for both these uses. This, coupled with the fact that

Weber uses *Herrschaft* in two distinct contexts, is the source of the confusion.

In Weber's initial use of the term *Herrschaft* he refers to it as 'the probability that a command with a given specific content will be obeyed by a given group of persons' (Weber, 1968, p. 53). This concerns the exercise of a particular type of power in a particular type of situation. This would be the situation where a 'given specific content' is applied to a 'given group of persons'. The group of persons will be given by the *Herrschaftverband*, as would the content of the command.

The *Herrschaft* referred to in this 'probability' concept concerns the exercise of legitimate *Herrschaft*. Parsons and Henderson (Weber, 1947) translate this as 'authority'. In its most literal translation *Herrschaft* means 'rule' (as is shown by the invariable translation of *Herrschaftverband* as 'ruling organization'). 'Legitimate *herrschaft*' would thus mean 'legitimate, or non-coercive rule' as Freidrich (1964, p. 180, note I) argues. *Macht* would thus mean 'coercive rule'.

This is not the only concept of *Herrschaft* that Weber uses. In his discussion of the concept on pages 217 to 226 of *Economy and Society* (1968), he distinguishes three types of legitimacy upon which *Herrschaft* may rest, in an ideal abstraction from reality. These are types based upon tradition, charisma, and rational-legal precepts. His discussion of each of these in terms of their internal dynamics is made in terms of the concept of 'rule'.

The confusion surrounding the meaning of the concepts *Macht* and *Herrschaft* diminishes, if *Herrschaft* can be translated as 'rule'.

In the previous chapter I argued that there existed a deep and underlying similarity between the seemingly different traditions of work that made up the 'strategic contingency' theory. In each instance it was necessary to use a concept of 'rule' to make any sense out of the concepts of power that these traditions proposed. For instance, it was only through a concept of 'rule' that Dahl's notion of 'power' could be interpreted meaningfully. Without it one is left in a meaningless world in which red lights and policemen have some inexplicable propensity to 'cause' traffic to stop. Any such interpretation of Weber would be totally at odds with his concerns (see Weber, 1949, pp. 159–60).

Underlying the 'authority' of policemen and traffic lights is a more 'meaningful' concept of 'rule' which makes reference to the interpretive work that people engage in, when they make sense of the world. This more meaningful concept of 'rule' is to be found in Weber's concept of 'rational-legal authority'.

Because of his discussion of the ideal type of legal-rational bureaucracy in terms of formal rules, it might be considered that Weber

meant by rule the formal codifications of courses of 'correct' behaviour. This is the case in his discussion of 'legal norms' and 'abstract
rules' (Weber, 1968, p. 217), but, this discussion occurred

> within the sphere of power in question – which in the case of
> territorial bodies is the territorial area – who stand in certain
> social relationships or carry out forms of social action which in
> the order governing the organization have been declared to be
> relevant (Weber, 1968, p. 217).

Power in the organization occurs within 'the order governing the
organization', the 'structure of dominancy':

> the validity of an order means more than the existence of a
> uniformity of social action determined by custom or self interest
> . . . the content of a social relationship (will) be called an order
> if the conduct is, approximately or on the average, oriented
> towards determinable 'maxims'. Only then will an order be
> called 'valid' if the orientation towards these maxims occurs,
> among other reasons, also because it is in some appreciable way
> regarded by the actor as in some way obligatory or exemplary
> for him (Weber, 1968, p. 31).

If a social relationship is not to be meaningless, and if it does not
rest on an incomprehensible statistical probability, there must be
some grounds for suggesting that one party to a social relationship
such as 'power' will fulfil the other's expectations. This grounding
is located in the party's belief that they are subject to an 'order', a
'structure of dominancy' which is 'regarded by the actor as in some
way obligatory or exemplary for him'.

This order presents features of a scene to which the actor orients
his action. As such, and in the tradition of an 'interpretive sociology',
it is a perceived order, rather than an external 'thing' to which the
actor reacts. This notion of an order is presented in the concepts of
'convention' or 'law' in so far as

> It is possible for action to be oriented to an order in other ways
> than through conformity with its prescriptions, as they are
> generally understood by the actors. Even in the case of evasion
> or disobedience, the probability of their being recognized as
> valid norms may have an effect on action. This may, in the first
> place, be true from the point of view of sheer expediency.
> A thief orients his action to the validity of the criminal law in
> that he acts surreptitiously. . . . Furthermore there may exist at
> the same time different interpretations of the meaning of the
> order. In such cases, for sociological purposes, each can be said
> to be valid insofar as it actually determines the course of action.

The fact that, in the same social group, a plurality of contradictory systems of order may all be recognized as valid, is not a source of difficulty for the sociological approach. Indeed, it is even possible for the same individual to orient his action to contradictory systems of order. This can take place not only at different times, as in everyday occurrence, but even in the case of the same concrete act. A person who fights a duel follows the code of honour; but at the same time, insofar as he either keeps it secret or conversely gives himself up to the police, he takes account of the criminal law (Weber, 1968, p. 32).

Weber implies by his use of the phrase 'different interpretations of the meaning of an order' that there is no one-to-one correspondence between an objectively real world and the ways in which people perceive that world. Members of the same organization are capable of holding the variety of interpretations which Schutz (1962) calls 'multiple realities'. What might seem to be the same object or events appear to have different meanings for different people. As Wittgenstein might have put it, different uses engender different meanings.

Weber (1968, p. 33) suggests that the reason why actors orient their actions towards a similarly defined order, despite these differences, is because their individual enactments are guided by collectively recognized and publicly available rules:

economic action, for instance, is oriented to knowledge of the relative scarcity of certain available means to want satisfaction, in relation to the actor's state of needs and to the present and probable action of others, insofar as the latter affects the same resources. But at the same time, of course, the actor in his choice of economic procedures naturally orients himself *in addition* to the conventional and legal rules which he recognizes as valid, that is, of which he knows that a violation on his part would call forth a given reaction of other persons (Weber, 1968, p. 33).

Given that the order is 'oriented to', then how one orients towards it becomes problematic. One can no longer consider that an 'order' is merely a formal codification, but rather that it is a 'structure of dominancy'. Power in the organization is embedded in such a 'structure of dominancy':

Without exception every sphere of social action is profoundly influenced by structures of dominancy. In a great number of cases the emergence of a rational association from amorphous social action has been due to domination and the way in which it has been exercised. Even where this is not the case, the structure of dominancy and its unfolding is decisive in determining the form of social action and its orientation towards a 'goal'.

61

Indeed, domination has played the decisive role in the economically most important social structures of the past and present.
Viz, the manor on the one hand, and the large scale capitalistic
enterprise on the other (Weber, 1968, p. 941).

A 'structure of dominancy', as an 'order' towards which one 'orients'
one's behaviour, does not necessarily

utilize in every case economic power for its foundation and
maintenance. But in the vast majority of cases, and indeed in
the most important ones, this is just what happens in one way
or another and often to such an extent that the mode of applying
economic means for the purpose of maintaining domination, in
turn, exercises a determining influence on the structure of
domination. Furthermore, the great majority of all economic
organizations, among them the most important and the most
modern ones, reveal a structure of dominancy. The crucial
characteristics of any form of domination, may it is true, not be
correlated in any clearcut fashion with any particular form of
economic organization. Yet the structure of dominancy is in
many cases both a factor of great economic importance and,
at least to some extent a result of economic conditions
(Weber, 1968, p. 942).

Weber has now moved from a discussion of the specific content
of *Herrschaft* where it is 'the probability that a command with a
given specific content will be obeyed by a given group of persons',
to a discussion of its 'form'. The formal structure of domination is
experienced in terms of differing substantive types of rule, which
make probable obedience to authority distributed substantively
according to type of rule. Different types of rule will exist in different
'orders' to which one 'orients' one's behaviour. This will thus afford
a differential 'probability' that differing types of command, under
differing conditions of 'rule' will be obeyed. Such commands would
be 'authored' by the 'rule'. They would be what we might call
'authoritative' commands. Submission to such a command we would
call 'authority'. The two types of *Herrschaft* as respectively, authority
and domination, seem to be somewhat similar to the two types of
power distinguished by *puissance* and *pouvoir*. Authority refers to
the 'exercise' of a 'rule' located in a 'structure of domination', in
which resides the 'capacity' to be able to 'exercise' that 'rule' more
or less authoritatively.

*Puissance* and *pouvoir*, and 'authority' and 'domination' appear
to re-present 'Two Faces of Power' (Bachrach and Baratz, 1971).
One face of power is that embodied in concrete decision-making.
This concerns the outcomes of specific issues. What the other face

of power presents is the possibility that these decisions are already 'authorized'. They are authorized because the issue which was decided actually reached the public arena. It need not have. It could have been suppressed, rejected, or simply never raised as an issue, perhaps because it was 'impossible', or simply 'taken-for-granted'. This second face of power would seem to present the kind of power that is meant by *puissance*. This is the prior capacity to be able to 'exercise' power at all. This Weber seems to have rendered as the 'structure of domination' articulated through different types of 'rule'.

Weber's discussion of domination was conducted in full knowledge of Simmel's (1971) parallel discussion (see Rex, 1971; Weber, 1972).

Simmel (1971), like Weber (1930) may be interpreted as arguing implicitly that domination is in part a function of the symbolic content of widely held traditional ideas which are expressed in the language in use in a particular situation. It is through this language and ideas that

Society confronts the individual with precepts. He becomes habituated to their compulsory character until the cruder and subtler means of compulsion are no longer necessary. His nature may thereby be so formed or reformed that he acts by these precepts as if on impulse, with a consistent and direct will which is not conscious of any law. . . . Or else, the law, in the form of a command which is carried by the authority of the society, does live in the individual consciousness, but irrespective of the question whether society actually backs it with its compulsory power or even itself supports it solely with the explicit will. Here then, the individual represents society to himself. The external confrontation, with its suppressions, liberations, changing accents, has become an interplay between his social impulses and the ego impulses in the stricter sense of the word; and both are included by the ego in the larger sense. . . . At a certain higher stage of morality, the motivation of action lies no longer in a real-human, even though super-individual power; at this stage, the spring of moral necessities flows beyond the contrast between individual and totality. For, as little as these necessities derive from society, as little do they derive from the singular reality of individual life. In the free conscience of the actor, in individual reason, they only have their bearer, the locus of their efficacy. Their power of obligation stems from these necessities themselves, from their inner, super-personal validity, from an objective ideality which we must recognize, whether or not we want to. . . . *The content*, however, which fills these forms is (not necessarily but often) the societal requirement. But this requirement no longer operates by means of its social impetus, as it were, but rather as if it had undergone a metempsychosis into a norm which must be satisfied for its own sake, not for my sake nor for yours (Simmel, 1971, p. 119).

Simmel makes the distinction between the 'form' of domination and its 'content'. We also found this distinction in Weber. The 'precepts' of 'society' inhabit the individual. These are the specific 'content' of the 'form' of domination. While domination as a 'formal' concept is a necessary feature of social life, its specific content is not. Simmel asserts of 'the spring of moral necessities' of formal domination, that in 'individual reason', in 'the free conscience of the actor', then we 'only have their bearer, the locus of their efficacy'. What is this 'their' that Simmel references here? Simmel says of it that it is 'the motivation of action' which 'lies no longer in a real-human, even though super-individual power', whose necessary form is filled by 'a social requirement . . . which must be satisfied for its own sake'.

Simmel (1971, pp. 100–6) has earlier discussed the topic of subordination under a ruler. What this subsequent discussion would seem to suggest is that we should re-think subordination under a ruler as a specific being, and regard it instead as a subordination under a 'bearer', a 'locus' of 'the spring of moral necessities, the motivation of actions'. Individual man, individual rationality is thus the site of a higher and more powerful rationality. According to Simmel, this most powerful rationality is that in which an 'objective principle' is regarded as a 'concrete object (which) governs the domination' (Simmel, 1971, p. 116).

In concluding this chapter on Weber and Simmel's use of concepts such as 'domination', I will pull together the strands that unite my discussion of their work, and the major discussion of power.

Weber defines the concept of 'power' in a way which is apparently not too different from Dahl's definition of the term. It is only seemingly so. It seems to be so only if one neglects the context of interpretive sociology in which Weber's discussion of *Macht* and *Herrschaft* took place. When one looks at this context it is confused by problems of translating these two terms into English. This difficulty is compounded by Weber's having used the word *Herrschaft* in two distinct ways. One of these can be translated as 'authority'. This is a special kind of power, 'legitimate' power exercised in a specifically limited setting, over a specifically given group of persons, concerning a specifically given content. In the roots of English usage this would be similar to the French term *pouvoir*, meaning the exercise of a capacity. Weber's other use of *Herrschaft* concerns the basis, or grounds, for that capacity. This is a 'formal' concept which concerns the structure of 'domination', as we would translate *Herrschaft* in this context. The particular form of domination in terms of its substantive content varies as to types of 'rule'.

The concept of 'rule' links the structural notions explicit in 'domination' to the actions of ordinary people. Different types of 'rule' provide differing 'orders' to which people orient their behaviour. Domination is socially significant as a structural phenomenon because people orient their behaviour towards it. This formal concept of domination is discussed by Weber in terms of three types of rationality. Simmel argues that the specific content of domination is formally that where 'an objective principle' is regarded by those subordinated to it, as a 'concrete object (which) governs the domination' (Simmel, 1971, p. 116). If we were to apply this to Weber's notion of the three types of substantive rationality, then we could say that each mode of rationality represents the juxtaposition of an 'objective principle' regarded as a 'concrete object', by those subject to it. They are subject to it because they orient their action towards a principle so regarded. A principle, an idea, takes on a concrete and governing function in reality.

In Weber, this rationality, 'in the vast majority of cases, and indeed in the most important ones' can be seen to 'utilize . . . economic power for its foundation and maintenance' (Weber, 1968, p. 942). Such 'economic power' as a 'concrete object' is the realization of an 'objective principle', as in a contemporary example, 'rational-legal bureaucracy'. In this type of organization an individual who wielded legitimate authority would do so on the basis of a

> legal norm . . . established by agreement or by imposition, on grounds of expediency or value rationality or both, with a claim to obedience, (to those) . . . who stand in certain social relationships or carry out forms of social action which in the order governing the organization have been declared to be relevant (Weber, 1968, p. 217).

These norms, usually intentions collected together, form a 'consistent system of abstract rules' whose administration consists of 'the application of these rules to particular cases' by a superior who is himself subject 'to an impersonal order by orienting his actions to it in his own dispositions and commands' (Weber, 1968, p. 217).

The codified, consistent body of abstract rules is the basis of authority. The 'impersonal order' that a superior is subject to would be the realization of an 'objective principle' in a 'concrete object'; that is 'economic power'. It is to his own understanding of this that the superior orients 'his actions . . . dispositions and commands'.

It would be in the superior's 'own understanding' of the 'objective principle' and 'concrete object' that is the realm of 'economic power' within which he works, that we can conduct research into the 'neglected face of power'.

In this 'understanding' we can locate what ethnomethodologists have called the 'background assumptions' of everyday life. We can investigate these to study the ways in which the particular issues over which power is exercised have their own mode of rationality in the organization.

But this is to move ahead before we have the means to do so. These matters must wait till the next chapter. Our return to Weber is completed. Next we must explore contemporary phenomenological attempts at a structural concept of rule, to see to what extent they provide the means to effect the research which is necessary to explicate Weber's analysis.

# 5  Social rules and the grammatical analogy

## Rules

In my interpretation of Weber (and Simmel) the concept of 'rule' provides the crucial link between the structural concept of 'domination' and the action concept of 'power'. 'Domination' refers to the form within which action is constrained. Weber regards 'power' as one of the specific social relationships which are within the scope of his definition of a 'social action' (Weber, 1968). The concept of 'rule' is the decisive link between the persons' social action of power, and the 'authorizations' of domination. It is these which define the arena in which power comes to be exercised.

What preceded this return to Weber was a critical look at some contemporary traditions of theorizing about power. These comprised exchange theory, behavioural theory and strategic contingencies theory. Each of these was found deficient. Their deficiency provided their seeming difference with an underlying unity. This unity was one of necessity. For these theories to be read as depicting a possible society like that of our ordinary common-sense world, in which people interpret phenomena, rather than react to them as if they were automata, then we have to supply some notion of people theorizing about their own existence in terms of commonly held criteria. These are 'interpretive rules' that people use to make sense of otherwise meaningless phenomena such as traffic lights. The failure of these traditions in this respect is the failing of any tradition in 'dialogue' solely with itself. Reasonable theorizing addresses not only itself, but also other traditions of thought, as well as everyday life. And everyday life articulates what the theory leaves unsaid.

## Power and intention

In our ordinary speech we distinguish between someone *having* power and someone *exercising* power. This is a similar sort of distinction to that between *pouvoir* and *puissance*. Using Weber's discussion of 'rules' some connections have been made between the two types of power. Within the type distinguished as an exercise of power, some discussion has taken place over whether or not to restrict the definition of power only to instances where intended effects are produced.

Bertrand Russell (1967) is perhaps the most distinguished proponent of the view that power is only exercised when an intended effect is secured. Other writers such as Wrong (1968) have followed Russell in this, on the simple grounds that almost all actions have unintended as well as intended effects. He cites the following as an instance: 'a dominating and protective mother does not intend to feminize the character of her son' (Wrong, 1968, p. 676). As White (1971) points out, the centre of debate on the topic has been 'whether or not an intention must be complied with for power to be exercised' (White, 1971, p. 749).

Consider the following example as an instance of power where the presence of intention might be thought equivocal. The directors of one firm decide to take over the business of another firm, a competitor in some of its markets. During the following years the vocabulary of 'shake-out', 'efficiency', and 'rationalization' is applied in an analysis of the new conglomerate. The result of this analysis is that very many thousands of former employees are made redundant. Have the directors of the new conglomerate (which after a recent example we might call 'G.E.C.') exercised power over these people in implementing the take-over in the first place? Did they exercise intention? Is the exercise of intention necessary for an exercise of power?

We might, if we could locate all of G.E.C.'s directors, and if they would agree to talk to us, ask them if they intended to produce such socially redundant labour. They may or may not agree, or they might equivocate, or deny it. It might be that they did not 'intend' it – really it was government action, or the restrictive practices of unions, or the bank rate, which precipitated it. Of course, we may not be able to locate them, or we might not be granted an audience.

From a Wittgensteinian (1968) perspective then, the way in which we assemble 'intention' would be the measure of its presence. 'Intention' would not be owned by the person, but would be a feature of our ordinary ways of granting or theorizing its presence.

To recommend that we should theorize the possibility of 'intention' in this way would not be to locate it as something possessed prior to an action, which somehow anticipated and predetermined the deed before its execution. Instead it would be to describe the grounds which are analytically prior for someone to even invoke intention as a method for making a scene seem recognizably power-full.

Intention in power may be as meaningful as it is in daily life. We somehow or other decide whether or not people intended to be rude, insulting, thoughtless, etc. through formulating people as intending or not intending the action in question. And we do this not on idiosyncratic, personal, or whimsical grounds, but on a more or less known-in-common and inter-subjective basis. The repertoires we display in doing something like ascribing an intention is thus a fairly routine and recognizable part of what any socially competent person takes for granted. We might characterize this knowledge as knowledge of a loosely conceived corpus of 'rules', that people typically use to theorize their ordinary interactions. Sociologically these rules may be located in the ways in which people treat occasions as an occasion for an intentional rudeness, insult, etc. The sociological import of intention would reside in repertoires for producing treatments of such things, as an occasioned activity, rather than in the thing itself.

As a sociological topic intention must be located not in the person (as it might be for psychology), but in discourse about the person, where such discourse continues on the basis of conventional social rules of behaviour.

To propose that power was exercised intentionally is to say that the people involved in its exercise may be defined by the sociologist as actors who orientate their actions towards rules which all may be said to partake of in some degree. If power were confined only to those instances where intended effects were achieved (then quite apart from knowing just what these would look like, or how they could possibly operate), important and everyday instances of power would be beyond our theoretical grasp. It would not be possible to say of Chancellors of the Exchequer that they had power over the economy because they can affect investment decisions through making investment grants more or less available. How could the Chancellor be in an intentional relationship with the people comprising the economy unless 'investment' is a rule-guided activity? Given that there are rules concerning investment, and that a number of key investors act on these, and that one rule is 'Invest at the best yield', then the Chancellor and investors can be assumed to know these and to act on them accordingly. Thus can Chancellors exercise power.

Introducing the concept of 'intention' in anything other than the way suggested by the notion of actors orienting themselves to rules, can only lead to confused and quite absurd analyses. The addition of 'intention' to stipulations concerning the theoretical presence of power, where 'power' is defined in terms of its 'exercise', adds to the initial causal chain, and merely compounds the errors of the definition.

The terms in which this discussion of 'intention' has been conducted derive from recent writings in philosophy (such as Ryle, 1949; Shibbles, 1967; Anscombe, 1957; Hampshire, 1959), particularly those of Melden (1961) and Hart (1960). In Hart's phrase, 'intention' would be a 'defeasible' concept, because our knowledge of 'intentions' is assembled in the light of our total knowledge of past, present and future situations. Our sociological knowledge of the 'intention' of another person is achieved by weighing whatever someone might tell us his 'intention' was, against our conventional knowledge of that 'intention' which would 'produce' a specific type of action. Where others do not inform us of their 'intention', then we rely on our conventional rule-guided means for ascribing 'intention'. 'Intention', as a sociological concept, could not be said to be a 'causally productive' notion, if only because, as Melden (1961) has observed, doing and acting are epistemologically prior to ideas, and ontologically inseparable from them. Thought derives from, and assumes, 'doing'.

Few sociologists have considered the implications of discussions . such as these for their models of social action. One exception is the early work on 'motives' of Blum and McHugh (1971; also see Blum et al., 1974). They argue, using 'motive' as their analytic example, that the rules that sociology deals with may be located as a 'public' phenomenon, displayed in particular in the ways in which people use language. Following Wittgenstein's (1968, par. 664) recommendation to look for the 'depth' and 'surface' grammar of an expression, Blum and McHugh (1971) argue that whatever motive is accomplished verbally is only the surface structure of motives. Motives have a deep structure. This deep structure concerns the grounds that could provide the analytic possibility of whatever it is that is actually said.

Cicourel (1973) provides the most articulated model of this deep/ surface distinction with regard to rules. If this model can provide us with some way of moving from what is said, in terms of specific issues that arise for power to be exercised over, to the deep structure that provides for these, then this would afford a means of analyzing the rationality of power in the terms suggested in the previous chapter. These concern the ways in which power may be seen in not only decision-making, but also non-decision-making.

## Deep/surface rules

The deep/surface structure model of rules has come into use in sociology under the impact of structural linguistics, and ethnomethodology. The use derives from a model of 'transformational grammar'. This suggests that the competence of a native speaker of a language to generate and understand grammatically correct utterances, is derived from a model of a deep structural grammar with which the pre-coded and 'intended' utterance is first formulated, according to base or phase structure. This is an elaborated model of what is actually uttered. The 'transformation' rules transform the raw material of the initial elaboration into a grammatically competent utterance. These transformation rules enable the creativity of linguistically competent members who generate novel utterances form a competent grasp of the deep structure.

Chomsky has noted that

several reservations are necessary when structural linguistics is used as a model in this way. For one thing, the structure of a phonological system is of very little interest as a formal object. . . . The significance of structuralist phonology . . . lies not in the formal properties of phonemic systems but in the fact that a fairly small number of features that can be specified in absolute language-independent terms appears to provide the basis for the organization of all phonological systems. . . . Furthermore, to a greater and greater extent, current work in phonology is demonstrating that the real richness of phonological systems lies not in the structural patterns of phonemes but rather in the intricate systems of rules by which these patterns are formed, modified and elaborated (Chomsky, 1968, p. 65).

Cicourel (1973) who has employed the deep/surface structure model also adopted by Chomsky (1968), has contrasted his ethnomethodological emphasis upon 'the interpretive work required to recognize that an abstract rule exists which would fit a particular occasion' with a linguistic emphasis (such as Chomsky's) which minimizes 'the relevance of interactional content sensitive features when stressing the importance of syntactic rules for semantic analysis' (Cicourel, 1973, p. 100).

Ethnomethodology views linguistic rules as

normative constructions divorced from the cognitive reflection and ethnographic settings in which speech is produced and understood. . . . The researchers context-free description or account, however, presumes and tacitly relies on an intuitive use of ethnographic particulars and interpretive procedures that are never made explicit, though occasionally touched upon in an abstract way (Cicourel, 1968, p. 160).

From the point of view of ethnomethodology, which stresses the contextual and situational nature of language,

grammatical or logical utterances retain their rule-governed structure because they have been cleansed and divorced from their occasions of use, and other particulars about the biographies of the participants, the features of the setting tacitly taken into account, the reflexive thinking and use of talk and so on. . . . Linguists prefer to live with different kinds of conveniently constructed glosses, while the ethnomethodologist prefers to treat the glossing itself as an activity that becomes the phenomenon of interest while recognizing that no one can escape some level of glossing in order to claim knowledge about something (Cicourel, 1973, p. 109).

Cicourel (1973) develops his model of the deep/surface structure of rules, from an ethnomethodological perspective which regards the 'deep structure' in terms of what he refers to as 'Interpretive procedures':[1]

'Interpretive procedures' as opposed to 'surface rules' (norms) are similar to, but in many ways different from Chomsky's distinction between 'deep structure' (for rendering a semantic interpretation to sentences) and 'surface structure' (for designating phonetic interpretations to sentences), for interpretive procedures are constitutive of the members sense of social structure or organization. The acquisition of interpretive procedures provides the actor with a basis for assigning meaning to his environment or a sense of social structure, thus orienting him to the relevance of 'surface rules' or 'norms' (Cicourel, 1973, pp. 44–5).

The acquisition of interpretive procedures is 'permitted' by 'language' and meaning principles which must allow for:

the operation of memory and selection procedures which are consistent with pattern recognition or construction, active (searching for documentary evidence) and passive (taking the environment for granted, until further notice, as 'obvious' or 'clear') hypothesis testing, and must be congruent with the actor's ability to recognize and generate novel and 'identical' or 'similar behavioural displays' (Cicourel, 1973, p. 30).

Cicourel suggests that these 'interpretive procedures' are analogous to Chomsky's deep structure in that

The interpretive procedures provide a sense of social order that is fundamental for normative order (consensus or shared agreement) to exist or be negotiated or constructed . . . the learning and use of general rules or norms and their long term storage, always require interpretive procedures for recognizing the relevance of actual, changing scenes orienting the actor to possible courses of action, the organization of behavioural displays and their reflective evaluation by the actor (Cicourel, 1973, pp. 31–2).

These 'interpretive procedures', in 'a more refined conceptual frame' will be a set of invariant properties governing fundamental conditions of all interaction so as to indicate how the actor and observer decide what serves as definitions of 'correct' or 'normal' conduct or thought. The interpretive procedures would suggest the nature of minimal conditions that all interaction presumably would have to satisfy for actor and observer to decide that interaction is 'normal' or 'proper' and can be continued. The acquisition and use of interpretive procedures over time amounts to a cognitive organization that provides a continual sense of social structure (Cicourel, 1973, p. 33).

Cicourel's version of 'surface features'

intend(s) the idea that we are dealing with a practice, policy, or institution which is justified by some collectivity or system of rules that confers powers and carries obligations which are binding upon some collectivity. Perceived adherence to the rules, practices, or policies on the part of someone, implies the fulfilment of membership in the collectivity (Cicourel, 1973, p. 80).

What are these 'invariant interpretive procedures' which 'orient' the actor to the relevance of 'surface rules'?

Surprisingly these do not connect with the 'interpretive tradition' of Weber, as one might have expected from such a concern with a 'system of *rules* that confers *powers* and carries *obligations* which are *binding on some collectivity*'.

Instead of these resonances we find that Cicourel's 'interpretive procedures' are formal aspects of *any* competent speaker's articulations; Schutzian 'reciprocity of perspectives'; Garfinkel's 'et cetera assumptions', and so on (Cicourel (1973), provides his most complete documentation on pages 52–8 of *Cognitive Sociology*).

In Cicourel's model speakers are *free* on the conversational market to exchange talk as formally equal members, because the focus is on the formal aspects of talk, rather than on the occasions that generate the necessity for any particular accounts, or the relation of the concepts of that account to particular forms of life.

If these invariant procedures enable *practices justified by rules that confer powers and obligations*, one might have thought that deep structure grammar would have addressed the possibility of these practices, rules, powers, and obligations, instead of taking them for granted as a peripheral feature of speech (what it says). Cicourel's analytic concern is with how whatever is said shows the formal structure of any speech.

The freedom of the conversational market is as illusory as the freedom of individual man on the market of materialism, or temporal

73

man in the stream of individual consciousness. The freedom of the conversational market in Cicourel's rhetoric is as illusory as is the freedom of the economic market in utilitarian economics. The inner freedom that a man retains to generate novel utterances, or particular meanings, in any situation, is a pure 'idealist hoax', because, on this basis, any one state of being is as good as any other; the slave is as free as the master, the workers' 'powers' as good as the bosses.

This 'freedom' is achieved through affirming the autonomy of thought under rules equally shared by, and constitutive of, all competent members of any speech community. In so doing it severs thought from action, grammar from form of life; the focus is on what we say as it is shown, rather than on our sayings as actions shaped in the context of what it is possible for us to say.

Cicourel's (1973) version of language achieves a happy synthesis between an external constraining (linguistically) social order, and a socially internalized (linguistically) compliant actor. The 'ghost' is legislated out of the 'machine' into a disembodied Mind – language – in which all who participate share in the deity's grant of social order.

Cicourel's social order is engineered by moving from its appearance – 'consensus statements' – to its possibility in 'deep structure', and then back to its 'reality'. It would be mistaken to consider this a journey from the world of appearance (the cave) to the world of light (the sun).[2] It would be more accurate to consider this a movement deep within the conventions of the cave, within the security of appearance. By starting with order and replacing subjectivity with linguistically willed obedience, where language becomes the source of order, Cicourel's method remains securely within the social order tradition of sociology (see Dawe, 1970).

Cicourel's *Cognitive Sociology* recalls an earlier search for the rules of pure reason. However, Kant (as did Wittgenstein) admitted the possibility of decisions which cannot be accounted for by any rules. Kant realized that no system of rules could prescribe the procedures by which the rules themselves were to be applied. In applying the rules there exists an 'ultimate agency', as Polanyi (1969, p. 105) puts it. Kant remarks of this agency that it 'is what constitutes our socalled mother-wit' whose application in concrete instances 'is a skill so deeply hidden in the human soul that we shall hardly guess the secret trick that nature here employs' (Kant, *Critique of Pure Reason*, A.133; A.141).

Cicourel (1973) seeks to hide from what Kant called his 'motherwit' by claiming that Wittgenstein has brought this 'mother-wit' into the open (Cicourel, 1973, pp. 77–8). This is achieved because of the public nature of language, and its rule-guidedness even in contextual use. Cicourel (1973) appears to want to use Wittgenstein's remarks on language as a warrant for the abdication by an author of his responsibility for what he says. Instead he wants to formulate the knowledge and competence that any such saying 'demands' for its generation. The saying itself might as well be babble as brilliance, because it no longer matters. With such nihilism, anything said, including one's own work, is reduced to the incidental status of chatter, with no redeeming grace of being responsible chatter aware of its own authority and that of the theorizing power it denies. With such nihilism the theorist no longer exists. One no longer exists. One has been removed from one's work and one's sayings. Science authors the work, and speech is wrenched from the speaker, and his context of theorizing. Such is to be disabled by the enablements of positivism.

To be disabled thus is to use one's theorizing as one *used* by the rule of whatsoever theorizing power one theorizes the world with. This is to be as unremarkably mundane as everyday theorizers in that one allows forgetfulness to rule one's speech. One rules through, and is ruled by, concepts whose origins one neglects, or of which one is too much membered, to be able to speak. The result of this is that one proposes theories which can only be read as conventions.

## Rules, theorizing and power

Winch (1958) has observed that unless one can say of someone that he does something correctly or not 'there is no foothold in his behaviour in which the notion of a rule can take a grip: there is then no *sense* in describing his behaviour in that way, since everything he does is as good as anything else he might do' (Winch, 1958, p. 33).

The 'competences' that Cicourel (1973) describes derive their 'good' from linguistic usage. To apply his model to an analysis of power by attempting to seek something other than his 'invariant' cognitive competences, we would seemingly have to see members usage of power. What is central to the debate surrounding 'The Two Faces of Power' is the consensus that is not articulated, because it is not questioned. There is thus a good sense in which any study of power which employed Cicourel's standards of membership and usage would be *unable* to move beyond the ordinary ways in which power may be either opaque to those who labour under it, or unproblematic – 'the way things have always been'.

Shwayder (1965) has distinguished rules which 'restrict' from rules which 'enable', as respectively: 'those which operate to modify independently existing forms of behaviour and activity, and those which create new forms of behaviour and activity. The first are called *restrictions* and the latter *enabling* rules' (Shwayder, 1965, p. 265).

If we transpose Shwayder's (1965) 'Enabling Rules' and 'Restriction Rules' to the context of Cicourel's 'Deep' and 'Surface Structure' respectively, it becomes clear why it is that Cicourel's model enables us merely to conform to usage. Restriction rules modify the manner in which anything is done, because the person does what he does in 'conformity with what he takes to be the expectations of others' (Shwayder, 1965, p. 265). Action subject to restriction rules is the behavioural display that deep structure enables, which may include 'the way things have always been' – what we might term 'conventional behaviour'. We could formulate the restriction rules for any such 'conventional' display by imagining other possibilities that might have occurred. By moving only from what is the case to what could have enabled it, if the case that we are focusing on is an instance of Weber's conventional, restricted non-decision-making, then the deep structure will only enable what is the case for members; what is already restricted.

Criticisms of concepts of power in terms of notions of 'non-decisions' offer prescription of conceptual use in terms of the topic to which the concept refers. Although it may seem so obvious as to be hardly worth saying, the concept of power is always distinct from the topic of power. None the less, using the concept of power as conventionally located in recent traditions of work, important aspects of (the topic of) power are overlooked. This could only be in order if those concepts provided all our topic. That we can make those criticisms that have been made of these works suggests that this can not be considered to be the case.

These criticisms have been used to stress the importance of formulating a model of power which can account for the restrictions on issues, as well as the outcomes of these. In Weber's (1968) terms these 'outcomes' would display power. However, as Weber (1968) emphasized, any power exchanges occur in a context of domination which he discusses in terms of the substantive rationality of these, typified in three modes of ruling; the traditional, charismatic and bureaucratic. The movement is from domination → rules → power.

Weber was aware of the consequences of remaining merely on the surface of this movement, when he ironically observed

> If, as has occasionally been done, one looks upon the claims
> which the law accords to one person against one or more others
> as a power to issue commands to debtors or to those to whom
> no such claim is accorded, one may thereby conceive of the
> whole system of modern private law as the decentralization of
> domination in the hands of those to whom the legal rights are
> accorded. From this angle, the worker would have the power to
> command, i.e. 'domination' over the entrepreneur to the extent
> of his wage claim, and the civil servant over the King to the
> extent of his salary claim. Such a terminology would be rather

forced and, in any case, it would not be of more than provisional value since a distinction in kind must be made between 'commands' directed by the judicial authority to an adjudged debtor and 'commands' directed by a claimant himself prior to judgement (Weber, 1968, p. 942).

Domination is discussed by Weber in terms of 'rationality', a rationality which Simmel locates as that in which an 'objective principle' is frozen as a 'concrete object' which 'governs the domination' (Simmel, 1971, p. 116). 'Domination' underlies the surface appearance of power-exchanges, mediated by members' interpretive rules with which they orient their behaviour towards the 'icon' of domination.

I have earlier suggested that 'form of life' can be seen as 'iconic': a material thing whose being is inexplicable apart from the idea(l) projected on to it. The behaviour glossed over by the phrase 'form of life' indicates that it is behaviour which may be seen as the embodiment of actions oriented towards a standard or measure of activity (p. 35).

This implies that for 'domination' to be 'iconic' it must similarly be a 'form of life' – 'some matrix of human activity considered as having point, purpose and regularity'. The point, purpose and regularity of this activity derives from the ways in which people orient their behaviour towards the 'icon'.

The form of life of domination is iconic because any theorizing is only possible under the auspices of some icon of what good, sensible and intelligible practice is. Lay members of organizations, just as much as employed sociologists, are theorizers. They theorize their existence under icons of domination as we do. Our icons may differ, and we may be more or less reflexive about the form of life which provides for our theorizing, but the formal aspects are the same. An icon auth(e)orizes. It legitimates domination. It allows us to remain secure within whatever standard of good speech our community (our tradition) proposes. For me to employ 'form of life' as icon is merely to practice a heightened reflexivity before both intellectual traditions and everyday life.

Domination in everyday organizational life is effected through both 'an objective principle' and a 'concrete object'. Theorizing under the icon of this provides a substantive rationality, having point, purpose and regularity, exhibited in the deep structure of rules which enable the surface display of exchanges.

The previous argument may be summarized as I have done in Figure 2, on p. 78.

Power is about the outcomes of issues enabled by the rule of a substantive rationality which is temporally and institutionally located.

Underlying this rule is a specific form of domination. The progression is from domination → rules → power.

In Figure 2, this is represented in terms of the schematic inter-relation of concepts, topics and examples. The figure may be scanned both horizontally and vertically. The vertical axis presents the structural inter-relation between and within each set of concepts, topics, and examples. The horizontal axis presents the relations between each concept and its appropriate topic and example.

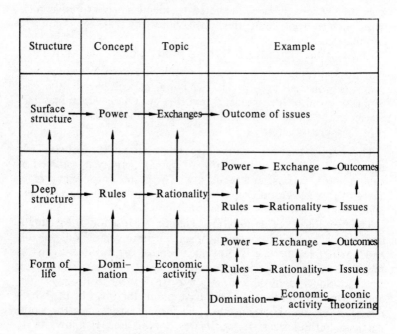

FIGURE 2   *The structure of power in organizations*

We can now recapitulate the return through conventional theorizing in these terms.

Under exchange, behavioural and strategic contingencies modes of theorizing power in the organization, analysis remains inveigled at the surface level of appearances, at power manifested in the outcome of particular exchanges. Cicourel's (1973) model allows us to make the move from the surface to the deep structure, but because of the direction of his movement (surface → deep structure) we would remain just as firmly within the concretely unproblematic world of (restricted) decision-making. The conventional theorizing of behavioural, exchange and strategic contingencies theory cannot possibly formulate the concrete society of everyday life, from which they have been criticized. The possible societies they propose can only be regarded as fictions pursued through method.

Using these modes of theorizing I found myself unable to address that which was my original reason for theorizing – the desire for knowledge of the neglected face of power. Under such traditions of theorizing, we relax our grasp of that desire which impulsed us, because our method will not assemble it. In the grasp of such theorizing power we find our theorizing fail us. Under the authority of usage our desire is similarly turned, away from the words to their production. To take the words themselves – the everyday speech – as our analytic authority is to find ourselves subject to the very same opacity which we might have wanted to penetrate with our theorizing – the opacity displayed in the omissions, the silences of our everyday life. The desire to theorize is lost to the babble of that which we might have wanted to penetrate. It would be as if we had become spectators lost in a film in which we had previously been extras, and having had a critical urge, had been desirous of knowing the directorial tricks which made the plot unfold as it did. But as spectators we only watch what we are allowed to see.

The argument summarized in Figure 2 suggests a movement from the analytically formulated depths to the world of·appearance as we can actually observe it and record it. In particular we can describe how decisions are arrived at, in terms of the substantive rationality of the organization and the explanatory schemata that this provides in terms of members' interpretive procedures. These organize and enable particular speeches in and about the organization, theorized under whatever icon of domination.

Analysis of power may be carried out in the way in which we can assemble members' speeches so as to provide for the possibility and the sense of these. They proceed on the basis of the common-sense understandings that participants share. Such understandings can be analysed by describing the deep grounds which make them sensible. These grounds provide the possibility of the surface display of action. They should not be considered as 'proofs'. They offer plausible accounts of the rationality of these actions, of what it is to be able to recognize that some things that people do may be stipulated as a doing of power, how it is that they are able to do so, and in so doing, how it is possible for us to recognize them doing such.

To begin to theorize thus is to complete the re-turn. Having made our return, it is not that power itself will be difficult or complex to grasp: it merely appears so for as long as our theorizing remains perspectively on the surface of things, rather than seeking to grasp what we see through formulating it. Vision requires distance. To see what is most clearly before our mind's eye, all that is necessary is to step back and look.

The following chapters do this by formulating the context of 'rationality' in which we see power in the organization.

# 6 Setting the scene

## Introducing the data

This chapter introduces data collected in the form of tape-recordings which were recorded over a three month period during the winter months of 1972–3. All these conversational materials were collected on a construction site in a northern town. I chose to conduct my field-work on a construction site because it was a setting with which I was already familiar.

During the summer of 1971 I had been employed by 'Construction Co.' as a joiner's labourer on one of their sites in 'Northern Town'. I used this acquaintance to gain access to another site in the same Northern Town, by making a request for research facilities through the Project Manager of the site on which I previously worked. In the winter of 1972 this was nearing completion at the same time that the other site was being started. This latter site (to which I gained access) was one on which a bus station and multi-storey car park were to be built as an integral development for the Corporation of Northern Town.

I came into the organization to collect field-work material for my research into 'power in organizations'. I concealed my purpose from people in the organization. To them I was researching into the ways in which people actually 'do organization' in organizations, as compared to the ways in which management books say they ought to do it. I struck a responsive chord. They told me that they also felt the lack of a certain fit between management theory and management practice. They applauded common-sense.

My access secured, my disguise constructed, I went to work. Because I was researching into what managers actually do, rather than what the books said they did, I requested that I might tape the daily proceedings in the project office. My request was granted. Some of these taped proceedings are to be found in the appendices.

Prior to attempting this field-work, I had spent nearly eighteen months reading some of the literature on 'power', as I attempted to formulate a strategy for my research. My reading, in particular as it led me into the area of 'theorizing', only served to convince me of the rhetorical function of such strategies in closing off lines of enquiry.

Strategies for data collection concern its policing rather than the production of the data themselves. We have no need to produce data because they surround us at every turn. Concern with strategies for collecting data is not so much a concern for production, because data is always at hand, but rather an affirmation of a tradition, a submission to the theorizing power of community. The collection of data is an assembly problem. How does one display the act of production in such a way as to affirm the law of community?

In earlier chapters I have argued that this affirmation of community has generated theorizing about power in which the 'real foundations of . . . enquiry' are consistently overlooked in theories 'entangled' in their own rules (Wittgenstein, 1968, pars 125; 129).

As an alternative to conducting research through the strategy of a particular tradition, I decided to employ the Wittgensteinian gambit (1968, pars 125–9) of disclaiming tradition in order to assemble 'reminders for a particular purpose'. In doing this one tacitly affirms commitment to a pragmatic strain which is shared by both interpretive sociology and ordinary language philosophy.

The structure of power in organizations did not seem to be a 'problem' when one came up close to it. What other people in the organization told me confirmed what I thought and what the Project Manager had said. He was the 'boss' on site. He had patiently shown me organization charts, and explained relationships, and it all seemed perfectly clear. The site was organized as a pyramid. He sat at the top of it. Below him on the 'staff' side were his Office Manager, Secretary, and Measurement Engineer. All other relationships were 'line' through the General Foreman. Below him were two foremen: the foreman joiner, and the foreman with responsibility for drains, sewers and concrete. Below these there were 'gangermen' with their respective groups of labourers, each 'gang' being assigned to a specific function.

The site was part of another pyramid. This pyramid was the company. At the top of the company was one man – he was the owner and managing director. Under his control were several special managers. Some of these were responsible for particular sites. Sites constantly change in location. The personnel change as well. Sites are usually organized around a project. In this way the company did not need to have a large rota of employees. Few employees 'belonged' to the company except more senior, loyal and trusted staff. Other men took the best paid jobs they could get, where and when they could find them. They travelled a lot. Sometimes they were unemployed.

Among the staff on site the organization functioned as a 'representative bureaucracy' (Gouldner, 1955). Rules were seen to be acceptable by staff members because they were 'expertly' promulgated by people with specific competences. The men on site often accepted these rules. Deviations from certain accepted ways of doing things would be considered to be the result of either momentary thoughtlessness, or ignorance.

This 'representative bureaucracy' co-existed with other 'modes of bureaucratic functioning' which Gouldner (1955) has identified. Some relationships between staff and the men on site could be best characterized as 'mock bureaucracy'. For example, the management was supposed to ensure that everybody on site was wearing a safety helmet. Many of the men on site did not wear them, although they received fifteen pence a week extra if they did so. This was regarded as a derisory amount by the men. Because the helmets were hot, uncomfortable and frequently a hindrance, both men and staff realized the inconvenience of *always* wearing them, thus it was that the company rule concerning safety helmets was often violated with impunity.

The most characteristic relationships between men and management were 'punishment-centred', where sanctions are used in an attempt to coerce the other side. These are usually exercised by management over men, but not always. Sanctions were usually financial, and hence positive rather than negative, and were most frequently administered through bonus schemes. However, much less subtle and more physical sanctions were applied in the context of the gang, where 'jacking' or being 'jacked' were frequent occurrences. (If a man *jacked* it signified that it was his decision to do so; if a man *had been* *jacked* then it signified that he had been fired. Frequently men were put in a position where they had no alternative to losing face other than to 'jack' voluntarily.) It was in such conflict as was generated by this mode of bureaucratic functioning that I expected to locate the exercise of power in the organization.

Where I would find this exercise of power seemed certain. In management.

It seemed very simple. There were managers who were managed. There were workers who were worked by the managed managers. It appeared to work satisfactorily. Buildings were built, strikes sometimes occurred, but after these were over, managers still managed and were managed, and workers still were worked.

Few people on site seemed to question this state of affairs. I was assured that all other sites were similar. Most other companies as well, I was told. Everywhere that people knew of seemed to be like that.

'Didn't I belong to a pyramid as well?' I was asked. Well, yes I did, and I told them about the University that I came from, and we agreed that it too could be seen as a pyramid of similar, if less squat, appearance.

Nobody could offer any reason why organizations should be like that. We just knew that they were, and that to question this was to invite suspicion of one's intentions. Still, I persisted in sampling opinion about the structure of the organization, only to be told more or less the same thing each time. The organization was a pyramid. The Project Manager controlled it. He in turn was managed from the Company Offices (as the Appendices show).

To persist in asking questions with such obvious answers is to risk censure of oneself – oneself as sociologist. A self indistinguishable from that of the fool – one who labours the obvious. And was that supposed to explain me?

My professional identity was in jeopardy. My mask was slipping. And so I ceased to question of members what members never question of themselves. Except that I was later to do this – but not directly.

I had reached 'bedrock'. I could go no further. My spade was turned. I had reached our form of life. For me to doubt our society would be as peculiar as for me to doubt myself (Wittgenstein, 1968, par. 217). Let me elaborate.

What would it be to doubt myself? Suppose I was in pain. Could I doubt that fact? Would I have to justify my feeling of pain as a fact? How odd it would be if pain were something like 'faith' or 'belief' – I could doubt my belief in some thing or other but could I doubt *my* pain? The very concept of doubt seems odd in this context. I could doubt my faith to myself without sharing my doubts with any other person. Clearly someone else might doubt my faith as they might doubt my pain – a referee in a football match, for instance, who suspects a player of 'feigning'. But could I doubt *my* pain to myself? Surely *I* would know if I was feigning or not? My pain is indubitably mine alone. Some other person could, or might want to challenge my claim to pain on the basis of their experience. And if we disputed the case, then there would be some socially available means of settling the dispute – an appeal to common sense, or medical opinion, perhaps, in terms similar to those of pp. 67–70.

Although others could doubt me, I would know myself.

Pain is claimed and ascribed on the basis of our recognition of what we call sensations (see Strawson, 1966). Power, unlike pain, is not a property that is claimed by the individual to be in him alone, although the recognition of either may be said to be social – a matter of the appropriate circumstances. Without criteria for ascribing pain to persons there would be no common language of pain, as Strawson

(1966, p. 47) puts it: 'It is because our common language-game must be that of ascribing pain to persons that symptoms, expressions of pain, assume such overwhelming importance.' In our language games, claims to power, although similarly social, are something different to claims to pain.

Consider some unrealized possibilities, suggested by Wittgenstein (1968, par. 312), and investigated by Strawson (1966, p. 47). Suppose that pain is associated with 'pain patches', and that we feel pain only and always under the condition that our skin is in contact with the surfaces of certain bodies. The pain would begin and end with the contact. In these circumstances, our pain language might be wholly different from the way that it is. Pain would be no longer ascribable to sufferers but would be a property of surfaces. Painfulness would then be much the same as that which we at present call rough, smooth, hard or soft. A person would feel pain if and only if every other normal person in that position or region also felt pain at the same time. Pain would no longer be a property of persons, but of regions or positions. We might ordinarily say things such as 'It's painful today', or 'What a painful thing', meaning not our subjective state of mind about some state of affairs, but the state of affairs itself. Pain would thus be non-personal.

Consider a further possibility. Let us see power as an embodiment of persons, a sensation that they possess. (It is the case that certain religions do commonly provide this way of seeing in their regard of power as an apperception in the individual of the Divine.) Those persons would be powerful who displayed certain behaviours and symptoms that we recognized as the actions of one who is powerful: these may include such phenomena as catatonic trances, hallucinogenic states, or a 'speaking with tongues'. Criteria would be publicly available for recognizing these as the appropriate display of power. Power would thus be personal.

But of course neither pain in persons, nor power in organizations is like that. If you have a pain, and I come near you, or touch what you are touching, this will not generally result in my being in pain as well (unless you are foolish enough to be touching something that does cause pain – a fire, or some such). If you are a powerful member of an organization, and I start to copy your dress, speech and behaviour, then this will not generally result in my also being in power. If a janitor apes a director he is a suitable case for treatment rather than for power.

If we were to consider these analogies reversed, then the possibility of any such claim to power or pain being warranted becomes more feasible. The warrant is the crux of the matter, in so far as if the janitor is then admitted to the position of director he would be powerful – but that kind of warranting which could routinely promote such acts is not at present a feature of our form of life. It could be. It might be elsewhere. For that to be so the form of life would have to be different to provide for the warrant of such acts. It should be evident that the warrant is the acknowledgement of the criteria of some phenomenon as it stands in our form of life.

In the previous chapter I suggested that forms of life provide their members with some very general social rules with which they orient their behaviour to its 'order'. This order is displayed in a particular substantive 'rationality'. Granted this, how should we research a form of life? Can we explain it by making it explicable in terms of something else, or being 'bedrock', can we only describe it in its own terms?

I suggest that it depends upon which 'face' of power we are investigating.

One face of power is that which is embodied in concrete decision-making. This concerns the outcome of specific issues, and is implied by the concept of *pouvoir*. (Here I am making reference to the argument of Chapter 4, where etymology was allied to a theoretical discussion of definition.) What the other face of power presents is the possibility that these decisions are already decided, because both the decision-maker (as a specific type of member of the organization), and the decision-area, are 'authorized'. This is implicit in the 'capacity' concept of *puissance*.

Particular decisions may be explained by retailing their history, thus explicating 'how' and 'why' they occurred.

One could explain 'how' a particular order in which a capacity is embedded may be historically located, as did Weber (1930). But can one explain 'order' in itself? We might make comparisons of how various peoples have attempted to impose order, or describe how they have done so, but can we say 'why' they should do so, without bootlegging some metaphysical, biological or psychological 'need'? I think not. If a form of life is 'bedrock' we can only describe it, as McHugh (1968) argues.

Such remarks as we might make about the form of life of 'power' are not to be regarded as 'findings' or 'proofs' – how could we doubt them? – but may be characterized as

> remarks on the natural history of human beings; we are not contributing curiosities however, but observations which no one has doubted, but which have escaped remark only because they are always before our eyes. . . . The aspects of things that are most important for us are hidden because of their simplicity and familiarity. (One is unable to notice something because it is always before one's eyes.) The real foundations of his enquiry do not strike a man at all. Unless *that* fact has at some time

struck him. – And this means: we fail to be struck by what, once seen, is most striking and most powerful (Wittgenstein, 1968, pars 415; 129).

Wittgenstein suggests that something may be so apparent as to be almost unremarkable. But Wittgenstein remarks that such facts can 'strike' one – what can he mean?

How do things attain an active being – one which can strike? Heidegger's (1962) *Being and Time* points a way towards grasping this metaphor of Wittgenstein's through its stress on our ordinary daily existence. In this daily existence we live in the world in a pre-reflective mode which is ontologically prior to any reflective theoretical knowledge that we may have of the world.

Heidegger (1962) argues that it is only when things are 'broken' or go wrong that we are struck by the nature of those things that we are ordinarily concerned with. Without treating this as an empirical proposition, it is evident that this may well be the case in certain instances. Garfinkel (1967), for instance, trades on the anomie of damage, stress, disruption and breakage, to reveal the fragile web of social rules and relations that bind us together. For both Heidegger (1962) and Garfinkel (1967), what calls us to reflection from unawareness is that moment when things strike us as they are, when we become aware of their breakdown.

In a view of the failing of the organization presented to me by some of its members we can locate the reality of the form of power in the organization, in our form of life. We can do so metaphorically, by formulating the world pictured by some simple remarks on the state of the organization.

### 'The Joiners' Tale'

Perrow (1970) has argued that organizations should be seen as the instrument or tool of men's purposes. Merton (1968) has stressed how the instrumentality can become a purpose in itself. I want to examine the way in which we can see the Heideggerian metaphor of the broken instrument being used by members of the organization in accounting for what they see as its failure. In examining their use of the metaphor in this way, then we find that it reveals the structure of power in the organization, much as one of Garfinkel's disruptions may reveal obvious, but unstated and unseen properties of everyday life.

The following piece of data, unlike that which follows it, is introduced out of sequence.

I had been engaged in field-work for several weeks when I recorded the following conversation between two joiners. The joiners were addressing these remarks to me.

On several occasions during a lull in activity in the site office, I would don my safety helmet and inspect the site. On this occasion I had wandered as far as the furthest perimeter of the site. Here I came upon three joiners who were kicking a football about on the concrete base which had been poured for the bus station. After their initial apprehension at seeing a white Construction Co. helmet approaching them (staff and visitors wore white helmets which differentiated them from site-men who had blue helmets), they started to chat about the job with me. Generally, they were dissatisfied as they were not earning the amount of bonus that they had expected – in fact, they were not earning any bonus at all, and were receiving a 'spot' bonus in lieu of the real thing. A 'spot' bonus was a figure arrived at by the Project Manager to compensate for the lack of bonus earnings. If no bonus was earned, it meant that not enough work had been produced for the Project Manager to relate output to a bonus system. The joiners laid the blame for the lack of bonus at the door of the Project Manager. As one of them put it, 'I mean, we can see how it should be done, but its not our place to organize it.'

As we spoke, the General Foreman and his Foreman Joiner approached – and as I might be thought to be keeping the men from their work, I retired from the scene, and continued my stroll.

A few minutes later, after the foremen had passed by without comment, I returned to the three joiners. Two of them then addressed the following remarks to me about the previous scene:

Joiner 1    See what I mean – there must be something wrong with this bloody job – when they see you standing around doing nothing, and they say nothing. Trouble is we're overstaffed – I mean, you can see that, we're hardly making any shutterage – what we do in a week here we did in a day at Tarmac.

Joiner 2    Aye, y'see there's no push, there's no organization from up there, they should be setting the job up properly so that there's an even flow of work and we're at it good and steady.

'The Joiners' Tale' comprises a number of 'pictures' which are 'collected' together in an account of the organization. Several themes may be constructed from the account. The first theme is that there is 'something wrong with the job'. Two further themes, which are subordinate to the first, may also be seen. These elaborate what it is that is specifically wrong with this particular job.

The three themes, the pictures they present, and the means by which they are collected together, may be reformulated as shown in Table 1.

TABLE 1

| Collection device | Theme |
|---|---|
| See what I mean | there must be something wrong/ with this bloody job/ they see you standing around/ doing nothing/ |
| and | they say nothing. |
| I mean | trouble is we're overstaffed/ |
| you can see that | we're hardly making any shutterage/ what we do in a week here/ we did in a day at Tarmac. |
| Aye, y'see | there's no push/ there's no organization/ from up there/ they should be setting the job up properly/ |
| so that | there's an even flow of work/ |
| and | we're at it good and steady. |

The diagonal lines represent the end of one picture, and the beginning of another. I use the term 'picture' in a loose sense, for the words and phrases present a picture only in as much as we are consistently invited to 'see' them in this way by the two joiners. The 'themes' are successions of pictures dealing with one aspect of the broken instrument that is the organization. These themes are 'collected' by devices which present no further pictures of the organization, but which invite our acquiescence in, and the continuation of, the dialogue, and the tale it tells.

The tale describes, at first glance, a realm consisting of three types of beings, who are described by an 'I' who invites 'you' (the listener; reader) to accept his description. These three types of being are pictured as 'they', 'we', and 'you'. Let us begin with some of the features of this 'you'.

What does 'you' do in the tale? He does nothing. He does this nothing in the sight of a 'they' who say nothing – 'There must be something wrong with this bloody job' when 'they see you standing around doing nothing and they say nothing'. So what is 'wrong' is 'they' *seeing you* 'standing around doing nothing', and ' *"they"* saying nothing'.

So the realm of beings in 'The Joiners' Tale', as the first theme develops it, consists of two beings. These begin to take shape not simply as two flat and unrelated figures in a landscape, but are related by being in sight, because 'they' see.

They are not equally in sight. 'They' do the seeing, and 'they' are also capable of commenting on the seeing. Part of what is 'wrong' seems to be that 'they' do not say anything, where 'they' might have

89

said something. So it would seem as if the relationship is not one of equality. So far we know that 'they' do the seeing, and that 'they' *ought* to do some saying, because their lack of saying is part of what is wrong.

The third theme in the tale tells us some more about 'they'. 'They' seem to be a higher type of being to 'you'. 'You' is now addressed plurally as any member of the organization distinct from 'they'. The tale has become more manageable, because more abstract. It now consists of two types of being, 'they' and 'we'.

'They' and 'we' are related by a division of labour. 'They' 'should be setting the job up properly' so that 'we' are 'at it good and steady'. The failure of this is a failure of 'organization'.

Before this scene one of the joiners had told me: 'I mean we can see how it should be done, but its not our place to organize it.' So both types of beings *can* see, but only 'they' are in a position, or have the 'place', to be able to implement sight in organization. 'They', if they were to be organizing correctly, 'should be setting the job up properly so that there's an even flow of work and we're at it good and steady'. It seems that if 'we' are to work, that this will be dependent upon the behest of 'they'. 'We' is subordinate to 'they' because 'we' depends for its activity on 'they' having done theirs. And the work that 'they' do is seeing that 'we' can (third theme) and that 'we' does (first theme) do *its* work. 'They' stand in a hierarchical relationship to 'we'.

This hierarchical structuring, as the structure of power in the organization, is self-evidently axiomatic. Without this bedrock assumption, one could hardly function as a normally competent member of such an organization.

Although the *form* of nearly all organizations known to us may be pyramidal in their structure, they will vary in terms of their substantive nature and functioning. This substantive variation and functioning will be found in the 'rationality' of our differing organizations.

The joiners theorize the organization as a 'bloody job', because 'we' (that is the joiners) do nothing, and are seen to do nothing by 'they' who say nothing. The second theme in 'The Joiners' Tale' elaborates the reason why this state of nothingness should exist, and in so doing allows us to grasp the 'rationality' of the organization's form of life.

The second theme that 'The Joiners' Tale' elaborates is that the failing of the organization is due to the low productivity of the labour force coupled with its excess capacity. What reasoning could ground this theorizing? As all theorizing is iconic by some standard or other, let us formulate the icon of this reasoning in its form of life.

If the implications of the joiners' theorizing about the organization's failings were explicated, then we can see that they might very well talk themselves out of a job. If the trouble with the organization, its nothingness, is that 'we're overstaffed', then 'we' who do nothing may well be among those who are surplus to requirements, given the unlikely prospect that 'they' who say nothing, whose job it is to say something, will talk themselves into redundancy. The joiners are theorizing the legitimacy of their own dismissal. It is evidently a powerful kind of theorizing which enables you to talk yourself out of a job.

Tarmac provides the standard of a good job, because of its 'efficiency'. A good job is one which is not 'overstaffed' and where plenty of 'shutterage' is made, because there is 'push' and 'organization from up there'.

If 'Tarmac' provides the ideal of a good job, in the way that it organized its economic activity, why should Construction Co. be any different?

'The Joiners' Tale' would seem to suggest that what is wrong with Construction Co. is its management – 'there's no push, no organization' – because they had allowed the site to become overstaffed. Some other data that I collected from elsewhere on site, on my first day in the field, also supported this assumption. I will introduce this at this juncture in order to propose that the 'failing' of the organization, as revealed in 'The Joiners' Tale', exemplifies an instance of the 'rationality' of Construction Co.'s economic activity. This in turn is an instance of the organization members' domination by a particular form of life, of which this 'rationality' is a particular instance. Both the 'we' of 'The Joiners' Tale', the joiners, and 'they' – management – the latter in the following example, theorize their respective versions of the organization under the iconic domination of a particular form of life.

The joiners do so by taking as the standard of their organizational reality an ideal approximation to a good job – 'Tarmac', with which they then compare Construction Co. 'Tarmac' then serves as an icon of good practice, because it is idealized out of their experience of its actual, material existence, to serve as the (idealized) standard which theorizes flawed reality. Iconic theorizing synthesizes the ideal standard with the reality that it flaws. The comparison of Construction Co. with Tarmac serves to formulate the latter as the (ideal) of the form of life of the organization. (Comparison with the appendices, particularly appendix three, will demonstrate that this 'iconizing' of one or more previous jobs is a common gambit for theorizing the organization.)

### 'Cooking the Books'
On the construction site that I observed, weekly cost figures were produced by the Project Manager, sometimes in conjunction with

other members of the organization, which he then forwarded in a weekly financial statement to the head office of Construction Co. The following is a transcript of one such meeting in which a crucial feature of the organization was initially revealed – its failing.

The conversational sequence begins with a query by the Project Manager (P.M.). He is speaking over the phone to the Construction Co.'s 'Estimator' at head-offices. Prior to this query he appeared to be having some difficulty in arriving at the figures for the weekly statement. Also involved are the Office Manager (O.M.), the Measurement Engineer (M.E.), and the General Foreman (G.F.) who enters shortly after the first transcribed utterance. The conversation took place in the Project Manager's site-office:

| | | |
|---|---|---|
| 1 | P.M. | ... did you include in your estimate an estimate for stop-ends in the shuttering concrete? ... (Foreman enters) |
| 2 | G.F. | Is this a meeting? |
| 3 | P.M. | You could say it's a liars' meeting. |
| 4 | O.M. | Best to say it's an adjusters' meeting. (Pause in the conversation as the estimator confirms over the phone that the stop-ends are included in the estimate. P.M. replaces receiver.) |
| 5 | P.M. | How the hell do we work this out? ... If we have $7\frac{1}{2}$p in t'square goes $6\frac{3}{4}$, so we've got 50p for stop-ends in concrete. |
| 6 | M.E. | Is this 50p correct? – that figure should be a lot smaller than what it is. |
| 7 | P.M. | Yeah – that figure of Al's includes stop-ends, but joiner's time has to go in against the costs – the measure and value stay. |
| 8 | O.M. | I take that one from there to there then? |
| 9 | P.M. | No it's not that one/ |
| 10 | M.E. | The only thing we're not sure about is F.3/ |
| 11 | P.M. | That's about two joiners for a week – that's about £40. We've got £78 costed against slab-edging, but according to Porton we didn't do any, so we've to correct that miscalculation. (I was unable to follow the next minute or so of conversation, but as I understood it, the problem was resolved by re-interpreting £98 as £9.8.) The conversation continued when the Office Manager said ... |
| 12 | O.M. | Just to keep you on your toes. |
| 13 | P.M. | You'll feel my toes soon (accompanied by mock |

|    |      | threatening gesture) . . . that's £36 instead o' thirteen. . . . |
|----|------|------|
| 14 | M.E. | You taking it one up or one below? |
| 15 | P.M. | It doesn't matter – one up. |
| 16 | M.E. | Yeah, one up. |
| 17 | O.M. | What about all those kickers? |
| 18 | P.M. | It doesn't matter about 'em, we can add 'em, or rub 'em off as we go along. . . . Ah ah, we're cooking it now nicely . . . let's allocate – if I put a hundred and fifty in there, that shows me – no that's the wrong way round, no if I put a cost of a hundred and nine in there, then its a loss of £90, take off twenty, so that's a loss of £70 as against four hundred – and there's that £12 – that's a cost not a loss – so if I put a value of £12 in I want a measure of nine hours – a joiner makes about £12 in nine hours, so it's 20p into £12 – that's sixty metres – it doesn't balance – we'd do better to leave that £12 out. I wanna have a word with Al, these codes here include all the extras – hey, that's a point, still got all those kickers to put in – leave the twelve pounds a moment, that's fifty-six metres of kicker is the same as fixing twenty metres of wall – the same effort – that gives me thirty-six, seventy-two, gives me a loss of thirty-seven quid. Uh, uh – that's it, isn't it, apart from that twelve quid? |
| 19 | M.E. | You want to scrub that £13 out. |
| 20 | O.M. | It's not bound to look ridiculous, you could be missing something out, added from next week. |
| 21 | P.M. | What I have to do to save these lads' skins – lost two hundred and forty quid, and had two joiners only doing seven metres a week. |
| 22 | G.F. | Aye, well you need to count teaman as well. |
| 23 | P.M. | Are these costs just a guide or do we follow them exact? What do the others do? If we code 'em after, it gives us more time to juggle 'em after. Have we cracked it yet? |
| 24 | M.E. | Where's the cost for F.13? We've no cost, where's F.13.1? – they're two different items. |
| 25 | P.M. | That nine hours at £12 should come out now/ |
| 26 | M.E. | There's a loss of £9, shouldn't be there. |
| 27 | P.M. | I can scrub that out altogether. |
| 28 | M.E. | If they spend all this time making kickers/ |
| 29 | P.M. | But we need this for two jobs, both bonus and cost codes. |

I was, to say the least, slightly bewildered by the above. I could not follow their 'analysis' of the costs at all, at least not in any clearly 'rational' way, such as my experience of accountancy practice recommended.

It was evidently not a 'straight' meeting in which 'correct' figures for the week were reported. As the Project Manager said, it was 'a liars' meeting', or as Al, the Office Manager, more delicately put it, it was 'an adjusters' meeting'.

In this instance it seemed that the Project Manager and his colleagues were creating the figures they reported. In creating the figures they appeared to have some guiding notion of producing a perceivedly rational outcome, warranted by 'correct' figures and procedures for achieving these – but 'correct' figures are not necessarily 'real' figures. As an example of this point recall the following remark:

6    M.E.    Is this 50p correct? That figure should be a lot
                  smaller than what it is.

The Measurement Engineer, Ken, knows that a 'correct' figure would be 'a lot smaller than what it is', and thus, that no matter how the figure was arrived at, it cannot be correct because it does not look right. The Project Manager tells us of some figures that:

18    P.M.    It doesn't matter about 'em, we can add 'em, or
                  rub 'em off as we go along. . . .

This is called 'cooking it nicely':

18    P.M.    if I put a hundred and fifty quid in there, that shows
                  me, no that's the wrong way round, no if I put a
                  cost of a hundred and nine in there, then it's a loss
                  of £90, take off twenty, so that's a loss of £70
                  as against four hundred –

At first glance those figures produced by the Project Manager appear to have materialized themselves in much the same way that rabbits do when conjured from the magician's hat. But although the figures themselves are somewhat less than indubitable, they are hardly random. If they were random then any notions of figures not being 'correct' or not being in 'balance' would be inapplicable. I have already observed that Winch (1958) has remarked of the notion of 'correctness' that it implies the use of a rule. What 'rule' underlies the production of these weekly figures?

The Project Manager knows the wage that a joiner would normally earn in nine hours, and how many metres of work a given number of joiners can produce in a given time. Such knowledge would be part of what every competent Project Manager ought to know. We might characterize this as 'rational' knowledge about the job.

Sociologists frequently equate 'rational' knowledge with scientific knowledge, but as Garfinkel (1967, pp. 262–83) has demonstrated, ten of the fourteen criteria of rationality which he derived from Schutz's (1953) inventory, occur not only as stable properties (and sanctionable ideals) of scientific activity, but also as features of daily life. Certain of these features appear to be present in the activity of 'Cooking the Books'.

Specifically, the Project Manager 'categorizes and compares' the figures he is producing with other instances such as the figures 'according to Porton' (Utterance 11). Further properties of 'rational action' suggested by Garfinkel's (1967, pp. 263–7) list of 'everyday' rationalities may also be found in this instance of 'Cooking the Books'. Notions of 'tolerable error' are obviously important in deciding the figures (i.e., Utterances 6, 18, 20). Garfinkel (1967, p. 264) also suggests that a particular action may be rational where it is one where a person 'reviews rules of procedure which in the past yielded the practical effects now desired'. This he terms a 'search for means'. To be able to make sense of the sequence (particularly Utterance 18) then we must assume that the Project Manager has some 'means' available to him for producing the figures, otherwise they would be purely random fictions. Different formulations are rehearsed in attempting to arrive at the 'correct' figures, in what Garfinkel (1967, p. 264) calls 'Analysis of alternatives and consequences'. The acceptance or rejection of these alternatives depends on what 'strategy' they are required for: the Project Manager asks 'if these costs (are) just a guide or do we follow them exact?', and he also notes that the figures are needed for 'two jobs, both bonus and cost codes' (Utterances 23; 29). In coding the figures the Project Manager exhibits a 'concern for timing' (Garfinkel, 1967, p. 265) in Utterance 23: 'If we code 'em after, it gives us more time to juggle 'em after.'

Garfinkel notes that 'Highly specific expectations of time scheduling can be accompanied by the person's paying concern to the predictable characteristics of a situation' (Garfinkel, 1967, p. 265).

The 'predictable characteristics of the situation' would appear to be that the meeting produces the 'correct' figures. It would appear to be some knowledge of what this ought to look like to which the Project Manager 'orients' his arithmetic. These 'correct' figures would seem to be dependent upon the judgement of the Project Manager. In particular they depend on an assumption that the organization *'ought'* to produce a particular type of outcome, the 'correct' figures. This assumption then serves as the warrant for the figures computed.

The Project Manager's skill in producing the figures seems to be displayed in what is essentially *normative* work, in that the figures are assembled as reportedly-correct-and-rational figures through his application of, and submission to, whatever conceptual rules could produce such a substantive rationality. To produce 'correct' figures one must make reference to whatever rule(s) sanction and legitimate *these* figures rather than any others that might be produced. One might have thought that in a simple instance of compiling a weekly financial statement of a week's work, then the correct figures would be those that represented the 'reality' of that week's work. Instead it seems that the 'reality' of the figures resides in their possibly being the 'correct' figures. The reality of the figures might be said to be located in their possibility. Their possibility resides in the rule that produces them.

It would appear that almost any figures might have produced the 'real' figures, and almost any figures might have been the 'correct' figures. That 'reality' and 'correctness' seem not to belong together appears to be evident from the conversation. The figures that are arrived at clearly 'index' something, but to what exactly does this indexicality refer? The underlying reality of the week's work? Well, hardly. What the members of the organization reportedly saw as actually happening seems to have little relevance for the bewildering display of figures computed.

Could it be indexical of correct ways of filling out forms? Well not if we mean by 'correct' the formally prescribed or formally ruled way. Whatever ruling is being accomplished it is not in the manner of that which is formally prescribed.

Perhaps the figures are nothing apart from the context in which they were produced, and they may thus be seen as indexical upon members' ways of 'bringing off' an appearance of the underlying 'reality' of the week's work, by displaying it, *post hoc*, as in accord with the ruling that such a reality *would* have produced, *had* it been accomplished. So the figures testify to the reality of the site-organization, by being in accordance with the rule(s) that such a reality would have displayed had it occurred. The perceivedly 'objective' index of this reality then stands as a warrant to the members' methods for displaying the site-production as being in accord with the figures that such a site ought to produce.

The 'correctness' of a 'true' figure appears to be irrelevant to what 'really' happened. Instead, the figures seem to depend on members' methods for producing them as if they measured something which really happened. The method used seems to be irrelevant to that method explicitly stated, and indeed it would seem to be subversive of formal rules and procedures. But none the less, it is supportive of a formally and recognizably 'correct' outcome.

The figures may not be the 'real' figures, and their 'correctness' may be in question, but they do seem to be 'rational'. Why should the Project Manager and his colleagues spend so much time constructing a rational fabrication, when they could have reported the 'real' figures?

'The Joiners' Tale' provides the answer. The joiners were not exaggerating, or grousing, when they claimed that the organization was 'overstaffed'. It was, by the standard that they measured it by. Tarmac stood as an example of this standard, which they understood in terms of cash. 'The Joiners' Tale' expressed their dissatisfaction with an organization in which they were unable to earn a 'good bonus'. The factors which limited the joiners' earnings, and necessitated the Project Manager 'Cooking the Books' were instances of the organization's rationality.

The Project Manager constructs his site's weekly financial statement in such a way as to make it appear as if the organization *were* showing a weekly profit. This is the 'objective principle' towards which he is orienting his actions in the data-example, 'Cooking the Books'. The figures only become rational if one considers this to be the outcome which he seeks to present, so that the figures' only function is to present *that* outcome, rather than to represent reality. Their fabrication is, in an ironical way, a testament to the 'rationality' of the organization. Let me elaborate this.

The conversational materials were collected a few months after a lengthy national strike in the construction industry which occurred during the summer of 1972. During the stoppage, many skilled tradesmen had secured themselves jobs outside the industry. Consequently there was a shortage of skilled labour for the industry after the strike had been resolved. This shortage was particularly acute where joiners were concerned. The boom in Improvement Grants from local authorities, coupled with the easy availability of mortgages, had led to a boom in the 'conversion' of old properties. After the strike was over, there were several major ringroad, motorway and construction sites which had been nearing completion prior to the strike in or near the Northern Town, which were paying top bonus rates in an effort to attract men from a diminished labour supply. By doing this they hoped to be able to complete more quickly, thus releasing capital, men and materials for other contracts which were due to have started during, or soon after, the strike.

It was because of this that the joiners were dissatisfied with the 'spot' bonus that they were receiving, because prior to this job they had been benefiting from the inflated rates that joiners were able to command immediately after the strike. But, as the 'normal' market condition re-asserted itself, and the urgent jobs were completed, the bonanza receded. In comparison to those earnings, as for instance with Tarmac, then the present rates were highly unfavourable.

The Project Manager's task is to orient his actions in the organization not only to the construction of a structure, but to the *profitable* construction of a structure. The payment of bonus rates to the joiners may help in this.

The Project Manager can readily calculate the contribution to profit that each joiner makes. Profit consists in obtaining more 'use-value' than 'exchange-value' from the joiners' labour. (Here I am introducing terms which have not yet been defined. For the reader who requires this, then their meaning may be found on pp. 120–1.) Disputes over the administration of this bonus-system were the focal point for many of the instances of the organization's 'punishment-centred' bureaucratic functioning.

The joiners' contribution to profit is readily calculable because each yard of wood-work that is produced for the contractor is paid at a rate per type of item as specified in the bill of works, by the client, to the contractor. This figure represents the joiner's use-value to the contractor. The joiner's exchange-value is his hourly wage plus bonus and 'perks'. This latter is a travel allowance of a pound a day which the joiners receive for each day they work. Hence the quicker the joiners work, the more money they will make for themselves. At the same time they will also be helping the contracting organization to maximize their profits. This is because the faster a job is completed, then the more profitable it is. This is so for a number of reasons.

If a job is finished after the contracted completion date, it is frequently liable to a 'penalty clause'. This means that for each specified period of time-unit longer than the specified time, the contracting organization has to pay a financial penalty to the client. So it is far more profitable to pay higher bonus rates to try and speed a job up, rather than suffer a penalty clause. Additionally, a rapid completion frees men and materials for other jobs, who have already been 'budgeted ahead' – that is they have been charged to the client for a tendered time-period, which is actually longer than the actual time, and so the variance favours the contractor. The 'freed' men and materials are now available for another job, to 'earn' a further profit. If a contractor has an early completion on his stage of a 'multi-contractor' contract, and client-utilization depends upon the completion of the total structure, then the period of guaranteed maintenance that the contractor offers on the structure will incorporate a period of time during which the structure is not being utilized, and hence not subject to claims arising from its utilization. This frequently occurs on motorway projects. Early completion cuts actual costs. It is in the contractors' interests to cut actual costs as much below tendered costs as possible, because that maximizes profit.

The Project Manager's 'Cooking the Books', and 'The Joiners' Tale', are instances of two differing types of accounts occasioned by the same feature of the organization, namely its failing. Both are theorized under the icon of capitalism.

Because joiners were a commodity in short supply the Project Manager was hoarding them, as other managements might hoard cocoa beans or copper as a form of commodity speculation, in commodities associated with their material form of life. He was storing them as a commodity in short supply until he knew exactly how many, at what bonus rates, were going to give him his best return – which with the delay caused by the strike and subsequent shortages, might be the quickest job.

'The Joiners' Tale' was occasioned by what was the organization's failing for the joiners – its lack of bonus. 'Cooking the Books' was occasioned by what was the organization's failing for the Project Manager – its lack of productivity. In their different ways, each of these two episodes helps to set the scene for the exercise of power in the organization.

'The Joiners' Tale' sets the scene for the exercise of power in the organization, because it provides us with a 'picture' of how the prior 'capacity' necessary for this exercise is distributed in the organization. It is distributed 'hierarchically'. We could use 'The Joiners' Tale' to formulate some rules for constructing an organization in accordance with that organization pictured by the joiners:

Rule 1. Stratify a population on a binary basis.
Rule 2. Make this stratification hierarchical.
Rule 3. Have the members of the organization accept this as legitimate.
Rule 4. Constitute the members as creators of value.
Rule 5. Divide value into wages and profits.
Rule 6. Relate greater profits to higher wages through the bonus.
Rule 7. Maximize profits and wages by minimizing labour and maximizing its productivity.

'Cooking the Books' also helps to set the scene for the exercise of power in the organization, because it provides us with documentary evidence that the organization was 'failing', that this organizational failing was one of less than projected profitability, and that this was clearly seen as a problem by the Project Manager. He attempts to hide this problem by presenting the weekly financial statement as something other than his understanding of the situation suggests that it is, enmeshed as he is in his (our) form of life.

In the following chapter I will argue that 'Cooking the Books' may be seen as an attempt to 'repair' indexicality. Using the 'failing' of the organization as the occasion, I will draw some illuminating comparisons between 'Everyday' and 'Weberian Rationality'. This will be developed into a discussion of 'rationality' in organization which lends empirical substance to Weber and Simmel's discourse on rationality as 'the juxtaposition of an "objective principle" regarded as a "concrete object" by those subject to it' (p. 65). In Chapter 8 this theme will be discussed in terms of the specific 'mode of rationality' of Construction Co., as this is displayed in the Project Manager's 'understanding'. Through the empirical study of this 'understanding' I will relate the exercise of power to the organization's 'mode of rationality'. This exercise of power will be seen to concern negotiations concerning this 'mode of rationality', negotiations which are managed by the Project Manager, and which occur within his willing submission to the structural power of his form of life, as willing cog and cipher. Thus, the exercise of power concerns the negotiation not of the taken-for-granted structure of power, which is typically submitted to without its overt exercise (legitimate authority), but the 'understanding' of its 'mode of rationality'.

# 7 'Rationality' in the organization

## Introduction

Data are always more 'innocent' than theory. In the context in which they are produced such data as those which I have used bear only those evident meanings taken-for-granted by the co-producers of the data. It is only with the perspective granted us by the distancing of theory, that we make of data what we will.

At the moment of data collection my thoughts had not yet been framed in the way suggested by the previous six chapters. I was still theorizing the organization, like any man in the organization, within a form of life so constitutive of membership that I (we) rarely have call to question it. My theorizing affirmed the frame through which we ordinarily look, rather than grasping the site of what is seen (Wittgenstein, 1968, pars 114–15).

When I questioned people in the organization, I was implicitly thinking in terms of power in its relation to 'uncertainty' as my line of enquiry. I had begun to conceptualize 'uncertainty' as 'indexicality' (see Wieder, 1974; Garfinkel, 1967), because it seemed as if a significant source of organizationally generated uncertainty arose in the differing ways in which the contractual documents – the 'bill of works' – could be interpreted. This would be 'indexical' because the construction put upon them would vary with who was speaking, to whom, in what context, and so on.

I asked a number of questions with these implicit ideas behind them. The answers that I received to these again stressed the 'failing' of the organization. Further questioning of this failing led to its being seen as a deficiency of bureaucratic rationality.

Through re-viewing this rationality through that which Weber (1968) formulated as the ideal type of rational-legal bureaucracy, and in the context of Weber's wider corpus, we can see that one can only characterize this 'rationality' with the name of reason through a heavy irony. Let me begin with some 'innocent' questioning.

101

### 'Them figures . . . are figures you can't argue with'

The following exchange took place two days after 'Cooking the Books'. The speakers are myself and Al, the Office Manager of the previous scene.

1 S. I was, uh, I was, uh, thinking about the other day, I was looking at, when you were, when you were having a talk in there the other day, there was you and uh, that chap in there with the reddish hair/

2 Al Ken.

3 S. Ken, Ken, is it, Ken, well you were talking about the figures and I was trying to relate that to the work I was doing, and it seemed to me that the most important thing, was, that you got the bill of works and the documents that went with it, like the technical drawings, and things, and those were what made this organization what it was, because, you know, depending on the kind of people that you get in like the number of concrete gangers and joiners, and things like that, and that the work then seemed to become a problem of interpreting that bill of works, and those things, so that they made sense on a day-to-day basis, in such a way that when you came to sort of write it up in your figures, and things, and sent them in, even if it wasn't the right figure, it still made sense in terms of the documents?

4 Al Well, I mean, them figures I gave him are figures you can't argue with, you see, if you've got a cost there, if you've got a cost there, well, then it's there, that's it. If you cut it off now and say 'Oh well, I'm not going to bother with it now' so as to show a weekly site profit,

5 S. Uh.

6 Al at the end of the job there'll be a big/

7 S. Yeah/

8 Al overhead coming in. I mean the costs, at the end of the job, the costs, you can't argue with 'em then, you know, at the end of the day, well this is what I was telling him. . . .

9 S. Yeah.

10 Al Except it's not a right good job this. . . .

11 S. Yeah?

12 Al If that's it, you can't help making losses.

13 S. What's a good job like?

14 Al Well, that I don't know, from my point of view, that what you put in you accept even if its bad,

15 S. Yeah.

16 Al bad from their point of view, they should accept 'em, and do something about them instead of cooking the books like.

17 S. Yeah, yeah. So that wouldn't be the normal thing that you'd do then?

18 Al In there?

19 S. Uhmm.

20 Al Oh no, you see the type of arrangement is that they allow us so much earth, say you're doing excavations, you see, y'get paid so much for taking the earth out, and if it's soft dirt, it's a lot easier to dig out than if it's rock, and if it's rock you get paid more for it.

21 S. Yeah.

22 Al So you might, say, be behind, and dig out earth, but book it as rock, I mean Mr H. (a Project Manager on a nearby Construction Co. site) did this once, but that was the only time he ever did it, he's spot on, he knows what he's doing.

23 S. Yeah, yeah.

24 Al I mean here, he just sits in there, when he comes in, on the phone all day, and so Ray (the Foreman) had to do it all, out there, it's all been on him, it's not surprising he's leaving. . . . I mean, any other job, they'd have had him in now so that Ray could hand over, working with him. I mean, Ray's a good foreman . . . you get a job, I mean, if another firm had taken this job on, basically they'd have gone about it in the same way,

25 S. Yeah.

26 A. but that's only basically, you know – I mean, it can be a hell of a lot of difference.

27 S. The way it was organized?

28 Al Yeah, it's not uniform, they don't go about the job uniform. . . .

29 S. How would it be different? What sorts of things?

30 Al Well, uh, we, you see, Ray's a good bloke, he should have never let him go, you see on this job, we've had no joiners, so what he's done is to keep 'em concreting, that slab, the base, to keep 'em concreting, he shouldn't have done, normally we'd have been up on the first floor by now, shuttering, but Ray's organized it like that to keep the men we have occupied/

31 S. And he did this because you couldn't get any more men?

| 32 | Al | Because we couldn't get joiners. |
| 33 | S. | And the way you'd do it would be – what? – To do one bit going up and then another bit going up? |
| 34 | Al | Well this is the way we work, the way we should've done it was to follow the joiners up, |
| 35 | S. | That's right, yeah. |
| 36 | Al | to get up on the first floor. |

Let me elaborate the ideas that prompted my inquiries on these lines. A version of ethnomethodology inspired my opening remark (Utterance 3) to Al. I was trying to use the distinction between an 'objective' and an 'indexical' expression in such a way that Al would understand it. An indexical expression is one which we treat as an index of an underlying reality, which is made explicable through locating it in its proper context. An objective expression is one which makes sense in itself, in terms of itself. It can be said to be explicable without reference to any specific context.

My long, rambling question (Utterance 3) assumed that in practice the purportedly 'objective' contractual documents were actually 'indexical'. The detailed and comprehensive instructions included in these documents (the plans, bill of quantities, etc. which comprise the 'Bill of Works') are supposed to stand as a blue-print for the process, the progress and the completed picture of the accomplished building structure (for example, see RIBA *Handbook of Architectural Practice and Management*). Such documentation is supposed to prevail on site, and to do so, it is supposed to be objectively clear.

'Cooking the Books' would seem to suggest that this documentation is not as unindexical as it is intended to be. For instance, the sequence begins with the Project Manager asking

| 1 | P.M. | . . . did you include in your estimate an estimate for stop-ends in the shuttering concrete? |

and he goes on to ask

| 23 | P.M. | Are these codes just a guide or do we follow them exact? |

The documents clearly do not speak for themselves.

In my initial question to Al (3) concerning what I had understood by 'Cooking the Books', I meant to suggest the following. The construction of the weekly figures that I had witnessed was an attempt by those participating in the discussion to make the figures reflect the site as it ought to be if it accurately mirrored the documentation concerning that week's work. What they were trying to do was to construct a purportedly 'normal' state of affairs in accordance with their necessarily indexical interpretation of the documentation from which they built. Their interpretation was necessarily indexical because they continually operate within the constraints of a specific context, many factors in which were unaccountable when the contractual documents were prepared. Thus 'Cooking the Books' could be seen as an attempt to 'repair' indexicality. That was the implicit theorizing behind my opening question to Al.

Al failed to connect with my question, other than to tell me that

4    Al    Well, I mean, them figures I gave him are figures you can't argue with, you see, if you've got a cost there, well then it's there, that's it.

It seemed that Al thought that the figures ought to enjoy some privileged position which 'Cooking the Books' had suggested that they did not.

I had intended that my opening question to Al would confirm that what might be loosely construed as the 'rules' for constructing the building-structure – the contractual documentation – were also the source of relationships within the organization, because of the nature of the work that had to be done. Find the author of these, I reasoned, and I would find the person who initially formulated the arena in which indexicality could be debated. If the documentation was central to the organization – if indeed it 'constructed it' – and if the indexical nature of this documentation was the primary source of organizationally generated uncertainty, then on the 'Strategic Contingencies' theory, control of this might point towards 'power' in the organization.

That I should have thought this was a measure of my 'entanglement' within the conventions of theorizing power in the organization. In the 'innocence' of my questioning, I had yet to understand this entanglement.

My enquiring of what a 'normal' job (17) would be like was similarly implicitly 'guided', but by some remarks of Wittgenstein's (1968) that

What we call 'descriptions' are instruments for particular uses. Think of a machine drawing, a cross section, an elevation with measurements, which an engineer has before him. Thinking of a description as a word picture of the facts has something misleading about it: one tends to think only of such pictures as hang on our walls: which seem simply to portray how a thing looks, what it is like. (These pictures are as it were idle.)

   Don't always think that you read off what you say from the facts; that you portray these in words according to rules. For even so you would have to apply the rule in the particular case without guidance (Wittgenstein, 1968, pars 291; 292).

The 'contractual documents' are 'instruments for particular uses' – 'rules' for constructing a building. But these do not present an 'idle' picture of a perfectly finished structure. They have to be interpreted. And on occasion this may require having 'to apply the rule in the particular case without guidance'.

Wittgenstein remarks that we can accept two types of criteria for a picture and its application, and asks

> Can there be a collision between picture and application?
> There can, inasmuch as the picture makes us expect a different use, because people in general apply this picture like this. . . .
> I want to say: we have a normal case, and abnormal cases (Wittgenstein, 1968, par. 141).[1]

It is because we are able to recognize 'normal cases' without necessarily being able to formulate exactly what is normal, that we can ordinarily apply a rule (see Wittgenstein, 1968, par. 142).

What Al says adds to the picture of the organization gleaned from 'The Joiners' Tale' and 'Cooking the Books'. He confirms that 'it's not a right good job this' (10). Part of what is wrong with the job is that 'you see on this job, we've had no joiners' (30).

Both the material collected for this section, and for 'Cooking the Books', to which it refers, were compiled several weeks prior to 'The Joiners' Tale'. On the earlier occasion, because the organization had been short of joiners the scheduled programme for building the structure had been modified, so that work could continue despite this shortage. By the time that the joiners had told me their 'Tale' this shortage had been overcome. A 'store' of joiners had been accumulated by the Project Manager so that he could 'cope' with this shortage. At the time of collecting this earlier material, the consequence of this shortage was that the job could no longer be regarded as 'normal' (30).

It is not only the sequencing of the job that is wrong; as Al remarks 'it's not a right good job this' (10). By finding out what a 'good job' would be, we are able to identify this further failing of the organization:

13  S.  What's a good job like?
14  Al  Well, that I don't know, from my point of view, that what you put in you accept even if it's bad,
15  S.  Yeah.
16  Al  bad from their point of view, they should accept 'em, and do something about them instead of cooking the books like.

We have come back to 'they' of 'The Joiners' Tale', identified here as the Project Manager – the embodiment of management on site.

It transpired that the performance of the Project Manager was central for analysing the job's normalcy – and the normalcy of a job proves to be of central concern for at least one member of the organization.

Al had compared the site with another site which Construction Co. were operating nearby. It occurred to me that if I were to re-open this comparison it might help me concentrate on the specific failings of the site. Some days later the occasion arose for me to do so. The full transcript of the conversation is to be found in Appendix 1, whence the following material derives.

### Al, the ideal typist

Al provides us with a layman's sociology of the organization which sounds remarkably Weberian. Weber writes of the modern organization that:

> There is the principle of fixed and official jurisdictional areas, which are generally ordered by rules. . . . The principles of office hierarchy and of levels of graded authority mean a firmly ordered system of super- and subordination in which there is supervision of the lower offices by the higher ones. . . . The management of the modern office is based upon written documents ('the files'), which are preserved in their original or draught form. . . . In private enterprise 'the bureau' is often called 'the office' . . . in general, bureaucracy segregates official activity as something distinct from the sphere of private life. . . . Office management . . . usually presupposes thorough and expert training . . . official activity demands the full working capacity of the official. . . . The management of the office follows general rules, which are more or less stable, more or less exhaustive, and which can be learned (Weber, 1948, pp. 196–8).

The job, as a 'fixed and official jurisdictional area', should comprise a 'continuous rule bound conduct of official business' (Weber, 1968, p. 218), a sentiment echoed by Al's idea(l) of a 'normal' job, which he theorizes in terms of his experience of similar jobs, notably the near-by job 'up there':

1.2*    Al  Yeah. I used to go in with Peter H. (the Project
              Manager on another Construction Co. site 'up
              there') he called me in, and had me in there all
              morning, and all we talked about was the job, and
              that was all I wanted to talk to him about. . . .

---

\* 1.2—this refers to Appendix 1, Utterance 2. Where there may be risk of confusion over the location of a cited utterance, I will adopt the convention used here: the first number references the appendix; the second number references the utterance.

1.3    S.    So that's what a job ought to be like?

1.4    Al    Uh.

1.5    S.    No chattering and gossiping, just getting on with it?

1.5    Al    Well you chatter and gossip between people of your own, you know, I chatter and gossip with some, but I don't go chattering and gossiping with Peter. You should be too busy, you shouldn't have time to chatter.

On an ideal job the Project Manager should not allow himself to be bothered with the everyday trivia of organization. He should delegate: 'The principles of office hierarchy and of levels of graded authority mean a firmly ordered system of super- and subordination in which there is a supervision of the lower offices by the higher ones', as Weber (1948, p. 197) put it. On an ideal job a Project Manager should not employ official time and resources to deal with matters falling outside of the 'official jurisdictional area': 'In principle, the executive office is separated from the household, business from private correspondence, and business assets from private fortunes' (Weber, 1948, p. 197).

In both these respects the 'Northern Town' job is deficient as it is theorized against the measure of the nearby job 'up there':

1.7    S.    The reps seem to take a lot of time as well.

1.8    Al    He won't have 'em up there. He doesn't have any bother, no. Tommy (the 'Buyer') looks after a lot of the reps admittedly, if Tommy thinks there's anything Peter ought to know he tells him, but he won't have bloody reps on't'job, cluttering it up. Half the time in there, they're just talking about his hobbies. Had a bloke here selling bloody clay once,

1.9    S.    Clay?

1.10    Al    bloody modelling clay, for his pottery, or his housekeeper.

1.11    S.    How did he get him?

1.12    Al    He just phoned up. One day, he went down to this hardware shop down town and asked for this tool, joiners use it, it's got a curved blade, it's what they used to use for chopping,

1.13    S.    Yeah.

1.14    Al    levelling pieces of wood. It's how you get the effect on an old table.

1.15    S.    Yeah.

1.16    Al    Went down there, and said have you got one, a small one about that big. They said no, don't know where to get one, or how much they'd cost – couldn't

get any in stock. So he came back, spent half the day
telephoning, found out where he could get some,
went back down t'shop, told him where to phone,
an' t'save him one. Well, he came back and said
'You know that firm down in Town – well they think
I'm a great bloke now'.

It is not only 'reps' who distract him from official business.
Personal troubles intrude upon professional practice:

| | | |
|---|---|---|
| 1.51 | Sec. | I could come in here about three days a week, and have everything done. He could dictate all his letters for the week. |
| 1.52 | Al | Yeah, but what would he dictate? 'Dear Madam . . .' |
| 1.53 | Sec. | (Laughs) Yeah, in answer to your advertisement/ |
| 1.54 | Al | What letters have you typed? |
| 1.55 | Sec. | I did five yesterday. |
| 1.56 | Al | For what? For Construction Co.? |
| 1.57 | Sec. | No, I haven't done a letter for Construction Co. for weeks. |
| 1.58 | S. | He still can't find a housekeeper? |
| 1.59 | Sec. | Oh, we restarted that yesterday. |
| 1.60 | Al | He'd . . . hundreds, he'd loads, and he was turning 'em down like flies – Not having her, because she said, 'Hello, this is, I'm answering your advert, how much money is it?' – but he wasn't having her – 'I don't like people who ask about money', he said. The next one phoned up and said, 'Well, is there much life in Harrogate, you know, what's Harrogate like? – well, he didn't want her – he's choosy. |
| 1.61 | Sec. | He'd boiled it down to two – he'd got one in Wakefield that was virtually going to be it – he took her out a few times, then all of a sudden she said, 'Well, I'm undecided, so I'll say no'. Then he got this other one from Newcastle, |
| 1.62 | S. | Yeah. |
| 1.63 | Sec. | and she came down for two weekends, |
| 1.64 | S. | Yeah. |
| 1.65 | Sec. | it was all set, everything planned, she was coming – she rang up on Sunday, and she said she didn't want to – well she got her mother to. . . . |
| 1.66 | Al | So we're back to square one again. And his original housekeeper's off on Saturday – so he's not going to be in on Friday. |

Weber (1968, p. 22) insisted that in an ideal bureaucracy its members should be 'subject to strict and systematic discipline and control', with which

1.24   Al   . . . you never get this feeling, look at your watch, 'Cor, is it that time already?'

1.25   S.   Yeah.

1.26   Al   You have a crap, push bits of wood about, start standing around. It just gets generally so that a job gets to a state of, you know. . . .

1.27   S.   Well, what should it be really like?

1.28   Al   Like I just said, blokes should be fully employed out there, that's what they're here for.

1.29   S.   I mean, if it was an ideal job, what would it be like?

1.30   Al   Well, we pay fifty-five and a half pence a labourer for working an hour, and we want an hour's work out of him. The rates, them rates have only been put in. . . . Like I was explaining before, you base your costs on doing a job, on him doing an hour's work,

1.31   S.   Yeah.

1.32   Al   for fifty-five and a half pence. If it's gonna take him two hours to do it you only want to be paying him two hours.

1.33   S.   And it's his job in there to see that you get an hour's work?

1.34   Al   Fully occupied – he's to keep 'em fully occupied.

But if the manager's task 'is to keep 'em fully occupied', at the same time he is supposed to exercise the same control and surveillance over himself. He should not shirk the office. The manager's 'continuous operation' (Weber, 1968, p. 219) on the written documents should constitute the duties of that office, which is not the case where

1.40   Al   I'll be in here, an' he'll have a pile on his desk, an' he'll say 'Oh, I've all this to get through' – a right bloody pile. Then the next thing you know, he's started chattering, it's half past six, and he'll say 'Oh well, time for t'off', you know, and he hasn't touched it, not just looked at it.

1.41   S.   Yeah, yeah, I suppose that on another job, a good job, there'd be a lot less talk?

1.42   Al   There would, yeah, you wouldn't have time to talk. Up there, I used to eh, I've worked through my dinner hour, and not known it, until after me dinner, and I've looked at my watch, and thought 'Oh God'.

1.43   S.   Because you've been so busy?

1.44  Al  I've gone in in the morning, you've got your work
          done, you're working on, and the sun's shining, the
          next thing I saw my wife walking on there ready
          to come home.
1.45  S.  Uhmm.
1.46  Al  I've checked what time it was, thinking she'd come
          early, but she weren't. And your day just lasted some-
          thing like, you'd think, 'Bloody hell', you'd think,
          'you've no sooner seemed to have come and you're
          ready for going home.' Well work didn't seem so bad,
          because you didn't seem to be there – on a day like
          you come here, you think you're here all bloody day,
          and you get sick of it.

The consequences of a bad job are viewed with dread:

1.71  Al  Well I tell you, I've prepared myself for this job
          folding up. The point is you see, what upsets me is,
          is that when I go on another job, say Construction Co.
          say, took me, want to take you off that job, take you
          on another job, and y'start talking amongst every-
          body, and they say, (laughingly), 'Oh yeah, you were
          on that Northern job weren't you – what went
          wrong?'
1.72  S.  It becomes a joke?
1.73  Al  Yeah, I'm classed as being 'You were on that
          Northern job – everyone was bad on that Northern
          job – that were a really bad job'.
1.74  S.  How would they know that this was, that it's going
          to lose?
1.75  Al  It's funny, you get good jobs and bad jobs, there's
          bad jobs going through the firm now that people
          don't forget. You see, he'll never, he's bloody useless
          sod now for Construction Co., they'll never give him
          anything, he'll never get another Construction Co.
          contract. Neither will I. Neither will Peter, the
          engineer, y'see because everything that goes wrong,
          he pushes it, he just pushes it.

In Construction Co. you are only as good as your last job. The last
job carries your 'career' (Weber, 1948, p. 203). And the job's only
as good as 'the bloke at the top'. And if he fails in either competence
or responsibility, it will soon become public knowledge; the figures
will tell the tale:

1.81  Al  ... It was Ken's job to check the steel, and it's also
          Peter's responsibility, because he's chief engineer to

111

check over Ken. Well that's as high as it went. It's
like I said before, y'know, the bloke at the top's
responsible for everything.

1.82   S.   So it was really the Project Manager's
           responsibility?
1.83   Al   Yeah, but he placed it just below him.
1.84   S.   But don't they know that up there, at Head Office?
1.85   Al   Well, it's like anything else, if you go back to your
           University, and they say to you 'What do you think
           to that Cashier on site?', and you say, 'Oh, he's a
           bit of a dosser, he does bugger all you know' – well,
           they'll take what you said.
1.86   S.   Yeah – but you said earlier, y'know you thought that
           they'd have that kind of opinion about him as well.
           I mean where would they get that from then?
1.87   Al   Well, they will because the job's not moving. When I
           put them cost figures in, and they say 'Oh there,
           bloody hell, we've eighteen joiners on that site and
           they've fixed between 'em twenty square yards of
           shuttering, that's one square yard each in a week.
1.95   Al   . . . and that's where it shows up badly for him you
           see, it's no one's fault but his then.
1.96   S.   And do you think it'll come home to roost?
1.97   Al   It's bound to do, another, just take it going ridiculous,
           another twelve months, and jobs no further on,
           there's bound to be, there's bound to come a time
           when they think, 'Well, what's going on' – and that's
           when they'll come in y'see, but, the only thing like
           I've said before, that I don't like about it, I'm not
           bothered if Construction Co. never get it built, but
           if I stick with Construction Co. I'll always be
           associated with this job.
1.98   S.   Why do you think it should be a bad job? Do you
           think they put in too low a price for it?
1.99   Al   No . . . it's like I said before – whatever bloke you've
           got in there, sets the tone – if he's a good bloke,
           sharp, quick, always here on time, everybody's the
           same.
1.100  S.   Uhmm.
1.101  Al   It does, it's true is that. John J., when he's on a
           motorway, you don't get people wandering in and
           out, bloody dinner times, half an hour longer than
           should be, coming and going when they want, even
           if he's not on site they're there – if they know he's
           not coming in tomorrow they don't think 'Well, we

don't have to come in' – they're bloody there. 'Cos, it's just instilled into you. McAlpine's are the same, you never, ever let 'em off, 'cos if you're coming in at five to eight, he's in at ten to, to make sure you're there at five to.

1.102  S.  Yeah.

1.103  Al  He'll never have more than half an hour for his lunch – it's so that you can never go and say, 'Oh, I'm too busy', 'cos he'll say 'You're too busy? I only have half an hour and it's good enough for you'. It's no good saying 'Look, I have three hours for dinner, and you only have half an hour'. It all comes from that room – it's like, rays, the sun and its rays, if the sun's bright, all its rays are bright aren't they? If the sun's dull, all your bloody rays are dull aren't they?

Normal experience of other jobs theorizes the ideal for Al. Other-than-normal experience on a job is murderous for 'career' (Weber, 1948, pp. 203–4). Career becomes 'fated'. And fate is cast by the control, or lack of control, that the manager has over the job. And the job includes your self.

For Al, the ideal job is normally like clockwork, staffed by precision-engineered puppets. And puppetry represents perfection unflawed by humanity, unless humanity flaws their production.

Essentially, the failure of organization for Al is a failure of 'control': control by the manager over his self and his site.

### Everyday and Weberian rationality

Al's analysis of the ideal organization recalls Weber's ideal type of the organization. This could be coincidence, or it might be that Al has read Weber at some time – but Al has never had that kind of sociological teaching, or management training.

The similarity may be neither fortuitous nor learnt. It may instead be characterized as a representation of our organizational rationality. Although the respective modes and traditions of theorizing which are embodied in Weber and in Al may differ, the message which each *appears* to bear would *seem* to be the same.

Firstly, let us explicate the context of Weber's ideal type of bureaucracy, before going on to a comparison of this with that advanced by Al.

Weber describes a system of economic activity as 'formally rational', 'according to the degree in which the provision for needs, which is essential in every rational economy, is capable of being expressed in numerical calculable terms, and is so expressed' (Weber, 1947,

p. 185). This 'Cartesian' conception of a 'mathematical rationality' underlies his analysis (see Rosen, 1969, pp. xv–xvi).

Weber does not collect rationality as the specific form of all industrial life, but a specific form of 'rationality' belonging to a particular epoch of capitalist industry, that of its world mastery and domination:

> Today it is primarily the capitalist market economy which demands that the official business of the administration be discharged precisely, unambiguously, continuously, and with as much speed as possible. Normally, the very large, modern capitalist enterprises are themselves unequalled modes of strict bureaucratic organization. Business management throughout rests on increasing precision, steadiness, and, above all, the speed of operations. . . . Bureaucratization offers above all the optimum possibility for carrying through the principle of specializing administrative functions according to purely objective considerations. Individual performances are allocated to functionaries who have specialized training and who by practice learn more and more. The 'objective' discharge of business primarily means a discharge of business according to *calculable rules* and 'without regard for persons' (Weber, 1947, p. 215).

This calculability is expressed in particular in the abstractions of 'capital accounting':

> Capital accounting is the valuation and verification of opportunities for profit and of the success of profit making activity. It involves the valuation of the total assets of the enterprise, whether these consist in goods in kind or in money, at the beginning of the activity; and the comparison of this with a similar valuation of the assets still present, or newly acquired at the end of the process (Weber, 1947, pp. 191–2).

This calculability is 'demanded': 'The peculiarity of modern culture, and specifically of its technical and economic basis, demands this very "calculability" of results' (Weber, 1948, p. 215). What is this 'peculiarity of modern culture, and specifically of its technical and economic basis'?

Weber answers this question in his *General Economic History* (1923) with a set of factors which include: the existence of a 'formally free' labour force; the appropriation and concentration of the physical means of production as disposable private property; the representation of share rights in organizations and property ownership; and the 'rationalization' of various institutional areas such as the market, technology, and the law. In particular, rationalization of the market would depend upon the existence of an economic surplus, and its exchange in monetary terms as 'normal preconditions' for this market. Thus, the foundation of rationalization, the market, is the historical product not of reason, but of might: 'money prices are the product of conflicts of interest and compromise; they thus result from systems of power relationships' (Weber, 1947, p. 211). 'Systems of power relationships' must thus pre-exist the market, and its rationally functioning organizations:

It is the most elemental economic fact that the way in which the disposition over material property is distributed among a plurality of people, meeting competitively in the market for the purpose of exchange, in itself creates specific life-chances. According to the law of marginal utility this mode of distribution excludes the non-owners from competing for highly valued goods; it favours the owners and, in fact, gives to them a monopoly to acquire such goods. Other things being equal, this mode of distribution monopolizes the opportunities for profitable deals for all those who, provided with goods, do not necessarily have to exchange them. It increases, at least generally, their power in price wars with those who, being propertyless, have nothing to offer but their services in native form or goods in a form constituted through their own labour, and who above all are compelled to get rid of these products in order barely to subsist. This mode of distribution gives to the propertied a monopoly on the possibility of transferring property from the sphere of use as a 'fortune', to the sphere of 'capital goods'; that is, it gives them the entrepreneurial function and all chances to share directly or indirectly in returns on capital. All this holds true within the area in which pure market conditions prevail. 'Property' and 'lack of property' are, therefore, the basic categories of all class situations. It does not matter whether these two categories become effective in price wars or in competitive struggles (Weber, 1948, p. 182).

But these 'material' factors alone are insufficient:

It is not sufficient to consider only the purely formal fact that calculations are being made on grounds of expediency by the methods which are amongst those available technically the most nearly adequate. In addition it is necessary to take account of the fact that economic activity is oriented to ultimate ends of some kind: whether they be ethical, political, utilitarian, hedonistic, the attainment of social distinction, of social equality, or of anything else. Substantive rationality cannot be measured in terms of formal calculation alone, but also involves a relation to the absolute values or to the content of the particular ends to which it is oriented (Weber, 1947, p. 185).

The 'ultimate ends' which initially sanctified capitalist activity were the religious values of Calvinism, in particular the stress on 'this worldly' asceticism, but

> Since ascetism undertook to remodel the world and to work out its ideals in the world, material goods have gained an increasing and finally an inexorable power over the lives of men as at no previous period in history. Today the spirit of religious ascetism – whether finally, who knows? – has escaped from the cage. But victorious capitalism, since it rests on mechanical foundations, needs its support no longer. The rosy blush of its laughing heir, the Enlightenment, seems also to be irretrievably fading, and the idea of duty in one's calling prowls about in our lives like the ghost of dead religious beliefs (Weber, 1930, pp. 181–2).

Now not even a ghost haunts the machine of 'victorious capitalism' as it stalks the withered souls of men:

> Already now, rational calculation is manifest at every stage. By it, the performance of each individual worker is mathematically measured, each man becomes a little cog in the machine and, aware of this, his one preoccupation is whether he can become a bigger cog . . . it is horrible to think that the world could one day be filled with those little cogs, little men clinging to little jobs and striving towards bigger ones . . . this passion for bureaucracy is enough to drive one to despair (Weber, in Mayer, 1956, p. 127).

Weber is not about to write a paeon to 'victorious capitalism' – although what seemed a conflation of reason to 'rationality' might have suggested so. Weber allows us to bracket this 'rationality' through his commitment to 'relate the events of the real world consciously or unconsciously to universal "cultural values" and to select out those relationships which are significant' (Weber, 1949, pp. 81–2).

Certainly, this despairingly angry and ironical conception of 'rationality' is significant. Its significance lies not in its 'universal "cultural value"' but in its pretence. It is a sham – a pretender to the title of rationality. None the less, historically it is significant enough to reach from the scholarly typification of Max Weber, to the everyday rationality of organization today, as Al presents it.

Weber developed his ideal type from 'experience' and from a 'technical point of view', 'in that it shows with what degree of approximation a concrete historical phenomenon may be in one aspect "feudal", in another "patrimonial", in another "bureaucratic", and in still another "charismatic"' (Weber, 1947, p. 110). The ideal type is constructed on the basis of experience, as a formal schema, whose meaning is to be understood objectively apart from those everyday or historical instances which ground it.

Weber's experience was gleaned not only from everyday life, but from a depth of reading and scholarship scarcely imaginable in this age of Nietzche's 'last man who makes everything small'. Before such a grasp of experience we can do little but 'blink'.

Al's experience is more limited, more in our grasp. His ideal type of organizational rationality derives from his knowledge and experience of a number of other, similar jobs. Yet both Al and Weber theorize the organization in similar typal terms.

Schutz (1962) shares with Weber a concern that such types should be subjectively meaningful, as well as being logically consistent. Additionally, he stresses that they are not 'adequate' unless any man, such as Al, can understand them:

Each term in a scientific model of human action must be constructed in such a way that a human act performed within the life-world by an individual actor in the way indicated by the typical construct would be understandable for the actor himself as well as his fellow-men in terms of commonsense interpretations of everyday life. Compliance with this postulate warrants consistency of the constructs of the social scientist with the constructs of commonsense experience of the social reality (Schutz, 1962, p. 44).

If we were to take Al as an example of an 'individual actor' then Weber's ideal type would be as capable of programming a person 'in terms of (the) commonsense interpretations of everyday life' which we need to pass as an organization member, as would any ethnomethodological study.

The type that both Al and Weber present would be a rational basis for identifying its substantive instances in daily life. As descriptions of (idealized) elements of reality, whose scientific rationality resides in their internal logic, subjective meaning (and usage-adequacy), these typifications could only represent the measure of everyday life in themselves, because the good of their reason, and that reason which they address, remains firmly within that life.

None the less, through anger and irony, Weber's despair transcends this reason. It allows us to note that he brackets this 'rationality' while admitting its power, as Dawe (1971) notes, and as he suggests that Marcuse (1971) ironically hints at. For Weber, in relating this 'rationality' to 'universal "cultural values"', could it have been possible that this 'rationality' represented a universal, cultural reason?

The distinction between Al's analysis, and that of Weber, does not rest in their substantive matter. It is what each makes of this analysis that is important. Any analysis which remains within the matter, as its topic and standard of speech, as does Al, only serves to allow itself to be ruled by the theorizing power of that matter. Thus, for Al, flawed rationality is a technical problem – the problem of control. And rationality is flawed by humanity. So, for Al, the problem of control is the freedom of humanity.

Weber was also concerned with the problem of control, as Alan Dawe (1971) has argued. Thus, the bureaucratic organization is a mechanical instrument of control:

> The decisive reason for the advance of bureaucratic organization has always been its purely technical superiority over any other form of organization. The fully developed bureaucratic mechanism compares with other organizations exactly as does the machine with the non-mechanical modes of production. . . .
> Precision, speed, unambiguity, knowledge of the files, continuity, discretion, unity, strict subordination, reduction of friction and of material and personal costs – these are raised to the optimum point in the strictly bureaucratic administration (Weber, 1948, p. 214).

The 'special virtue' of this instrument, like all machines, is its 'dehumanization': 'Its specific nature, which is welcomed by capitalism, develops the more perfectly the more bureaucracy is 'dehumanized' . . . this is the specific nature of bureaucracy and it is appraised as its special virtue' (Weber, 1948, pp. 215–16).

So for Weber it might also seem that the problem of control is the suppression of any remaining vestiges of humanity in the machine, so that the more perfectly rational, the more perfect the control, then the less flawed the machine. And thus the least flawed machine would be the most inhuman (the Concentration Camp as the apotheosis of rationality).

But we could not make Weber say this, no matter how hard we tried, because of the relevance of value, and the value of reason, to his analysis of the 'scientific calling' (Weber, 1948; Dawe, 1971). His 'Reason' transcends our 'rationality'.

For Weber, the decreasing limits of personal freedom, the compulsion of our material form of life, and its usurpation of reason, represent the 'problem of control'.

Al has no such problems. His problem of control is the mirror image of Weber's. And this is the measure of domination.

Al does not work as the Protestant once worked, 'for the highest spiritual and cultural values'. There are no ascetics on site.

Al works for the (ideal of) organization as one where control is fully extended and exerted, where men become machines, and where machines serve this ideal. Men do not do this for any over-riding ethical purpose, but because 'career' is served by the job (1.97).

Self-interest serves organizational-interest; organizational-interest serves self-interest. I shall now consider this 'interest' as it is expressed in the 'rationality' of the organization.

## The 'rationality' of the organization

The organization is the juncture of materials with ideas about the relationship of these to each other. These materials comprise not only the site, plant, capital and raw materials, but also labour, regarded descriptively as a commodity (Macpherson, 1973, p. 10). The organization as the amalgam of materials and ideas is the site of an 'objective principle', frozen as a 'concrete object' which 'governs the domination' in the organization (Simmel, 1971, p. 116). This domination is expressed in the 'rationality' of the organization (Weber, 1968; Karpik, 1972).

This 'rationality' may be seen in the deep structure of organizational strategies and tactics, expressed in speech, and produced through members 'understanding' of their iconic form of life, in the domination of the ideal of profitability.

The organization as the locus of domination represents our economic form of life – that system of relationships between production, exchange, and consumption of goods and services. Where the icon of capitalism stands as that which gives this activity its point, purpose, and regularity, then the prices of these are directly or indirectly fixed by the market, as opposed, for example, to exchange based upon rules of reciprocity, which characterized pre-capitalist society (Weber, 1968). In capitalist society, the price mechanism governs exchanges, the rationality of which is oriented towards an ideal of profitability as a general rule.

The ideal, a mode of being profitable, co-exists as an 'objective principle', towards which members orient their actions, with different modes for achieving the production of our material life. These we may characterize as, for example, the material life of 'construction', or 'mining', or 'shipbuilding' or whatever. This material life will concern the application of specific techniques and technologies in the service of the particular economic form of life – in this instance these would be beholden to the icon of capitalism.

The material life, or what Karpik (1972) has termed the 'logic of action', of the enterprise may be categorized in two further ways – the 'collective' logic of action, and the 'distributive' logic of action.

The collective logic of action consists of different strategies for transforming material life into profits, such as a policy of innovation in goods and services offered for sale; the presentation of products as particularly prestigious in order to try and increase sales, or a policy of asset-stripping the materials of the organization.

119

The distributive logic of action concerns the way in which whatever the collective earns is distributed either as surplus-value for profit, or as exchange-value for wages and salaries. The distinction between 'exchange-value' and 'surplus-value' derives from Marx (1973).

Marx (1973) argues that what the worker sells to the capitalist, in return for his wages, is his labour-power. This cannot be a 'fair' exchange. If it were, then the capitalist would quickly have no money left, because if the capitalist did not share in the labour, then all the money would soon pass to the labourer. Marx (1973) argued that where there existed profit there could be no fair exchange:

> The surplus value which capital has at the end of the production process . . . signifies . . . that the labour time objectified in the product . . . is greater than that which was present in the original components of capital This in turn is possible only if the labour objectified in the price of labour is smaller than the living labour time purchased with it (Marx, 1973, p. 321).

Raw material and machinery represent fixed amounts of objectified labour as components of capital. Where the price paid for labour, the wage, is exactly equal in labour time payments to the amount of labour time the labourer has added to the raw material and machinery,

> then the capitalist would merely have exchanged exchange value in one form for exchange value in another. He would not have acted as capital . . as far as the capitalist is concerned, it has to be a not exchange. He has to obtain more value than he gives. Looked at from the capitalists' side, the exchange must be only *apparent*; i.e. must belong to an economic category other than exchange, or capital as capital and labour as labour in opposition to it would be impossible (Marx, 1973, p. 322).

The labourer exchanges his creative labour, which for Marx was the source of value, 'for a predetermined value, regardless of the result of his activity'. Labour has two types of value: 'use-value' and 'exchange-value'. The worker sells his labour power (use-value) for an exchange-value, the wage. Exchange-value refers to the value a product has when it is exchanged with other products. As such, it presupposes a definite structure of economic relations, in which the value of the product is produced by the labour necessary to produce it. The use-value of labour creates the capitalists' value. This is profit, which is that part of the labourers exchange-value which is retained by the capitalist after deducting his costs of production, the raw materials, machinery and the use-value of labour – wages. Marx (1973) thus argues that profit is unpaid labour, (although technically, profit need not always be the same as unpaid labour's surplus-value).[2]

Surplus-value may be distributed either as profit to the owners of an organization, or distributed as a dividend to share-holders, or perhaps it may be re-invested either in the enterprise, or elsewhere in the market. Exchange-value may be distributed according to three criteria (Karpik, 1972). These may be on 'liberal' principles according to individual or collective bargaining (which may be subject to State intervention); on bureaucratic legal-rational criteria according to age, experience, qualifications, etc., as specified in the 'files' (see Weber, 1968); or on a 'control' basis which links together the ideal of profit with means of achieving the particular material production: examples of these would be productivity bonus; profit-sharing; or a bonus for harmonious industrial relations. These agreements will be policed by professional and trade union bodies. Not every feasible distributive logic of action would cohere with every possible collective logic of action. To asset-strip and promise a bonus payment for increased growth would not cohere, for instance.

This approach to the organization puts into perspective the 'entanglement' in which I initially approached the organization.

The basic form of power relations in organizations are hierarchical: as Weber put it,

No special proof is necessary to show that military discipline is the ideal model for the modern capitalist factory . . . organizational discipline in the factory is founded upon a completely rational basis. With the help of appropriate methods of measurement, the optimum profitability of the individual worker is calculated like that of any material means of production (Weber, 1948, p. 261).

The joiners (in 'The Joiners' Tale') appear to think that this hierarchy is stratified on a binary basis, into 'organizers' and 'organized'. Weber argues that within these categories of organization many levels of 'cogs' exist, but that 'The bureaucratic structure goes hand in hand with the concentration of the material means of management in the hands of the master' (Weber, 1948, p. 221). It is this basic distinction between 'masters' and 'men' which 'The Joiners' Tale' represents. The relationships between 'masters' and 'men' are governed by an 'objective principle' (Simmel, 1971, p. 116), the abstractions of 'capital accounting' which are 'demanded' by 'the market'. It is this abstraction which, in a very real sense, explains the exercise of power in the organization over and above the pyramidal control structure that Weber discusses.

This abstraction stands as the measure of the organizational ideal – the production of profit. This ideal is oriented towards by executive members as that to which they orient the instrument of their purpose – the organization. The particular mode of rationality of the organization will be a result of the interaction between the particular material form of life, and the requirements of a wider economic framework; the juxtaposition of choices in technology with choices in markets, for example. The choice of these involves specific policy decisions, or reactions to 'market forces', which entails a variable commitment of organizational resources, which will involve management in more or less reversible 'management for objectives'.

My 'entanglement' in initially theorizing about power in the organization in terms of the 'strategic contingency' theory of Hickson *et al.* (1971) was in thinking that the consequences of this 'management for objectives' could provide the grounds for a theory of power in organizations, as the 'strategic contingency' theorists suggested. At the most, the 'strategic contingency' theory could provide a theory of managerial influence in the organization and not a theory of power. I will argue why this should be so.

First we have to consider the hierarchical structure of the organization. This is the context to which any theorizing about power in the organization must orient itself. Second, we have to consider the ways in which this might be subverted, so that there would exist a definite pattern of power over and above this structure, which was in need of explanation. Theorizing in a 'strategic contingency' mode neglects the former, and over-states the possibility of the latter in those terms which it proposes (which is not to deny the possibility of an alternative theory about the subversion of power in organizations – but that is another matter).

The crucial error in my initial entanglement in 'strategic contingencies' was to neglect the concepts of domination and rule, and also the topics of economic activity and rationality. By restricting power solely to the determination of outcomes to issues, one forgets the context in which this occurs. The crucial point becomes: which issues?

'Strategic contingencies' theory implicitly assumes the correctness of the 'managerial thesis', that power no longer resides in ownership but in management (e.g. Burnham, 1941). It then takes it one stage further by assuming that the pure type of general manager has disappeared only to be replaced by different sub-units of specialists (see Galbraith, 1967). Thus power is initially assumed to have shifted to these sub-units: the question then is – which sub-unit? The answer is presumed to be that which manages to cope with more strategic contingency than the others. Now we can bring our two preceding questions together.

The first question was – which issues? By assuming that there has been an effective managerial revolution, and by neglecting structural power, domination and rules, the theory presumes that, one, the crucial issues to be decided are settled at the level of departmental managers, and that, two, the outcomes to these then decide their power. This was our second question – which sub-unit?

On the construction site there were no 'sub-units' as such, but there were 'issues' over which power was exercised as people attempted to impose their different definitions of situations upon other people's actions. I found on the site-organization that the exercise of power was invariably managed by the Project Manager. This is what one would expect from the structure of power in Construction Co.'s site-organization. Had it been otherwise then it would have been something 'peculiar' to explain, something which was contrary to what we might have expected.

How might something contrary to what we had expected occur in an organization? I have argued against a 'strategic contingencies' explanation, with one strand in my argument being that the concept of 'uncertainty', from a sociological perspective, cannot be described as a property of a determining 'environment', but must instead be described as something located in 'member's knowledge'. I have also noted how, after having been in the organization for a while, I began to think of the concept of 'uncertainty' in this context in terms of the concept of 'indexicality'. 'Indexicality' achieves its importance on site because it is the means by which the organization manifests its 'mode of rationality', as I will argue in the next chapter.

I have suggested that organizations pursue a 'mode of rationality' as something constructed by their managers in the way they orient their actions towards the ideal of profitability. The 'mode of rationality' of Construction Co.'s site-organization would be their particular way of achieving the ideal of profitability. As a sociologist I was not concerned with the economic concepts of profit and loss, or the accountancy of the balance-sheet. What interested me was the sociological possibility of these. And this means examining the ways in which profits and losses, for example, are made, not economically, but sociologically. This involves seeing how such a phenomenon as a 'profit' is constructed out of the understandings that members of the organization share concerning the ways in which 'profit' may be made.

It is through the empirical study of this 'understanding' on the construction-site that the exercise of 'power', the functioning of power in the organization, may be related to the organization's 'mode of rationality'. This 'mode of rationality' concerns the means by which the organization pursues the ideal of its economic/material form of life. On the construction-site, as in any other organization, this rationality provides an area of 'significant issues'. A 'significant issue' will be one which effects the ideal of profitability as it is manifested in the organization's 'mode of rationality'. The major exercise of power in the organization, because it is generated by members orienting themselves to the iconic domination of the ideal of profitability, which they do in a concertedly 'rational' way, will concern issues that effect the 'rational' functioning of this form of life. Thus, if we were to have a theory of 'significant issues' we would implicitly have a theory concerning the functioning of power in the organization. The position(s) that exercised power over 'significant issues' would then be the positions with the effective functioning 'power' to act on 'issues'. But this 'power' depends upon one's submission to the iconic domination of one's economic form of life which grants one this 'power'.

As the market differentiates 'issues' so it differentiates the members of organizations in a hierarchical structure. Where this 'axiomatic' structure of power, and its functioning, no longer cohere, because of the emergence of new 'issues' – perhaps because of the development of new technologies, or products, or markets – we might expect a political process of incorporation into the structure to be underway. The 'power' granted to deal with 'issues' would, in any case, give its functionary an 'influence' over the formulation of organizational policy and strategy, concerning the persual of the icon, precisely because of the expert's limited specialist knowledge. But because of the control exercised by the iconic domination of the organization's economic form of life, it could hardly subvert the structure of power. (This is not to suggest that it cannot be subverted. It can. But only through a rejection of the dominant icon, as has happened – as a temporary 'aberration' – during factory occupations which have occurred after the icon has been shattered by the facts of bankruptcy and subsequent loss of jobs. But the market has usually reasserted itself.)

# 8   Issues from organizational life

## Construction: this research and previous research

AI suggests that the failing of organization is a failing of control: control by the manager over his self and his site. Previous research suggests that this is a 'normal' feature of the industry. In 1966 the Building Industry Communications Research Project received the results of research that it had commissioned from the Tavistock Institute into 'communication problems' in the industry. This was published as a digest titled *Interdependence and Uncertainty: A Study of the Building Industry* (Higgin *et al.*, 1966). In the introductory remarks on sampling are to be found the following comments:

> In selecting projects for study we concentrated on those which seemed likely to go well. No purpose was seen in criticizing projects which were obviously inefficient.
>
> Throughout, informants have emphasized that what was observed was normal and that the contracts studied were regarded as 'good' by those concerned. Yet none of the projects studied seemed to live up to expectations. The experience of the team has been of an industry in which misunderstandings, delays, stoppages, and abortive work result from failures in communications, and impressions of confusion, error, and conflict have provided the starting point for an analysis of the operational characteristics of the building process (Higgin *et al.*, 1966, p. 17).

The Tavistock researchers observed that,

> Although the reasons for these situations are commonly seen in personal terms – incompetence, laziness, or financial greed of others for example, and although bitterness, and even hurt, can be given by accusations in such terms – these behaviours are seldom crucial (Higgin *et al.*, 1966, p. 52).

125

Instead, we are told that the 'real' reason lies in a disjuncture between a 'formal' and an 'informal' system of organization. The formal system is characteristically that which we encounter in formal texts about the building process, such as the RIBA *Handbook of Architectural Practice and Management*. It stresses the independence and sequential application of tasks such as briefing, designing, design quantification, construction planning and control, manufacturing, sub-contracting, and so on. It is assumed that these tasks have a 'sequential finality' which

> does not seem suited effectively to control a process character-
> ized by the interdependence of its operations, fraught with
> uncertainty and requiring carefully phased decisions and
> continuous application of all control functions (Higgin *et al.*,
> 1966, p. 45).

The Tavistock researchers located this 'interdependence', and 'uncertainty' in the functional demands of the building process. Interdependence arises from the 'relevance of different streams of information to each other in particular contexts' (Higgins *et al.*, 1966, p. 22), because of the differing types of members' knowledge required in building a structure. On a processual and interdependent task, then any decisions which have to be taken may well have wider implications than those of the immediate time and place. This introduces some uncertainty into decision-making. However, the researchers also noted that uncertainty could be introduced into the process from two further sources:

> First, there are the uncertainties engendered by the action of
> those not directly involved in the building process, such as
> government departments, planning authorities, public bodies,
> client organizations, and even the general public (see Appendix
> 2). Second, there are the uncertainties which stem from resources:
> labour, equipment and materials (Higgin *et al.*, 1966, p. 34).

The researchers saw the failing of the (formal) organization as a corollary of the efficient functioning of the (informal) organization:

> the characteristics of the formal system are so much in conflict
> with the control functions required to achieve effectiveness in
> the system of operations that, in practice, the formal system
> cannot be closely followed. Rigid adherence to the procedures
> of the formal system would not be possible, under normal
> conditions, without unacceptable expenditure – particularly of
> time. In practice, reality forces a recognition of interdependence,
> uncertainty, phased decision-taking, and the continuous
> application of functions. It forces members of the building team
> to adapt themselves (Higgin *et al.*, 1966, p. 46).

They then go on ironically to juxtapose what (formal) organization recommends with that (informal) organization which occurs:

In formal theory, design is complete at an early stage. Not only is information expected to be complete at this time, but it is also considered to be feasible in terms of 'buildability' and cost.

In practice, this is not possible, and even the formal system recognizes this by provisional items in the Bill of Quantities. But there are many other aspects of the design – not covered by provisional items – that are incomplete. This particularly applies to the design of services: the reason for this is related to the sequential manner in which the design process is usually handled. . . .

In practice, many details of services design are worked out on the job, during tours of the work after site meetings, for example. . . .

In theory, the quantity surveyor preparing for full competitive tender should quantify the design in full detail. In practice, of course, he seldom, if ever, has sufficient information. He has to extemporize and include what he expects architect and client may want.

Now the formal system requires that, before Bills of Quantities are prepared, full working drawings shall be completed. According to the RIBA handbook, these drawings will embody: 'Final decisions on every matter related to design, specification, construction and cost, and full design of every part and component of the building'. Then, in heavy type, comes the warning 'any future change in location, size, shape, or cost after this time will result in abortive work'. . . . Informal practice . . . follows procedures the reverse of the formal theory. . . .

The contract, in theory, is arrived at as a result of tendering procedure which is considered to be a legally and commercially rational bargain between the client and the builder – generally the builder who can undertake the work most cheaply. This view is based on the assumption that all details of the project have been finally decided and are specified in detail in the tender documents, and that the contractor can anticipate accurately at this time what all his costs will be. This is not so and it is not surprising, therefore, that the builder's pricing and the client's acceptance of any competitive tender must always be acts of faith (Higgin et al., 1966, pp. 47–8).

The idea that the contractual documents are a series of instructions, or formally complete and binding rules for constructing a

127

structure from its 'detail', cannot be sustained for long after one has observed a site in progress. My own observations of the site supported the general impression of the Tavistock researchers. Such contractual documents are inherently indexical, in that apart from the use that members make of these, and the occasions of their use, they remain potent, if unenacted, symbols. They exist as 'the ground for negotiation' (Strauss *et al.*, 1963), the constitutional grounds for achieving the eventual structure.

The problem for members (and the Tavistock researchers) is precisely this indexicality, which gives rise to what they describe as 'communication problems'. These are features exhibited in particular during site-meetings by 'misunderstandings, delays, stoppages, and abortive work . . . confusion, error and conflict' (Higgin *et al.*, 1966, p. 17) which they say are caused by the disjunctive effect of 'uncertainty' on the (formal) organization. This formal organization includes not only the idealized structure of relations, but also the idealized (as unindexical) constitutional grounds of the organization. It is when these are challenged by some member of the site-organization, over some specific detail or matter of interpretation, that what are termed 'communication problems' occur. These are occasioned by 'uncertainties'. These exigencies then modify the (formal) organization into an adaptive (informal) organization.

I do not see this 'uncertainty' in terms of anticipated, if specifically unforseeable, informal modifications of a formal machine, wrought by a reality recalcitrant before the plans of men. Nor do I seek to treat organization members' theorizing of this disjuncture simply as an occasion for 'scientific' irony at the expense of whatever members might say (as the Tavistock researchers do in recommending sociotechnic reason over everyday reasons). Nor do I feel bound by whatever members might say. (As if membership of the community one investigates provided the criteria not of orthodoxy, but of correctness. Consider the problems this would create in the Criminal Courts.)

'Misunderstandings, delays, stoppages, and abortive work . . . confusion, error and conflict' represent not 'communication problems' but the organization in its form of life. To argue as the Tavistock researchers do that these 'problems' are the result of a collision between two entities – 'uncertainty' modifying the 'formal' organization – is to argue as if they were both something apart from the (informal) organization which emerges from their impact. What is the status of this 'formal' organization, and of the disturbance (informal organization) wrought on it by 'uncertainty'?

The Tavistock mode of theorizing regards the 'formal' organization as a normative idealization which is unadapted to the functional imperatives of the socio-technic system. Their knowledge of the 'informal' organization derives 'from direct observation of the building team at work and from talks with them about what they were doing' (Higgin *et al.*, 1966, p. 46). This is in distinction to the 'formal' organization, which

> is not very directly manifested in actual behaviour and, if our information were based only on the behaviour of the building team on the job, we might never have become aware of the formal system in its true form. It is easily understood, however, from what people say when describing their jobs as distinct from what they do. It is even more readily understood from writings about the building process (Higgin *et al.*, 1966, p. 45).

The 'informal' organization is what people do. In contrast, the 'formal' organization is what people do not do. Thus, the formal organization is nothing, while the informal organization is everything!

Formal organization is nothing because of the existence of uncertainty. But what is 'uncertainty'? I have suggested earlier that 'one plausible interpretation of the concept of uncertainty would locate it in member's knowledge for predicting future states of affairs ... as a situation in which rules for remedying surprise had yet to be enacted' (p. 48).

Where the future holds out the possibility of surprise, then the formal organization must come to nothing. It must always be somewhat 'flawed' by a lack of present certainty, or predictive control in the future. The 'future-perfect' (Schutz, 1967; Weick, 1969) is flawed by the present, temporally shifting day.

But nothingness can only be a metaphor. In daily organizational life we find that members *do* make something out of the nothingness to which socio-technics would consign the formal organization. By enquiring of what it is that is done with the notion at this bedrock level, we are able to bracket distinctions between the (informal) organization and the (formal) organization. We are left only with the organization as 'an organization of social actions' (Garfinkel, 1956, pp. 181-2; Garfinkel and Sacks, 1970, p. 342; also see the similar formulations of such diverse writers as Tussman, 1960, pp. 6-7, 26; and Weber, 1968, pp. 48-50).

The 'formal organization' is regularly and routinely invoked as a part of the organization of social action on site. It is contained, in particular for the site, in the detailed contractual documents comprising the 'bill of works' on which the contractor tenders. As I had earlier suggested to Al (3; p. 100; also pp. 104-5), these are constitutive of the types of members, their special skills and knowledge, and those inter-relationships which occur on site, as well as containing the intendedly unindexical blueprint for the completed building. Members use these to make sense of the (informal) organization. This organization is not what uncertainty makes of the formal organization. The organization is what members make of uncertainty and the formal organization. The latter provides the constitutional (and constitutive) framework within which members *make* uncertainty out of their grasp of the indexical nature of the documentation of the 'formal' organization. This thus provides an occasion for members to reflexively theorize this indexicality by way of their form of life.

On these occasions where members employ the 'formal' organization as a resource for theorizing their indexical grasp of whatever-matter-is-at-hand, then one is confronted with

> a rich and ambiguous body of background information that normally competent members of society take for granted as commonly known. In its normal functioning this information furnishes the tacit foundation for all that is explicitly known, and provides the matrix for all deliberate considerations without itself being deliberately considered. While its content can be raised to the level of analysis, this typically does not occur (Bittner, 1965, p. 244).

On the construction site, those instances on which this particularly comes into play are specifically occasioned conversations. These we may regard as empirically occurring language games. These are taken, by all participants, to be about the 'problem' of issues – which are defined by using the resources of the 'formal' organization. Members call these 'site-meetings'. Site-meetings are members' socially organized procedures for constituting, formulating and discussing 'issues'. Issues are instantly recognizable as such because they are addressed as something formulated as a problem. They are the subject of members' concerns in site-meetings. They provide a focus for practical reasoning about the issue of issues: that is, what is to count as an issue, and how it is to do so. They are thus inherently reflexively generative, in that they provide occasions which members address precisely in order to formulate what it is that these issues consist of. (It is interesting to contrast this with Garfinkel, 1967, pp. 7–9.)

The procedural aim of the remainder of this investigation is to raise the content of this 'lay theorizing' of issues to the level of analysis. The reason for doing so is to display the apparently distinct contexts of surface speech in which issues reside, in their mode of rationality of the organization's form of life. Then we will have grasped power in the organization, not only in its structure but also in its functioning.

This functioning includes more than just the site members of

Construction Co. A number of other organizations are represented on site through some of their members. The 'inter-organizational' relationships which occur on site between these various organizations, in an official capacity, are usually conducted through the Project Manager.

A contract is initiated by a client. This is invariably an organization, rather than a person, although negotiations may occur through one or more key people. In this instance the client is the Corporation of Northern Town, with the key man being the architect, from their own Architect's Department, who is handling negotiations with Construction Co. He will usually be present at site-meetings. On this contract a firm of consultant structural engineers had been engaged, and their representative to the site was also frequently involved in negotiations. Not all the work that is done on site can be accomplished by members of the construction company engaged to build the structure, unless perhaps the contract has gone to a consortium, and so the site will usually have a number of sub-contractors present to deal with areas such as steel-fixing, heating and ventilation, electrical services, plumbing and gas, as well as any labour involved in the supervision of specialist equipment or materials that have to be sub-contracted in. Additionally, there may also be people on site who represent supplying organizations – salesmen, delivery drivers, etc. And of course there is the Clerk of Works. He is the client organization's permanent representative on site, whose task it is supposed to be to 'police' the site. Police-work, in this context, means seeing that the law is observed on every occasion, unless there exist good reasons for its not being so. And the 'law' is the prescriptions contained in the contractual documents concerning design, specification, construction, and cost of each item in the projected structure.

When I came into the organization I had anticipated that the exercise of power would mostly concern matters connected with the discipline and functioning of Construction Co.'s workforce. But I was surprised. Although this did occur, by far the most significant exercises of power were 'inter-organizational'. They occurred between members of Construction Co. – usually the Project Manager – and members of these other organizations, in particular, the architect, Clerk of Works, and consulting structural engineer. Why should this be so? And why should these be the most 'significant'?

When a contractor tenders for a job one typically assumes that he does so in order to have his bid accepted. Furthermore, one assumes that the bid, should it be accepted, would be one which would allow the contracting organization to make a contribution to its profitability. Once accepted, and a site commenced, a primary consideration of the project manager is to see that this contribution is not risked through the 'uncertainties' of the building process, such as a shortage of a specific type of labour (see 'The Joiners' Tale', Chapter 6). I shall argue that 'significant' exercises of power concern these considerations of profitability, and that these focus on questions concerning the constitutional grounds of the organization – the contractual documents. Discussions of these occur primarily within site-meetings, as occasions for conversation about what practical actions have got to be done, have been done, and will have to be undone.

## Constructing a gloss

Following a rule is analogous to obeying an order. . . .
'There is a gulf between an order and its execution. It has to be filled by the act of understanding.'
'Only in this act of understanding is it meant that we are to do THIS. The *order* – why, that is nothing but sounds, ink-marks. –'
(Wittgenstein, 1968, pars 206; 431).

Ideally, according to formal recommendations (such as the RIBA handbook), the contractual documents ought to function as an unambiguous order for a structure which the contractor is supposed to deliver. Constructing the structure should be simply a process of obeying the orders given in the documents concerning design, specification, construction and cost for each item of the projected structure. But, as Wittgenstein remarks, such an 'order' requires 'understanding' for it to be activated. Without this, it remains mere sounds, ink-marks.

This 'understanding' consists of what we might term 'glossing practices' (Garfinkel and Sacks, 1970). These are methods that members of 'natural language' communities employ to achieve objective, observable and reportable 'understanding' of a phenomenon, to make it 'account-able'. One such gloss would be the 'paradigm' (Kuhn, 1962). This would locate correct 'understanding' in a grasp of community sanctioned method and 'ways of seeing'. This 'understanding' grounded much of the conversation that I heard in site-meetings. I frequently found these conversations difficult to grasp in their more technical aspects. This difficulty was exacerbated by the frequency with which these site-meetings would discuss some detail relating to the contractual documents, with the relevant documentation in front of them. Any report of this type of conversation, without having the documents in front of one, or without the skills necessary to interpret them, would be largely unintelligible to an audience unfamiliar with the technical aspects of the construction industry.

Sometimes the practice of using the documents to try and settle an issue would be taken further. The drawings and bill of quantities were supposed to function as a 'blue-print' for the completed structure. I quickly found that issues revolved around what seemed to be either 'ambiguity' in the text of these documents, or conflicting 'ways of seeing' these. Sometimes, in order to try and settle the issues, 'mock-ups' (Garfinkel and Sacks, 1970, p. 363) would be used to point-up features of the text or drawing that they were supposed to be describing. This is one glossing practice that the Project Manager uses in attempting to enforce 'understanding':

3.24    P.W.    . . . I've got a situation at the moment where the, eh, . . . the two big external ramps he's not quite certain, the architect, whether his drawing is correct or not, whether the two ramps might clash together, would I mind setting it out on the ground, so that he can see.

3.25    S.    Uhmm,

3.26    P.W.    All right, I mean, well there's no skin off my nose really, in doing it, but I'm not doing it now, I will do it, if he gives me a V.O. to cover it, and thereby, it means he pays me extra . . . for doing it.

3.27    S.    Yeah.

3.28    P.W.    By the same light he's, like all architects he draws in two dimensions, he cannot visualize in three dimensions . . . he would not agree last week at the meeting when I told him that these ramps, geometrically, must be a spiral. Something which is circular on plan, and is rising, like that, must be a spiral. He said, no it's flat, I said, no it's a spiral. So I built a model, to show him that you cannot bend plywood in two directions, and, eh, we're having a meeting this afternoon, him and the consulting engineer. Now, not only am I right, but secondly, the bill of quantities, you get, various items on it, so much, . . . of, . . . a . . . description, soffit shuttering, so much per square metre, ditto circular on plan, at an enhanced rate. Now they've billed the soffit to those ramps as circular on plan. Well it might be circular on plan, but they're inclined, and the standard method of measurement which is a standard book, tells you that that's an extra item, so that they haven't allowed for it in their bill of quantities, which means now that I can submit what I call a star rate, a new rate for doing this work. And anything

133

> that's in the bill of quantities bears no relationship
> to it whatsoever, so as far as he's concerned he's
> going to be paying about fifteen quid a square
> metre for that now, uh, I'll have him!

What I find particularly interesting about the above is not that
it re-affirms the fact that indexicality is a cardinal fact of (everyday)
life, but the use to which this indexicality is put. The Project Manager's
'understanding' extends not only to enforcing agreement on the
'correct' way of interpreting the drawing, according to the geometri-
cal paradigm, but also seems to involve certain corollaries; as he
puts it

3.26    P.W.    ... well there's no skin off my nose really, in
                doing it, but I'm not doing it now, I will do it, if
                he gives me a V.O. to cover it, and thereby, it
                means he pays me extra . . . for doing it.

A corollary of 'understanding' seems to be that it will cost money.
It is not that the details cannot be understood. They will not be
understood, unless 'he gives me a V.O. to cover it'. A V.O. is a
'variation order', that is one which varies some element in the contractual documents. But that is not the end of the additional cost to
the client. Through making an issue of re-interpreting the drawings
the Project Manager is able to

3.28    P.W.    ... submit what I call a star rate, a new rate for
                doing this work. And anything that's in the bill of
                quantities bears no relationship to it whatsoever,
                so as far as he's concerned he's going to be paying
                about fifteen quid a metre for that now, uh, I'll
                have him!

The 'star-rate' will include the 'bit of profit' which is normal, plus
some 'extras' such as the 'buggeration factor':

3.30    P.W.    Yeah, all right then, say I reckon, say allowing for
                a bit of profit it's going to cost eight quid a metre/
3.31    S.      Yeah/
3.32    P.W.    I'll say right, what the hell. I'll put ten quid in,
3.33    S.      Yeah,
3.34    P.W.    Plus, that by and large with a thing like that your,
                what I call, buggeration factor,
3.35    S.      Hmh, huh, what the, eh, stress, the strain?
3.36    P.W.    No, that, a you never know I mean, something
                like that, you get one job, and the radius and such
                might be such that you can use three-quarter-inch
                plywood, cut in strips, 'cos you gotta set each one,
3.37    S.      Uhm,

3.38    P.W.    this job might be, the radius might be too sharp, and I might find it doesn't work with three-quarters, and so I've got to get some half-inch ply, I've got to use that many more bearers underneath it to stop it deflecting, you know, so you want something in for your buggeration factor.

P.W.'s gloss, as Project Manager, involves an indexical reformulation of the contractual documents in order to serve the interests of Construction Co. This interest is served by the profitable construction of the projected structure. Once a contract has been signed, one of the most significant means of achieving either additional profit to that contracted for, or of securing that profit contracted for against exigency, is to renegotiate the contractual documents at any instance that occasions itself. These instances are not simply 'communication problems' (although they may be seen as such) occurring because of some exogenous causal factor, such as the prevalence of 'uncertainty', but are specifically *constructed* as such by the Project Manager as potentially profitable 'issues'. This is the mode of rationality of the Construction Co.'s form of life, in the site organization. Its mirror-image is presented in the mode of rationality of the client organization. For the client organization, issues that may cost them money are to be resisted, while issues that risk quality and design are to be raised.

From what the Project Manager says, it seems that it need not have been the case that the 'ramps' should have been an issue. They did not have to be, except that

3.26    P.W.    . . . but I'm not doing it now, I will do it, if he gives me a V.O. to cover it, and thereby, it means he pays me extra . . . for doing it.

'Now' something is different. 'Now' the 'ramps' will be built correctly only at a cost to the client, a cost which will be billed against the incorrect detail supplied by the architect. Why is 'now' different from some other time when presumably the 'ramps' need not have become an issue? P.W. argues the case in 'personal' terms, terms which refer to another matter of textual exegis of the indexical documentation. P.W. may see this as a personal trouble, which for him it is, but additionally, I would see it as an exemplification of the site-organization's form of life. What makes 'now' different from some other time is the trouble of 'normal clay'.

### 'Normal clay' and other issues

Clay – sticky, yellowish-brown stuff that I find when I dig the garden. Normal clay, whatever that could be, had never crossed my mind until I came onto the site. In my gardening at home, I had no use for knowing whether clay was normal or not. Unlike the site-members. They knew what clay could be. It could be 'sandy, stony clay' – and that was a good foundation to build on. Or it could be 'puddle clay' – which was of no use as 'normal clay' for building purposes. And these distinctions proved to be crucial on site.

The site is mapped out on the architect's and engineer's drawings, on a grid-line system, rather like an ordnance survey map. A reference thus enables one to locate any spot on the map that someone else may be referring to. The engineer's drawings instructed Construction Co. to excavate a number of spots on the site as bases into which concrete would be poured for foundations. These were in a straight grid-line across the site. On the engineer's drawings there was an excavation instruction which *instructed* the contractor to excavate to a minimum of 600 mm. into 'sandy, stony clay'. It did not specify the depth at which this 'sandy, stony clay' occurred. Accompanying these drawings was a consultant's bore-hole report of a site-survey of ground conditions. This *recommended* that the contractor should excavate to two metres into clay. It did not specify that there was any clay other than 'clay' (2.77), and did not differentiate between 'puddle clay' and 'sandy, stony clay' (2.70-7). P.W. excavated the bases according to his interpretation of these details, which was to excavate to 'normal clay' – the 'sandy, stony clay'. The resulting depth of his excavations, and the way in which he organized them, became the subject of an acrimonious letter from the architect to Construction Co.:

| | | |
|---|---|---|
| 4.9 | P.W. | Hey, here you are, read that letter, I'll, here, y'are, where is it, where is it? . . . You're mentioned in here so, |
| 4.10 | G.E. | Am I? |
| 4.11 | P.W. | (reading from letter) 'they clearly state they eh . . . when work commenced the first two or three bases were excavated, the formation at the bottom of the excavations was approved by the consulting engineer', |
| 4.12 | G.E. | Is that you saying that, or? |
| 4.13 | P.W. | That's them, |
| 4.14 | G.E. | Yes. |
| 4.15 | P.W. | All right? – 'with the knowledge of the clerk' – which you did, which you did you came and looked and said if that's/ |
| 4.16 | G.E. | Aye/ |
| 4.17 | P.W. | the sort of formation you're digging, fine. |
| 4.18 | G.E. | Uhm. |

4.19   P.W.   'and the bases constructed. Thereafter work progressed on the excavations, the Clerk of Works being asked to approve the formation exposed. At no time, however, was his attention drawn to the fact that additional excavations had been carried out below the specified levels, . . . uh, I've also been informed by consulting engineer that he was not made aware of the, eh, additional extractions'

4.20   G.E.   No, no, nono, that's . . . quite true as well,

4.21   P.W.   Yeah, that's true, yeah . . . uhm . . . but that first bit . . . 'Clerk of Works being ah, at no time was the additional extraction made explicit' – we asked him to take levels, that's the first point, and then it goes on – 'It would appear that a general instruction, general instruction, was given by your site-staff to the excavator driver to go down as far as he considered necessary, irrespective of the consulting engineer's drawings',

4.22   G.E.   Just, just hang on, now then, he says – It would appear – is it right or is it not right? Did you tell him to do that?

4.23   P.W.   Course not! I don't turn a, a machine/

4.24   G.E.   Well now, where's he got that impression from?

4.25   P.W.   Norman, said that to Brian – It looks as though they've been tear-arsing around on site. . . .

4.26   G.E.   Well, all right, y'know this/

4.27   P.W.   It then goes on, ahblahblahblah. . . . 'My clerk of works was also not informed that your staff considered the basement-levels as shown on my drawings to be incorrect! – That is untrue, we said, all right, those levels, we'll take those levels as correct as the buildings were there. What we, or we said, we never found any basement bottom intact, to agree with that, they were just smashed to pieces. 'I therefore consider it unreasonable blahblahblahblahblah, investigation of the claimed actual excavation levels reveals little or no consistency, thus leading one to assume that either the satisfactory bearing strata varied from base to base' – well it does, strata/

4.28   G.E.   You would expect it to vary.

4.29   P.W.   'or as is more likely' – he's coming a bit harder now – 'the excavator driver carried out his work with wrong instructions and/or inadequate supervision. My assistant inspected the excavation for

the bases to column B.2 to B.5. inclusive and was
satisfied that these bases were at the correct level,
approximately two metres into stony clay', well
you cannot argue it was two metres into stony
clay, that clay's never stony. . . .

4.35     P.W.    . . . . 'It is therefore unreasonable to assume that
in view of this and the site-investigation report,
clay was not encountered at anything other than
the expected levels' – clay was encountered, but
not the correct stuff.

The points at issue result from 'investigation of the claimed actual
excavation levels' by the Architect's Department revealing 'little or
no consistency' (4.27). The architect's letter advances as reasons, that
first, additional excavations were made to the first two or three bases
after they had been checked by the Clerk of Works as being at the
'specified levels', without his being explicitly informed (4.11–4.21).
Secondly, 'that a general instruction' was given by Construction
Co.'s site-staff to the excavator driver to go down as far as he considered necessary, irrespective of the consulting engineer's drawings'
(4.21). Third, the architect's letter proposed that there was an inconsistency in levels because Construction Co.'s 'staff considered the
basement-levels as shown (on the architect's drawings) to be incorrect', and had not informed the Clerk of Works of this (4.27). That the
'satisfactory bearing strata varied from base to base' (4.27) is not
considered as likely a reason as those previously advanced, with the
'more likely' explanation being that 'the excavator driver carried
out his work with wrong instructions and/or inadequate supervision'
(4.29).

P.W., the Project Manager, obviously feels strongly and personally
about the whole issue. As he said to Ray, who had previously been
his foreman but who has left to work for the Corporation as a Clerk
of Works,

2.31     P.W.   I'm still. . . . Yesterday when I got that letter,
yesterday morning, I got the shakes, believe it, you
know, I was so angry, and I'm still feeling a bit
that way.

Later, during the course of his conversation with G.E., the consultant
engineer, the source of P.W.'s anger becomes more specific. It is the
Clerk of Works whom he is especially singling out for having made
accusations of incompetence concerning the management of the job:

4.132   P.W.  Eh, . . . well straight off, before we get into the,
the nitty-gritty, of, the claim, we, Construction
Co., or me, are writing a strong letter to the

Corporation about the tone in which that letter was sent, the accusations of, incompetence,

| 4.133 | G.E. | Uhm. |
| 4.134 | P.W. | I've also got Norman's Clerk of Works memoes, it refers to, not so much, he doesn't use the word incompetent, but he says it's about time you had a competent person, on site, which is/ |
| 4.135 | G.E. | Same thing/ |
| 4.136 | P.W. | same thing, |

Reciprocally, the Project Manager's view of the Clerk of Works similarly questions his competence:

| 2.25 | P.W. | I mean, I've said it three times to Brian (Borough Architect) verbally, about Norman (Clerk of Works) and levels, it's now going in writing/ |
| 2.26 | Ray | Yeas, you might point out that he can't read a . . . level. Had Ken not helped him out there, which I were very annoyed with, we'd 'ave proved it that day. |
| 2.27 | P.W. | Well, I already said, when I said to Brian yesterday, I said, you know, your Clerk o' Works can't even read a level, he said 'Oh, can't he?'. |

If we were to believe the tales that the Clerk of Works and the Project Manager tell of each other, then we should hardly believe our eyes as we drove through Northern Town and saw the completed bus-station and car park. But, one can understand that P.W. would feel personally upset by the allegations of incompetence, especially if, as has been suggested, he failed to properly exercise managerial control:

| 2.59 | P.W. | . . . the thing that's upset me more than anything else, is those two references to the fact that we just turned a machine-driver loose. . . . |
| 2.60 | Ray | Yeah, but I mean, what, that's only Norman's is that int it, that's no official statement is it? It's no, it's the attitude of the Clerk o'Works is that/ |
| 2.61 | P.W. | What turning/ |
| 2.62 | Ray | Yeah, 'cos he said that, he said that/ |
| 2.63 | P.W. | alright, he said it, he said it yes, but it has now been recorded/ |
| 2.64 | Ray | Yeas, but it's only hearsay by the Clerk o'Works is that. . . . |
| 2.65 | P.W. | Maybe it's hear . . . no it's an accusation/ |
| 2.66 | Ray | Yes, I know, but it int sub . . . there's no grounds for it. . . . |

| 2.67 | P.W. | They can't substantiate it/ |
|------|------|------|
| 2.68 | Ray | No/ |
| 2.69 | P.W. | but the Borough Architect of Northern Town has accused us, of/ |
| 2.70 | Ray | which is wrong/ |
| 2.71 | P.W. | giving wrong instructions, inadequate supervision, turning a man loose, and/ |
| 2.72 | Ray | You might use me and say that I gave the driver the instructions to dig down to this stony, sandy clay, not to the first layer of clay, which were only puddle-clay anyway, and that's the instruction he got, and when he found that level/ |
| 2.73 | P.W. | Uhm/ |
| 2.74 | Ray | that were when we, the bases were taken. |

Machine-drivers, like Joiners, are not regarded as beings with the 'place' of organization. But this does not make them wholly irresponsible beings:

| 2.85 | P.W. | But the other thing that absolutely proves that we did not turn a machine driver loose, if you take the levels/ |
|------|------|------|
| 2.86 | Ray | Yeah/ |
| 2.87 | P.W. | off that sketch on our bases/ |
| 2.88 | Ray | Yeas/ |
| 2.89 | P.W. | they're pretty constant throughout the site, |
| 2.90 | Ray | Yes, yes. |
| 2.91 | P.W. | but ... oh, sorry, they're not constant, some are up, some are down according to local conditions/ |
| 2.92 | Ray | Yeah/ |
| 2.93 | P.W. | it's the other way around/ |
| 2.94 | Ray | Yeas/ |
| 2.95 | P.W. | but if we'd turn a man loose he'd have dug 'em all to the same bloody level, he wouldn't have, he's not going to go down an extra metre on one hole just 'cos it suits him. |
| 2.96 | Ray | No ... well your only way to prove it's to get a statement off the driver int it? I'd threaten to do that. |
| 2.97 | P.W. | They wouldn't accept that. |
| 2.98 | Ray | No, well that's the position you're sitting int it? |

To be irresponsible would be to begin behaving willfully, as one who exercises a choice, where no choice is necessary. But, whatever the machine-driver did or did not do is of little moment. What is of moment is what claims can be verified, and what accounts can be discredited?

Hearsay can be discredited, because it is personal attitude, not 'official statement'. But when it has been 'recorded' it becomes an 'accusation'. Accusations are open to negotiation. One ground for negotiation is to evoke features of a setting which are investigable matters that can be settled by documents, as Zinnerman (1971) has suggested. Hence P.W. has to try and present some grounds for his actions which are not simply a personal statement which 'They wouldn't accept' (2.96). Without these he can only tell tales of what happened, without being able to prove it:

| | | |
|---|---|---|
| 2.151 | P.W. | Yes, but one thing that is missing out of here is that when we dug that hole, |
| 2.152 | Ray | Yeah. |
| 2.153 | P.W. | Brian went down it, George went down it, and George said to Brian, that stuff at the top is no bloody use. If Construction Co. have gone into this stuff then they've gone into the right stuff. |
| 2.154 | Ray | Yeah, this is it, this is what he approved and what he agreed/ |
| 2.155 | P.W. | Yeah, uhm/ |
| 2.156 | Ray | this is the sort of bottom we want – now, them's the exact words of him, of George, and Norman were standing around him/ |
| 2.157 | P.W. | But according to Brian, because the/ |
| 2.158 | Ray | Yeah/ |
| 2.159 | P.W. | ground level's like that, the clay should be like that, he doesn't allow for the fact that clay/ |
| 2.160 | Ray | Well, ask him a question, why they've gone right, so deep with that, if clay's so high up, why has that base gone down there, then, when it's in perfectly good clay, as you say? |
| 2.161 | P.W. | Uhm. |
| 2.162 | Ray | 'Cos that's why I said to Brian in that hole, I said, well if, if, if, stru . . . structural engineer thought this clay was good Brian, why's he gone right down here then? We're down six foot, you could have knocked three foot of that off. Aye, and Brian made no comment – you know? – the reason why he's going down here Brian, he's going down for this sandy, stony clay, which is what we're on, and it started just about there didn't it, when we were in' hole/ |
| 2.163 | P.W. | Yeah/ |
| 2.164 | Ray | it were a bit, anywhere like. . . . |
| 2.165 | P.W. | In view of the contour of the clay, the sandy clay |

in that hole, it just about proves that you can't
have a level bed of it across the site.
2.166    Ray    No, oh no.

George, the consultant structural engineer, may have told Brian, the Borough Corporation's architect, that the top clay (puddle clay) was no good, and that what was needed was the 'sandy, stony clay', and Norman, the Clerk of Works, may have heard him say so. But it amounts to nothing if it can not be proved. Even that 'in view of the contour of the clay, the sandy clay in that hole, it just about proves that you can't have a level bed of it across the site' (2.164), this will not in itself be sufficient. Nearly proof is not proof. Proof must counter the suggestion that 'the bottom that we showed them, that we could've in fact rooted out, two or three foot above' (2.82).

Where P. W. had 'slipped up' (4.91) was in not ensuring that the levels to which Construction Co. excavated were checked and agreed by the Clerk of Works. There would then have been documentary proof of the levels excavated to, and of the Corporation's agreement to these:

3.1    S.    You been having bother with that agent again?
3.2    P.W.    And how!
3.3    S.    What is it this time?
3.4    P.W.    Oh, arguments about a claim over the level to which we excavated the site.
3.5    S.    Have you taken out more than on the estimate, and they're claiming you didn't do it?
3.6    P.W.    We, we took out more than was on the drawings/
3.7    S.    Yeah/
3.8    P.W.    because we damn well had to. The ground conditions were such that we had to.
3.9    S.    It was soft and/
3.10    P.W.    Uhm/
3.11    S.    Yeah/
3.12    P.W.    And they're claiming that, eh, they're not going to pay us extra, because we never notified them that we were taking out extra dig.
3.13    S.    And is it their job to be there to know that you're doing it?
3.14    P.W.    I am wrong, in so far as I did not say specifically 'I have gone down deeper', but what I did say to Clerk of Works on the very first base we dug, I said 'Right Norman, there it is, there's the formation level, I want you to approve the formation and agree the level with me, so that we can do it on every base in the future so that

| | | |
|---|---|---|
| | | there's no argument at a later stage, as to what level we went to'. |
| 3.15 | S. | Uhm. |
| 3.16 | P.W. | And he said, 'I won't bother to do it now, I'll check one or two later, you know, as the job goes on', and he never checked one 'cos he can't use a ruddy instrument . . . that's my honest opinion. |

Had Norman, the Clerk of Works, been present to check and agree the levels excavated to, then P.W. feels that he would not have had this dispute on his hands:

| | | |
|---|---|---|
| 2.175 | P.W. | All that they're, what they're doing, and I can't understand it, they seem to be going to great extremes in that letter, well, all they're doing, they're protecting Norman. |
| 2.176 | Ray | Uhm. |
| 2.177 | P.W. | That letter is a cover for the inadequacies of their own Clerk of Works. |
| 2.178 | Ray | Yeah, yeah, . . . well they was given all the facilities, and all the chances to check them levels/ |
| 2.179 | P.W. | They were asked, they were asked/ |
| 2.180 | Ray | they was asked to do when the first one came out, and Norman's exact words was, I'll check 'em now and again, I'll do one or two, which he never did . . . and that's what I said to Brian this morning. . . . |

The crux of the issue is that, firstly, the Corporation have accused Construction Co. of excavating to a greater depth than the bore-hole report recommended as necessary:

| | | |
|---|---|---|
| 2.75 | P.W. | The corporation are ignoring, they're choosing to ignore that note on the engineer's drawings/ |
| 2.76 | Ray | Yes/ |
| 2.77 | P.W. | and are working to the bore-hole report/ |
| 2.78 | Ray | Yes |
| 2.79 | P.W. | which just states 'clay', does not differentiate between the two types of clay, |
| 2.80 | Ray | And they're not bearing in mind that, that George and the Clerk o' Works has agreed that was the bottom we wanted, |

The Corporation are able to do this by exploiting the inconsistency between the bore-hole report and the consultant's drawings. While the latter specifies 'sandy, stony clay', the former only notes the

143

existence of 'clay'. The Project Manager claims to have followed the instruction on the drawing, rather than the recommendation on the bore-hole report, and to have excavated to 600 mm. into the 'sandy, stony clay'. The Project Manager's retort is that had the Clerk of Works checked the excavations he would have seen that it was necessary to have excavated to a greater depth than that recommended by the bore-hole report. He accuses the Clerk of Works of not checking the levels, because he does not know how to do so! It is now too late to check some of the excavations, because they have had concrete poured into them, and have been 'backfilled' around the pour with a composition of pebbles and gravel.

Second, the Corporation have made their formal 'accusation' that an unnecessarily large amount of earth has been excavated because Construction Co. have put in a claim for additional work involved in doing these excavations, over and above that which the bore-hole report recommended they would have to do. As G.E., the consultant engineer puts it –

| 4.93 | G.E. | You'd think that, it all comes back to this, if you were asking for ten quid they'd give it to you rather than haggle with yer, |
| 4.94 | P.W. | Uhm. |
| 4.95 | G.E. | but because you're asking for, probably three thousand to eight thousand, or whatever the figure is, that's where you're coming unstuck. |

'Normal clay' is raised as an issue by the Corporation's representatives, because if conceded, the claim will cost them a considerable amount of money. (And, of course, if conceded it will also earn Construction Co. an additional sum.) It is the Corporation who raise 'clay' to the level of an 'issue'. They are able to do this because they were not specifically asked by the Project Manager to check and agree all the levels, and because they have found that some of the excavated bases which have not yet been poured and filled are deeper than the level recommended by the bore-hole report. They thus have one interpretation of the indexicality of the documents which proposes that two metres ought to have been the depth of the excavations. Using this 'documentary evidence' they are able to point to the actual excavations, and the claimed depths, and say that there was no reason for digging out to these depths. This is denied by the Project Manager in terms of his interpretation of the indexicality of the documents. He uses the engineer's drawing instruction to excavate to 'sandy, stony clay' as 'documentary evidence' for the need to excavate more than the recommended two metres, because this 'sandy, stony clay' was not encountered until a greater depth than this two metres:

| 4.202 | P.W. | We don't pour on any old kind of clay we dig up, it, it all comes down to what is clay, we couldn't have rooted out any higher on those bases, it was only puddle clay, we wanted that sandy, stony clay, whereas you say we can't differentiate between the two types of clay. |
| 4.203 | B.S. | Well, this, this has been my whole point all along, what is clay, what is stony clay, and what will basically take three tons? |

B.S., the Corporation's architect, continues to maintain an interpretation in terms of the bore-hole report, while P.W., the Project Manager, continues to argue his interpretation in terms of the drawings, and the necessity of on occasion having to dig deeper than the two metres recommended, if he was to fulfil the instruction of excavating to 600 mm. into the sandy stony clay. He seeks to support his claim by invoking some investigable features of the dispute. These are that it was necessary to dig deeper, due to variation in the strata, variation in ground conditions – that some of the excavations were in old cellar bottoms, and because of the 'unreasonable' assumptions about the machine-drivers behaviour which would be necessary to sustain the fact of the different depths excavated:

| 4.250 | B.S. | and I asked specifically, ehm, you know, what was the difference between clay and what was the difference between sandy, stony clay, |
| 4.251 | P.W. | Uhm. |
| 4.252 | B.S. | this, this was all questionable and we were arguing all down the hole. |
| 4.253 | P.W. | This hole, that we went down the ladder, uhm, now you made another point, about the clay being at a sort of constant level across the site, |
| 4.254 | B.S. | I said I would expect it to be, yes. |
| 4.255 | P.W. | Yes, right, we went down that hole yesterday and we took one, two, three, four, five, six, seven, eight readings, admittedly it's just round the perimeter of one hole, |
| 4.256 | B.S. | Yeah. |
| 4.257 | P.W. | we got a variation of six hundred mill, up and down, up and down, all around the hole, from the line of the stony clay, which gave us an average depth, of ninety eight one five O, that's for the top of it, I then deducted off my six hundred and ten mill, and gave me an average level of ninety seven five forty, and if you look at this sheet of paper that I've drawn here, I drew a line |

|       |       | across it, representing ninety seven five forty, and I plotted in my bases in relation to it, the half that come underneath that line, all the one's in blue, are in basements, so they don't count they would be below, anyhow, |
|-------|-------|---|
| 4.258 | B.S.  | No, uhm. |
| 4.259 | P.W.  | and, the others, like D.11, I've dotted, that's a debateable one, 'cos that came right on the edge of a ruddy cellar, yer know, in the fill material, and if you, I've got Ken, at the moment, he's drawing me sections, of the site, on each grid-line, superim – eh, to an enlarged scale, super-imposing the basements, the original formation level, our bases, and you'll find, and this is your other point, if we turn a machine-driver loose on that site, he's not going to dig this hole up, that one down, he'd have dug the whole bloody lot to a level, but as soon as you plot those in, in relation to those basements, you can see, that they all relate, to the bases, that we haven't gone tearing down a common level, |

What the final outcome of the claim over 'normal clay' was I do not know. Nor is it of particular concern to this analysis. What is significant about the episode of 'normal clay' is the way in which it displays the rationality of the site-organization, and some tactical moves in its language games.

Let us review the episode from the time of the claim having been made by Construction Co. for the additional work involved in excavating 600 mm. into the 'sandy, stony clay', excavations which were in excess of the anticipated two metres. I do not know whether the additional excavation on Construction Co.'s part was necessary or not. It may have been an initial tactical move on their part, or it may not.

The Corporation, on the other hand, were the initiators of the move that made 'normal clay' the issue that it became. This was to question the claim for additional payments (of between £3–8,000, according to G.E., the consulting structural engineer) which the Project Manager had made for Construction Co. Once that move was made, then it became a major issue.

Why did the architect raise 'normal clay' as an issue? It wasn't just because the contractor had excavated deeper than the bore-hole report recommended. It was because the contractor had done so without explicitly having approval to do so, and because in so doing, the contractor was seemingly in breach of contract and cost. Had there not been the bore-hole report, and had the Clerk of Works checked and agreed the levels, the Corporation would have had no grounds for disputing this claim. Given these grounds, then it is not surprising that the Project Manager should attempt to challenge these with documentary evidence to the contrary. One would expect these tactics.

But these are not P.W.'s only tactics. These we may say are defensive tactics. They are essentially a reaction to the Corporation's moves. As such they seek to negotiate the 'understanding' of the documents that the Corporation have, by indexically interpreting them alternatively. And so we have the stress on using the documents to support his action, by documenting his evidence in relation to them, and by stressing that the bore-hole report is not an instruction, but only a recommendation (4.244), and 'that this bore-hole log is not worth the paper it's printed on, because there's no datum given, for the start of the bore' (4.41). This re-formulation of the documents is exactly the same tactic which the Corporation's architect uses in raising the issue of 'normal clay' initially. Without the indexical interpretation of the documents, the issue would have to rest on the personal bickering of the Project Manager and the Clerk of Works.

The Project Manager does seem to react to the issue in what appear to be 'personal terms'. Consider the following episode, which P.W. begins by saying to Ray:

2.95    P.W.    . . . if we'd turned a man loose he'd have dug 'em all to the same bloody level, he wouldn't have, he's not going to go down an extra metre on one hole just 'cos it suits him.

2.96    Ray    No . . . well your only way to prove it's to get a statement off the driver int it? I'd threaten to do that.

2.97    P.W.    They wouldn't accept that.

2.98    Ray    No, well that's the position you're sitting int it?

A certain resignation to 'the position you're sitting' seems to be Ray's advice to P.W., after P.W. has outlined this position:

2.98    Ray    No, well that's the position you're sitting int it?

He poses this in the form of a question more rhetorical than open, almost as a summation of what has just been said. But P.W. answers the question with a 'No', and proceeds to outline why he is not just simply resigned to a defensive position:

2.99    P.W.    No, what's his name, John, were here this morning – you know we cast that little upstand along the front of the operator's office/

2.100    Ray    Yeah/

| 2.101 | P.W. | and also there's another one coming up the ramp/ |
|-------|------|---------------------------------------------------|
| 2.102 | P.W. | Yeah/ |
| 2.103 | P.W. | They've now realized that they should've had inserts in there/ |
| 2.104 | Ray | for fixing/ |
| 2.105 | P.W. | for fixing the windows to. |
| 2.106 | Ray | Yeah, well, I mean, we may have put them in, but it's only a fact of fixing a screw straight through, or something/ |
| 2.107 | P.W. | No, but he's on about they should've been in/ |
| 2.108 | Ray | But there's no windows int drawings, where should they've gone? |
| 2.109 | P.W. | Well, I said, all right . . . no, he's not accusing us, of, a, they should have gone in/ |
| 2.110 | Ray | Ah, they should a gone in/ |
| 2.111 | P.W. | and he wanted to know if we'd cast the upstands, and I said yes we have, ehm, I said, bearing in mind that letter that you sent me yesterday, to put those in there's going to cost you a small bloody fortune. |
| 2.112 | Ray | Aye. |
| 2.113 | P.W. | I said I'm not doing any favours, |
| 2.114 | Ray | No. |
| 2.115 | P.W. | and I said, you can't drill 'cos that's only three inches wide, you'll split it right off. |
| 2.116 | Ray | Yes, yes, well there's no window drawings. |
| 2.117 | P.W. | I told him, you either jack the whole bloody lot out, and cast a new strip, with the inserts in, or you pay us for expensive drilling as opposed to percussion . . . hammering. |

A representative of the Corporation's Architect's Department, John, has informed P.W. that the drawings from which some 'upstands' were to be constructed have been insufficiently detailed by the architects concerned. This means that some changes will be required of the upstands which have already been cast, to which P.W. replied that 'bearing in mind that letter that you sent me yesterday, to put those in there's going to cost you a small bloody fortune . . . I'm not doing any favours' (2.110–2.112).

We might think this carrying a personal dispute too far. John had nothing to do with the trouble of 'normal clay'. But, on reflection, P.W. cannot possibly have meant his remarks to have been taken 'personally' by John. The modifications and additions required are not wanted by John personally, nor is their inclusion going to be any personal cost to him. The 'you' who will bear the cost is not any man personally, but the Corporation as an entity, represented on site by a number of specific people.

We ought not to let the personal pronouns fool us. This may seem to be the expression of a petty personal bicker, but it is one which is developed as a definite strategy by P.W. in his reaction to the troubles of 'normal clay'. And in so doing it takes us beyond 'normal clay', into a wider range of issues.

How does P.W. orient towards the issue of 'normal clay'? Initially, I have discussed his defensive tactics – the attempts at documenting the 'correctness' of his actions, by interpreting the indexicality of the bill of works in a particular way. But, as an offensive, this tactic is capable of being strategically deployed as a move which exemplifies the rationality of the organization in its form of life.

If we take as the key feature of 'normal clay' that if the Corporation succeed in their claim, then they will have cost Construction Co. quite a considerable amount of money, one can see that this can only be replaced on a fixed-price contract, by either obtaining more 'use-value' from labour, or somehow varying some other costs in the contractor's favour. My experience of working on construction sites is that once a job has got properly under way one works, and is worked, hard. Additional effort, where it can be bullied, cajoled or induced, would not make a major difference in itself. It is rare that equipment and material costs can be directly renegotiated. The major grounds of such negotiation are usually to be found in the contractual documents which form the bill of works, and the 'understanding' involved in interpreting these.

This 'understanding' has been characterized as 'misunderstanding' by other researchers, for instance, the Tavistock researchers. If the behavioural episodes which surround issues such as 'normal clay' are glossed as 'communication problems', or 'personal troubles', then it becomes extremely difficult to see power in action in organization. Instead, we are confronted with bickering or lack of understanding which just seems to keep on recurring. We may then express pious hopes that such 'blemishes' may be eradicated by more perfect communication, the nirvana of unindexicality.

For me, 'normal clay' exemplifies the functioning of power in the organization that I researched, because power is exercised in a concertedly rational manner, to maintain the organization on the planned, projected course whose smooth progress signifies 'control'. 'Normal clay' threatens that control, because it threatens its measure – profit.

After 'normal clay' has occurred, then the grounds of P.W.'s 'understanding' of the documents become apparent. 'Now' he will not do any 'little favours' like setting out some 'ramps' for the architect, unless 'he pays me extra' (3.24–3.26). 'Now', unlike some time

149

before, he has both a grudge against the Corporation, because of the letter, and he has to find some additional profit to cover the losses he is likely to sustain on 'normal clay'. 'Now', any equivocality, contradiction or confusion in the bill of works becomes (for me) an occasion to recollect his form of life, exhibited in the rationality of his 'understanding':

P.W.   The only fly in the ointment, is George, he's adamant that we can't do it. Now, I've got a meeting, they should be here now, Brian and George, I'm going to put it to them again, because George is hanging his hat on, oh, a phrase in the bill, about you know, maximum pours of twenty-five metres, eh, square on deck – but the phrase starts off, 'recommended size of pour', it is not an instruction. . . . Well, I was going to say, I'll see what happens in the next hour or so, but I think I was going to hang my hat on this, it would solve me, with a lot of problems on stop-ends – I would save a day per pour, in other words I'd save two weeks a floor, and if I add that to my two weeks I've already saved on reduction curing time, and the fact that I'm now pushing George to go from three days to two days, I could pick up six weeks if I can get this . . .' (Clegg, 1974, 9.1).

The above was a monologue over the phone, by P.W., to his boss at Construction Co. head offices, concerning the strategy he is going to adopt in a site-meeting which was shortly to begin. In it he explicates the 'background assumptions' to his 'understanding' of a particular piece of the formal documentation contained in the bill of works. The issue concerns the size of pour that is to be used in pouring the concrete floors for the car park. P.W. wants to renegotiate the quarter of a bay, 25 m, which is at present being poured, into a pour of two bays at a time. The ensuing discussion (reported in Clegg, 1974, Appendix 9) largely consists of the architect, consultant engineer, and the Project Manager, P.W., arguing this issue.

This issue, like that of the 'ramps', the 'upstands', 'normal clay', and all the other issues that may be found in the transcripts of site meetings, resolves around the 'understanding' of the bill of works. Here, perhaps more clearly than anywhere else, because of the way that the 'background assumptions' are explicated beforehand, the underlying rationality which enables these to be constructed as issues is apparent. We could, if we wished, concretize this as a rule: '*Always make (out) of the bill of works what you can.*'

This is not always made for direct payment for the 'buggeration factor', and any other extras, through star-rates, variation orders, and the like. It may more readily be made by 'speeding up the programme', thus reducing some of the 'variable costs'. These would be costs such as the length of plant-hire time, and the period over which a full wages bill has to be paid.

These various issues, and the many that I have left unaccounted, are strategies employed by P.W. to try and reassert control. His 'understanding' of the bill of works that he is to build from varies with the state of play in the site organization. After 'normal clay', issues are a transparently ruled phenomena, because 'normal clay' makes them so. Issues are constructed as a concerted offensive against the possibility of eroded profitability. 'Normal clay' presents P.W. with the view of himself that others had presented to me: as (a) being out of control. As Al has observed, the job and the man are intertwined, so that a profitable job displays a worthy self. Where profit is attacked or eroded, its preservation becomes a personal matter.

This, to me, seems to be the crux of power in the organization, that it's exercise, its display – rather than its outcome – is the most significant sociological feature. Certainly, its outcome will be of importance for the people concerned, or for chroniclers of past events, but for the sociologist concerned with the features of power in this organization at the present time, it matters little. Only the faces change, while their theorizing remains constant. Issues serve as occasions for the powerful to flex their 'muscle'. Issues are constructed by the submission of the powerful to that which gives them their power – the iconic domination of their, in this instance, capitalistic form of life. Issues as a specific something or other are constructed through members orienting their actions towards the primary categorial concept of profitability. Their actions in displaying this orientation serve to exhibit the mode of rationality of the organization's form of life. Their actions are a ritualistic reminder of the domination of our form of life.

Issues may be (concretely) about many substantive things, but for me they are all about one thing: their own possibility. The issues that arise do so because they share a common 'rationality'. They are constructed out of the constitutive basis of the organization as a rational occasion for re-negotiating the formally contracted-for-profit, by re-negotiating the formally-contracted-for building. This is the 'mode of rationality' of that organization, there and then.

*

My analysis stops at this juncture. It could be elaborated almost indefinitely – but what would be the point of that? To overwhelm you with evidence? And would surfeit be proof? I would rather you took my analysis as a point of departure for your own, rather than as a substitute. The possibilities of your reading have been an ever-present feature of my writing. While I have read myself (my tradition) in others, others will read themselves (their tradition) in me. And thus my conclusion must be interpreted not as a closure but as an opening – an opportunity for us (thought) to find our way.

# 9    Concluding remarks

I began this study by attempting to give a rational account of some problems encountered in theorizing about power. I had hoped to conclude by giving a rational analysis of power in (an) organization. What would have been the criteria of a rational account according to the conclusion reached in chapter three? Let me reproduce these:

> a rational speech would be one in which the form of life of theory would be taken to be an account of both itself (albeit necessarily partial), and of its subject. Where its subject consisted of everyday accounts, then rational theorizing would be that which accounted both for itself, and those accounts it accounted. It could thus intelligibly provide for its agreement or disagreement with other competing traditions accounts of the 'same phenomena'. The notion of 'phenomenon' invoked here would thus serve as an occasion for theorizing which addressed both the rationality of itself and other accounts of the phenomenon, and the rationality of the phenomenon itself (pp. 39–40).

I have attempted to account for my own theorizing in terms of an itinerary which involved exploring the tradition(s) of sociological theorizing about power, in order to explicate the use of the concept of 'power'. This involved grasping the work of Weber and Simmel on the concepts of 'power', 'rule' and 'domination'. I then employed this trinity of concepts in order to demonstrate that recent work in the area of 'organizations' was flawed in its neglect of these as related concepts. Behavioural, exchange and strategic contingency theories had all dealt only with the 'surface' concept of 'power'. They failed to explicate how 'power' was underlain by 'rule' and 'domination'.

I then had to attempt to use these distinctions to account for those 'everyday accounts' which I had collected by tape-recording daily proceedings in an office on a construction-site. I had to hear these in a 'power-full' way. I deliberately used ordinary conversational material as my 'data', rather than any form of more elaborate, and consciously designed method (such as questionnaires), because I wanted to be able to point to 'power' in the material of the social world. By presenting this material as faithfully transcribed conversations, I hoped to present the opportunity for dialogue beyond the covers of this work. I wanted to be able to say 'this is what organizing was actually like in one organization. Here is how I have seen "power" in it. This is my way of seeing, as opposed to any other. Here are the materials I used. Now it is your turn to begin dialogue with my dialogue. I have presented you with the facilities.' And the rest would be up to the reader. My concern was not to cover my reasoning by hiding it under the cover of unquestioned 'methods', but to present an 'open book'.

My accounting of the accounts that I collected in 'Northern Town', on the construction-site, attempted to formulate these in their form of life. That is, if I was to hear 'power' in the surface of speech, in the way that members attempted to do 'ruling' and 'over-ruling' on each other, then I would have to regard this as merely the surface expression of the rational mode of a form of life. But how? My solution to this came from the data with which I had occasioned my theorizing.

When I began to collect the data, I had no idea what I would do with it, or whether or not it was 'good' data. It had to be, given the constraints on presenting the 'everyday performance' which I had set myself as a criterion of rationality. I had no option other than to make something out of this data.

When I first started attending at the construction-site, I went almost every day for several weeks, sometimes remaining in the site-offices, sometimes walking around the site. I found that the kind of material which pertained most closely to my chosen topic of 'power' was most readily encountered where conflict occurred. And conflict occurred most frequently in site-meetings. And the issues over which it occurred were most frequently concerned with questions of 'understanding' the formal documents that the contractor was to build from. These conflicts became more noticeable after the episode of 'normal clay'.

At the same time, nearly everyone that I talked to on site was concerned to tell me that this was not a 'good' job. Different reasons were advanced by different people as to why this should be. The joiners thought it was a 'bad' job because of their lack of bonus earnings, the Office Manager, Al, thought that it was a failing of organizational 'control'. Previous research (Higgin *et al.*, 1966) suggests that this is a general, normal feature of construction sites.

'Normal clay' seemed central to the failing of the organization, because if the claim for additional costs incurred in excavating to the 'sandy, stony clay' were not met by the Corporation, then the job could be as much as eight thousand pounds on the debit balance for this one item alone. If the job was to yield the anticipated profit, then this meant that somewhere or other, an additional profit of up to £8,000 may have to be found. In a phrase, 'something had to give'.

In a situation where the scope of operations is limited by a contractually binding agreement, then the contract, as a formal document which constitutes a 'formal organization', has a profound symbolic value. It stands as a token of the projected structure for its designers. It protects the client against unforeseen cost. But it also limits any subsequent disputes, or negotiations, within the parameters of that documentation. To attempt to secure any profit in excess of that contracted for, then the contractor has to attempt to re-draw those parameters. Hence the usefulness of indexicality on site. The contract has to 'give'.

'Power' was being exercised in attempting to implement different 'understandings' of these documents. This 'understanding' was constructed on the contractor's side by the way in which he oriented towards these documents. His 'understanding' of these documents was not a solitary or idiosyncratic affair, but one which was arrived at in close collaboration with his superordinates at Construction Co. head offices. This 'understanding' consisted in re-formulating any indexical matter in the documents to the advantage of Construction Co., in terms of either additional payments, or lower operating costs. Some of these I have discussed. This strategy, I argued, displayed this organization's 'rationality' (within the standards of its own community), or 'collective logic of action'), as Karpik (1972) has termed it. In turn, this 'rationality' was something produced in speech as a public and rule-guided phenomenon, which I argued, could be formulated as producable by members dominated by the icon of capitalistic notions of 'profitability' as an ideal – because that is their (our) form of life.

There is no interest for me, or I suspect for sociology, in pointing the finger at a specific individual as a powerful person. The sociological question concerns his identity as an 'historic individual' – in Simmel's reformulation of the Kantian question, the interest resides instead in the 'possibility' of any such person as a social being. And so I have sought to answer the question 'How is such a society (as that which I have recorded on my tapes) possible?' My answer has been that what maintains the order of this society is its members' unthoughtful (and thus willing) submission to the iconic domination of a form of life in which the ideal of profitability is King Harvest

– it must be reaped. And hence I do not display any one person as the 'most powerful' in the situation – for me, from this perspective, they are all equally enmeshed in a web which provides their working lives with its rationale, and which gives some of the meaning to their lives. Of course it does not provide all the meaning – King Profit is not omnipotent in the minds of men, and so they talk of, and do, other things whilst at work, than those that I have attended to. You may find instances of these in the tapes.

All of the data that I have used, apart from 'The Joiners' Tale', shows how members of the organization orient to this iconic ideal, how it is harvested and reaped, and how pervasive it is – even the members' sense of social time in the organization is constituted in terms of it, as is exhibited by the issue of 'normal clay'. Before, and after, this issue, are critically different times. This difference manifests itself in one primary way. This is through attempts to reassert profitability through the indexical reformulation of the formal organization as it is contained in the bill of works, etc.

Earlier drafts, and comments on these, tend to be suppressed features of a text's biography, but not on this occasion: 'The rules of the communication-with-others-in-writing game lead the receivers, the readers, to expect a conclusion that arrives with a thump.'

This reader says that I have no conclusion to *thump* about – I agree. To my way of thinking it would be surprising if there were. I have only represented some familiar things in a rearranged guise, in order to try and present them more clearly. If sociology were a more honest practice then I would think it difficult to do anything else. Criticism of my disinclination to conjure up novelty (as if novelty were the criteria of worth – the values of the ad-market) says more about the practice of sociological writing, than it does about my instance of it.

Should the reader require a 'thump', then this is the writing itself, its movement within the circle of the story. The writing is a slice of me making my sense for other people of some conceptual and empirical problems as I found them. My presentation of this progress is not that of an epic movie – I have no pretensions to be Cecil B. De Mille, and hence I have sought neither to shock nor amaze with a cliff-hanging conclusion. Instead I have tried to produce something which is almost circular in construction, a whole which might teem with sufficient detail such as to invite you to re-enter the text.

The text may have a certain interest as an intellectual object – as a canvas on which someone has tried to display their artistry – but I should like it also to exhibit a certain interest in the way in which it reproduces people caught in their everyday affairs as 'men at work'. And in these people, and in this work, we have just an ordinary slice of time, in which people are engaged in their mundane daily affairs.

Part of my conception of this as a circular text involves you, the reader. In Chapter 1 I explained that you were not to be thought a passive 'receiver' of news, but were instead rather more like an active collaborator. As a collaborator I can point out routes which further work on this theme of 'power' might follow. One possible route would be to return back into my text and tapes, and to take up the dialogue contained in my writing. Your very act of reading begins this task, and should point to the unfinished nature of my analysis of the taped materials (which by the criteria of this work must always remain 'unfinished'). The appendices are at hand.

Another route would be to take this analysis out of these covers and to try and formulate it elsewhere in other ways.

Historically, one might be able to use the concept of organizational 'rationality' to analyse the changing patterns of influence within specific organizations, or types of organizations, and to analyse the interplay between these (in the functioning of power) and the structure of power in that organization.

I have dealt here with only one organization at one point in time, and have analysed only one type of language in use in that organization, with only one theoretical interest: that of pursuing the iconic form of life of capitalist domination in one mode of rationality. Many more modes of rationality must exist within the one icon. Many other types of organizations exist, premised on other forms of domination.

In order to attempt such an analysis then the hermeneutic style which I have used may not be practical. It requires both slow and careful collection and interpretation of a large amount of conversational material which will rarely conform to one's conceptual niceties, and which is typically inimical to any comparative intent. Happily, this work is atypical, because of the existence of a previous large-scale research (Higgin *et al.*, 1966) which substantiates that the 'failing organization' is a normal feature of the construction industry. None the less, the reconciliation of this style of work, and the possibility of a comparative, as well as an interpretive, sociology, must be faced.

In conclusion, I believe it is customary for one to point towards the practical implications of one's work for an audience wider than that of one's academic community. At a superficial level my discussion of the ways in which indexicality may be profitably reformulated on site may be taken as realistic, if slightly cynical, advice to aspiring Project Managers as to how they might manage their affairs. But if I were to advance an interpretation, then it would be that such an analysis allows us to see ourselves as the people that our

157

form of life recommends. Not in order to 'Know thyself', but in order to revolt us against the selves we have become. When each man becomes a reflexive theorist, then might be the opportunity to 'Seize the time'. And then this work would have surely become redundant as anything other than a chronicle of past confusions and events.

# Appendix 1    Al, the ideal typist

I had been at the site for about two or three weeks, going in about three or four days a week, taping material in the site-office and wandering around the site, watching people at work that I knew well from my experience as a joiner's labourer. Occasionally I would talk to men at work on the site, but not too often, for to do so was to risk us both getting into trouble with the Project Manager.

This Project Manager occasioned the following conversation:

| | | |
|---|---|---|
| 1 | S. | I suppose up there, most of the talk is issuing commands and getting them done. That's normal? |
| 2 | Al | Yeah. I used to go in with Peter H. (the Project Manager on another Construction Co. job, 'up there') he called me in, and had me in there all morning, and all we talked about was the job, and that was all I wanted to talk to him about. . . . I mean, on that job alone, up there, and it's a small job compared to motorway jobs, there's the Project Manager Peter, John C, the Assistant Manager, he's got a car, Dick B., he's got a car, Colin G.'s got a car. Dick S. had a car when he was there. |
| 3 | S. | So that's what a job ought to be like? |
| 4 | Al | Uh. |
| 5 | S. | No chattering and gossipping, just getting on with it? |
| 6 | Al | Well you chatter and gossip between people of your own, you know, I chatter and gossip with some, but I don't go chattering and gossipping with Peter. You should be too busy, you shouldn't have time to chatter. |
| 7 | S. | The reps seem to take a lot of time as well. |

| 8 | Al | He won't have 'em up there. He doesn't have any bother, no. Tommy (the 'Buyer') looks after a lot of the reps admittedly, if Tommy thinks there's anything Peter ought to know he tells him, but he won't have bloody reps on t'job, cluttering it up. Half the time in there, they're just talking about his hobbies. Had a bloke here selling bloody clay once, |
|---|---|---|
| 9 | S. | Clay? |
| 10 | Al | bloody modelling clay, for his pottery, or his housekeeper. |
| 11 | S. | How did he get him? |
| 12 | Al | He just phoned up. One day, he went down to this hardware shop down town and asked for this tool, joiners use it, it's got a curved blade, it's what they used to use for chopping, |
| 13 | S. | Yeah. |
| 14 | Al | levelling pieces of wood. It's how you get the effect on an old table. |
| 15 | S. | Yeah. |
| 16 | Al | Went down there, and said have you got one, a small one, about that big. They said no, don't know where to get one, or how much they'd cost – couldn't get any in stock. So he came back, spent half the day telephoning, found out where he could get some, went back down t'shop, told him where to phone, and t'save him one. Well, he come back and said 'You know that firm down in Town – well they think I'm a great bloke now'. |
| 17 | S. | Yeah . . . well, the blokes on site they're not happy about it, they're not earning what they could be are they? |
| 18 | Al | No, but, there again y'see . . . but it's the same, if you work out there. . . . You've worked on a job haven't you? |
| 19 | S. | Yeah. |
| 20 | Al | If you've got nothing to do . . . |
| 21 | S. | You get bored stiff. |
| 22 | Al | Yeah, how long does your day last? |
| 23 | S. | Twenty-four hours – I mean it just goes on and on – you just live for snap time and break time and snap time. |
| 24 | Al | Yeah . . . you never get this feeling, look at your watch, 'Cor, is it that time already?' |
| 25 | S. | Yeah. |
| 26 | Al | You have a crap, push bits of wood about, start |

standing around. It just gets generally so that a job gets to a state of, you know. . . .

27 S. Well, what should it be really like?

28 Al Like I just said, blokes should be fully employed out there, that's what they're here for.

29 S. I mean, if it was an ideal job, what would it be like?

30 Al Well, we pay fifty-five and a half pence a labourer for working an hour, and we want an hour's work out of him. The rates, them rates have only been put in. . . . Like I was explaining before, you base your costs on doing a job, on him doing an hour's work,

31 S. Yeah.

32 Al for fifty-five and a half pence. If it's gonna take him two hours to do it you only want to be paying him two hours.

33 S. And it's his job in there to see that you get an hour's work?

34 Al Fully occupied – he's to keep 'em fully occupied. Ray was good at that. He'd have J.C.B. on one job, and he'd have labourers preparing the next job for the J.C.B. when it'd done that, to move straight to there, and they could move back – none of this 'that was stood there' and 'they were stood here' – he came across here, he couldn't do anything, so he brings some labourers, and then the machine's standing for two hours at three quid an hour.

35 S. Yeah.

36 Al Y'see, it's just not productive is it?

37 S. No, you must organize things.

38 Al It's same as, if you've done that house up at home . . . you must know that there's things, when you've got a job to do, you got to think about it, you can't fix the bloody roof on before you built the walls.

39 S. That's what the blokes out there are saying – I've told 'em I'm studying work organizations, an' they say 'You whaaaat? – You've come to a right bloody place here – work disorganization's more like it'.

40 Al I'll be in here, an' he'll have a pile on his desk, and he'll say 'Oh, I've all this to get through' – a right bloody pile. Then the next thing you know, he's started chattering, it's half past six, and he'll say 'Oh well, time for t'off', you know, and he hasn't touched it, not just looked at it.

41 S. Yeah, yeah, I suppose that on another job, a good job, there'd be a lot less talk?

| 42 | Al | There would, yeah, you wouldn't have time to talk. Up there, I used to eh, I've worked through my dinner hour, and not known it, until after me dinner, and I've looked at my watch, and thought 'Oh God'. |
| 43 | S. | Because you've been so busy? |
| 44 | Al | I've gone in in the morning, you've got your work done, you're working on, and the sun's shining, the next thing I saw my wife walking on there, ready to come home. |
| 45 | S. | Uhmm. |
| 46 | Al | I've checked what time it was, thinking she'd come early, but she weren't. And your day just lasted something like, you'd think, 'Bloody hell', you'd think, you've no sooner seemed to have come and you're ready for going home. Well, work didn't seem so bad, because you didn't seem to be there – on a day like you come here, you think you're here all bloody day, and you get sick of it. |
| 47 | Sec. | Can I please agree with that? |
| 48 | Al | You know, you get fed up, you get fed up with everybody, there's no, 'cos you've seen 'em too much. |
| 49 | Sec. | My work finished at twenty past nine this morning. Phone's only gone once. |
| 50 | Al | I seem to have been here about bloody eight hours already. |
| 51 | Sec. | I could come in here about three days a week, and have everything done. He could dictate all his letters for the week. |
| 52 | Al | Yeah, but what would he dictate? 'Dear Madam . . .'. |
| 53 | Sec. | (Laughs), Yeah, in answer to your advertisement/ |
| 54 | Al | What letters have you typed? |
| 55 | Sec. | I did five yesterday. |
| 56 | Al | For what? For Construction Co.? |
| 57 | Sec. | No, I haven't done a letter for Construction Co. for weeks. |
| 58 | S. | He still can't find a housekeeper? |
| 59 | Sec. | Oh, we restarted that yesterday. |
| 60 | Al | He'd . . . hundreds, he'd loads, and he was turning 'em down like flies – Not having her, because she said, 'Hello, this is, I'm answering your advert, how much money is it? – but he wasn't having her – 'I don't like people who ask about money', he said. The next one phoned up and said, 'Well, is there |

|     |      | much life in Harrogate, you know, what's Harrogate like?'–well, he didn't want her–he's choosy. |
|-----|------|--------------------------------------------------------------------------------------------------|
| 61  | Sec. | He'd boiled it down to two – he'd got one in Wakefield that was virtually going to be it – he took her out a few times, then all of a sudden she said, 'Well, I'm undecided, so I'll say no'. Then he got this other one from Newcastle, |
| 62  | S.   | Yeah. |
| 63  | Sec. | and she came down for two weekends, |
| 64  | S.   | Yeah. |
| 65  | Sec. | it was all set, everything planned, she was coming – she rang up on Sunday, and she said she didn't want to – well she got her mother to. . . . |
| 66  | Al   | So we're back to square one again. And his original housekeeper's off on Saturday – so he's not going to be in on Friday. |
| 67  | Al   | Well, I don't think I'll be in either. |
| 68  | Sec. | Neither am I. Let's close the site. Well, what use is there, I've no work to do unless Peter's here. |
| 69  | Al   | The only work you do is what I give you. |
| 70  | Sec. | Yeah, the orders . . . |
| 71  | Al   | Well I tell you, I've prepared myself for this job folding up. The point is you see, what upsets me is, is that when I go on another job, say Construction Co. say, took me, want to take you off that job, take you on another job, and y'start talking amongst everybody, and they say, (laughingly), 'Oh yeah, you were on that Northern job weren't you – what went wrong?' |
| 72  | S.   | It becomes a joke? |
| 73  | Al   | Yeah, I'm classed as being 'You were on that Northern job – everyone was bad on that Northern job – that were a really bad job' |
| 74  | S.   | How would they know that this was, that it's going to lose? |
| 75  | Al   | It's funny, you get good jobs and bad jobs, there's bad jobs going through the firm now that people don't forget. You see, he'll never, he's bloody useless sod now for Construction Co., they'll never give him anything, he'll never get another Construction Co. contract. Neither will I. Neither will Peter, the engineer, y'see, because everything that goes wrong, he pushes it, he just pushes it. They, probably, at Head Office think, oh, – when they interviewed Peter at Head Office they'd think, because he's a |

|     |      | right canny lad, he's a University lad, not an ordinary site engineer/ |
|-----|------|---|
| 76  | Sec. | and he's got the gift of the gab as well |
| 77  | Al   | He's what? |
| 78  | Sec. | Got the gift of the gab. |
| 79  | Al   | They probably thought – oh, we've set on, got quite a good catch here – Peter already has got us into trouble with that column. It was his job to make sure that that was checked, Peter said on the phone, |
| 80  | Sec. | I thought he said Ken? |
| 81  | Al   | Both of them. It was Ken's job to check the steel, and it's also Peter's responsibility, because he's chief engineer, to check over Ken. Well that's as high as it went. It's like I said before, y'know, the bloke at the top's responsible for everything. |
| 82  | S.   | So it was really the Project Manager's responsibility? |
| 83  | Al   | Yeah, but he placed it just below him. |
| 84  | S.   | But don't they know that up there, at Head Office? |
| 85  | Al   | Well, it's like anything else, if you go back to your University, and they say to you 'What do you think to that Cashier on site?', and you say, 'Oh, he's a bit of a dosser, he does bugger all, you know' – well, they'll take what you said. |
| 86  | S.   | Yeah – but you said earlier, y'know you thought that they'd have that kind of opinion about him as well. I mean where would they get that from then? |
| 87  | Al   | Well, they will because the job's not moving. When I put them cost figures in, and they say 'Oh, there, bloody hell, we've eighteen joiners on that site and they've fixed between 'em twenty square yards of shuttering, that's one square yard each in a week.' |
| 88  | S.   | How much does a joiner normally fix in a week? |
| 89  | Al   | He should be fixing twenty a day, each joiner. |
| 90  | S.   | Twenty square yards a day! |
| 91  | Al   | It depends y'see. On a big job, a bridges structure where you've got big walls to go at, like works on there, they can fix anything, you can get two hundred bloody square yards a week, off a gang of joiners, but the money's coming in then. |
| 92  | S.   | Yeah, for the firm and the joiners? |
| 93  | Al   | Yeah, for the firm and its covering the joiners. One week we'd seven square yards of shuttering fixed on this job with nine joiners. |
| 94  | S.   | That was that week when you were having that dispute over that figure? |

| | | |
|---|---|---|
| 95 | Al | Yeah . . . and that's where it shows up badly for him you see, it's no one's fault but his then. |
| 96 | S. | And do you think it'll come home to roost? |
| 97 | Al | It's bound to do, another, just take it going ridiculous, another twelve months, and job's no further on, there's bound to be, there's bound to come a time when they think, 'Well, what's going on' – and that's when they'll come in y'see, but, the only thing like I've said before, that I don't like about it, I'm not bothered if Construction Co. never get it built, but if I stick with Construction Co. I'll always be associated with this job. |
| 98 | S. | Why do you think it should be a bad job? Do you think they've put in too low a price for it? |
| 99 | Al | No . . . it's like I said before – whatever bloke you've got in there, sets the tone – if he's a good bloke, sharp, quick, always here on time, everybody's the same. |
| 100 | S. | Uhmm. |
| 101 | Al | It does, it's true is that. John J., when he's on a motorway, you don't get people wandering in and out, bloody dinner times, half an hour longer than should be, coming and going when they want, even if he's not on site they're there – if they know he's not coming in tomorrow they don't think 'Well, we don't have to come in' – they're bloody there. 'Cos, it's just instilled into you. McAlpine's are the same, you never, ever let 'em off, 'cos if you're coming in at five to eight, he's in at ten to, to make sure you're there at five to. |
| 102 | S. | Yeah. |
| 103 | Al | He'll never have more than half an hour for his lunch – it's so that you can never go and say, 'Oh, I'm too busy', 'cos he'll say 'You're too busy? I only have half an hour and it's good enough for you'. It's no good saying 'Look, I have three hours for dinner, you only have half an hour'. It all comes from that room – it's like, rays, the sun and its rays, if the sun's bright, all its rays are bright aren't they? If the sun's dull, all your bloody rays are dull aren't they? |
| 104 | S. | Yeah. |
| 105 | Al | That's one way of putting it I suppose. That's it, if you got a bloke in there, full of it, bags of bloody energy, it goes through all the bloody site. That's why Ray left. |

| 106 | S. | Because it was so badly set up? |
|---|---|---|
| 107 | Al | Well, Ray thought he was, Ray, y'see, Ray said, after he'd been here a few months, he knew Peter pushing it all on to him. He just said that were it, he'd never get anywhere with Construction Co., he knew he wouldn't. |
| 108 | Sec. | He said, well, at the end of the job, after it'd been a dead loss, well all the blame'd go on t'him, wouldn't it? |
| 109 | Al | They'd be saying, 'Oh, that Ray, he were on that Northern job weren't he?' They'd be looking for another job for him you see, and they'd say to a project manager somewhere, 'How about this fore-man from t'Northern job?' And they'd say 'Oh no, that Northern job, I'll hang around for something better'. |

# Appendix 2 Normal clay

A conversation is in progress between Ray, the General Foreman, and P.W. the Project Manager. The discussion, in the form of an impromptu meeting, was about an incident with the Clerk of the Works, and the Corporation architects. The latter had argued that Construction Co. had excavated earth for the foundations for some bases to a greater depth than that specified in the 'bill of works'. P.W. is arguing that this is an attack on his integrity and capability, especially as these accusations have been committed to a letter sent to his boss at Construction Co.

| 1 | P.W. | I'm going to write a letter, you know, item by item, what I've got Ken (Assistant Measurement Engineer) doing at the moment, I roughed it out on there, an enlarged vertical scale, so you can see what you're talking about, a section through the site of each grid line/ |
|---|------|---|
| 2 | Ray | Yeah/ |
| 3 | P.W. | with the basements plotted in, and the ground levels as known/ |
| 4 | Ray | Yeas/ |
| 5 | P.W. | and then plot in our bases, and soon as you do that you start seeing that, we haven't gone down deep as they're saying, eh, if you look at the picture I drew yesterday, said he, said he (searching) . . . this hole here, this inspector's office base, that they looked at the clay, we took a check all around it yesterday, and in fact, just around the one hole, |
| 6 | Ray | Yeah |
| 7 | P.W. | that sandy clay was up and down anything/ |
| 8 | Ray | Yeah/ |

167

| 9 | P.W. | up to/ |
|---|---|---|
| 10 | Ray | Yeah/ |
| 11 | P.W. | six hundred mills around it, so we take the average, ninety eight one five-O |
| 12 | Ray | Yeah/ |
| 13 | P.W. | take the six hundred and ten that we've got to go into it, gives us an average level of ninety seven five forty/ |
| 14 | Ray | Yeah/ |
| 15 | P.W. | that's the run. And I've plotted in all the base levels we've got, – all the ones ringed in blue are the basements/ |
| 16 | Ray | Yeah/ |
| 17 | P.W. | so they're bound to be below that line/ |
| 18 | Ray | Yeah/ |
| 19 | P.W. | and above that you get one or two in basements/ |
| 20 | Ray | Yeah/ |
| 21 | P.W. | that must've been hard bases, but um', now I'm getting Ken to put this onto one drawing/ |
| 22 | Ray | Yeah/ |
| 23 | P.W. | also drawing the uh, clay line, for what it's worth, through, that you get from the bore-holes 'cause you only get three fixes, but at least that'll give you something to go on,/ |
| 24 | Ray | Yeah/ |
| 25 | P.W. | I mean, I've said it three times to Brian (Borough Architect) verbally, about Norman (Clerk of Works) and levels, it's now going in writing,/ |
| 26 | Ray | Yeas, you might point out that he can't read a . . . level. Had Ken not helped him out there, which I were very annoyed with, we'd 'ave proved it that day. |
| 27 | P.W. | Well, I already said, when I said to Brian yesterday, I said, you know, your Clerk o'Works can't even read a level, he said 'Oh, can't he?' |
| 28 | Ray | Yeah, can't even read a metric. |
| 29 | P.W. | No. . . . I put it to Brian, and I said it to John J. (a Construction Co. member, who is P.W.'s immediate boss, having responsibility for, among others, the Northern Town job), last night as well, that, I'm still quivering/ |
| 30 | Ray | Mentioned it to me this morning, did Brian/ |
| 31 | P.W. | I'm still. . . . Yesterday when I got that letter, yesterday morning, I got the shakes, believe it, you know, I was so angry, and I'm still feeling a bit that way. |

| 32 | Ray | Well, I said to Brian this morning, I said, well Brian, in all fairness, I said, Norman were given the facilities to check these, he were asked to check them/ |
|----|------|---|
| 33 | P.W. | He was asked to check them/ |
| 34 | Ray | you can't take a man by his hand/ |
| 35 | P.W. | and the operative word was, will you check these/ |
| 36 | Ray | Yes/ |
| 37 | P.W. | so that we can establish records/ |
| 38 | Ray | Yes/ |
| 39 | P.W. | for the job/ |
| 40 | Ray | Yes . . . yes/ |
| 41 | P.W. | now we're on the first one. |
| 42 | Ray | Yeah. |
| 43 | P.W. | Uhm, now, I said it to Brian, I said it to John J. last night, either Norman bloody goes, or I go. |
| 44 | Ray | Yeah . . . take some moving'll Norman, you know. |
| 45 | P.W. | I know it'll take some moving, but, eh . . . well, |
| 46 | Ray | . . . But you certainly gotta fight it all the way through, aren't you? |
| 47 | P.W. | I am/ |
| 48 | Ray | Aye/ |
| 49 | P.W. | I am that. |
| 50 | Ray | Yeah. |
| 51 | P.W. | I mean, 'cos one of the things, Ron C. (another Construction Co. 'boss') came in last night/ |
| 52 | Ray | I think Brian agrees with, there's errors on both sides if you'd like me to say that/ |
| 53 | P.W. | Ron C., last night, came in, and one of the questions he asked me was, he said, has Brian been a bit clever here, I said no, he was clever with N.S.M., but he hasn't been clever on this lot/ |
| 54 | Ray | No/ |
| 55 | P.W. | I said, I'm quite happy to, I'll dig the whole bloody job up/ |
| 56 | Ray | Aye/ |
| 57 | P.W. | and show everyone/ |
| 58 | Ray | Yeah/ |
| 59 | P.W. | that . . . the thing that's upset me more than anything else, is those two references to the fact that we just turned a machine-driver loose. . . . |
| 60 | Ray | Yeah, but I mean, what, that's only Norman's . . . attitude is that int it, that's no official statement is it? It's no, it's the attitude of the Clerk o' Works is that/ |

| | | |
|---|---|---|
| 61 | P.W. | What turning/ |
| 62 | Ray | Yeah, 'cos he said that, he said that/ |
| 63 | P.W. | all right, he said it, he said it yes, but it has now been recorded/ |
| 64 | Ray | Yeas, but it's only hearsay by the Clerk o'Works is that. . . . |
| 65 | P.W. | Maybe it's hear . . . , no it's an accusation/ |
| 66 | Ray | Yes, I know, but it int sub . . . there's no grounds for it. . . . |
| 67 | P.W. | They can't substantiate it/ |
| 68 | Ray | No/ |
| 69 | P.W. | but the Borough Architect of Northern Town has accused us, of/ |
| 70 | Ray | which is wrong/ |
| 71 | P.W. | giving wrong instructions, inadequate supervision, turning a man lose, and/ |
| 72 | Ray | You might use me and say that I gave the driver the instructions to dig down to this stony, sandy clay, not to the first layer of clay, which were only puddle clay anyway, and that's the instructions he got, and when he found that level/ |
| 73 | P.W. | Uhm/ |
| 74 | Ray | that were when we, the base were taken. |
| 75 | P.W. | The Corporation are ignoring, they're choosing to ignore that note on the engineer's drawings, |
| 76 | Ray | Yes/ |
| 77 | P.W. | and are working to the bore-hole report/ |
| 78 | Ray | Yes/ |
| 79 | P.W. | which just states 'clay', does not differentiate between the two types of clay, |
| 80 | Ray | And they're not bearing in mind that, that George, and the Clerk o'Works has agreed that was the bottom we wanted, |
| 81 | P.W. | Um, um, |
| 82 | Ray | George, George E. told me that, and stood next to me and said, 'Yes Ray, that's, that's what we wanted', and that were when we got to this sandy, stony clay. The rest is only clay, int it? |
| 83 | P.W. | Yes, what, what they're suggesting now is that the bottom that we showed them, that we could've in fact rooted out, two or three foot above. |
| 84 | Ray | Well, we'd have seen that wou'n't we? |
| 85 | P.W. | But the other thing that absolutely proves that we did not turn a machine-driver lose, if you take the levels,/ |

| 86 | Ray | Yeah/ |
|---|---|---|
| 87 | P.W. | off that sketch on our bases,/ |
| 88 | Ray | Yeas/ |
| 89 | P.W. | they're pretty constant throughout the site, |
| 90 | Ray | Yes, yes. |
| 91 | P.W. | but, . . . oh, sorry, they're not constant, some are up, some are down according to local conditions,/ |
| 92 | Ray | Yeah/ |
| 93 | P.W. | it's the other way around/ |
| 94 | Ray | Yeas/ |
| 95 | P.W. | but if we'd turn a man lose he'd have dug 'em all to the same bloody level, he wouldn't have, he's not going to go down an extra metre on one hole just 'cos it suits him. |
| 96 | Ray | No, . . . well your only way to prove it's to get a statement off the driver int it? I'd threaten to do that. |
| 97 | P.W. | They wouldn't accept that. |
| 98 | Ray | No, well that's the position you're sitting int it? |
| 99 | P.W. | No, what's his name, John, were here this morning – you know we cast that little upstand along the front of the operator's office/ |
| 100 | Ray | Yeah/ |
| 101 | P.W. | and also there's another one coming up the ramp,/ |
| 102 | Ray | Yeah/ |
| 103 | P.W. | they've now realized that they should've had inserts in there/ |
| 104 | Ray | for fixing/ |
| 105 | P.W. | for fixing the windows to |
| 106 | Ray | Yeah, well, I mean, we may have put them in, but it's only a fact of fixing a screw straight through, or something/ |
| 107 | P.W. | No, but he's on about they should've been in/ |
| 108 | Ray | But there's no windows int drawings, where should they've gone? |
| 109 | P.W. | Well, I said, all right . . . no, he's not accusing us, of, a, they should have gone in/ |
| 110 | Ray | Ah, they should a gone in/ |
| 111 | P.W. | and he wanted to know if we'd cast the upstands, and I said yes we have, ehm, I said, bearing in mind that letter that you sent me yesterday, to put those in there's going to cost you a small bloody fortune. |
| 112 | Ray | Aye. |
| 113 | P.W. | I said, I'm not doing any favours, |
| 114 | Ray | No. |

| | | |
|---|---|---|
| 115 | P.W. | and I said, you can't drill 'cos that's only three inches wide, you'll split it right off. |
| 116 | Ray | Yes, yes, well there's no window drawings. |
| 117 | P.W. | I told him, you either jack the whole bloody lot out, and cast a new strip, with the inserts in, or you pay us for expensive drilling as opposed to percussion . . . hammering. |
| 118 | Ray | Yeas, . . . well all fixings come in window, in t' window details, anyway, don't they?, |
| 119 | P.W. | Uhm, |
| 120 | Ray | all variable, there's nothing in our drawings say we supply any fixings at all |
| 121 | P.W. | No |
| 122 | Ray | Whose gonna drill 'em on? We've to do all t' ordinary door frames for fixing walls t'curtains, y'know, dies to put in, |
| 123 | P.W. | Well, they could've, they could argue, they could have argued back, that, 'em, they haven't done as yet, they could say that as Williams are our sub-contractor it's up to us to have obtained/ |
| 124 | Ray | Yes, but their drawings haven't been approved or anything/ |
| 125 | P.W. | No/ |
| 126 | Ray | yet have they?/ |
| 127 | P.W. | and as it has already been agreed to expedite the job, that Heywood Williams and Architects Department will talk direct, about design, |
| 128 | Ray | Yes, yeah . . . aye |
| 129 | P.W. | have to get round that one. . . . Eh, dunt that coat suit him Ian? |
| 130 | Ray | It's a right 'un is this, very warm, I put it on other day, an' I thought, I'll put coat that on |
| 131 | Ian | Huh, huh. |
| 132 | Ray | Lovely 'n warm, aren't they? |
| 133 | Ian | Not bad are they really? |
| 134 | Ray | No, no it is, better'n donkey jacket y'know. |
| 135 | Ian | Now, you're in a, ehm, position of respectability |
| 136 | Ray | Huh ha ha, that's a funny one . . . aye, . . . I thought I'd have a bite t'eat with ter, like. |
| 137 | P.W. | Wheaah, |
| 138 | Ray | It dawned on me yesterday, yer know, as I left, I thought I'll get back t'it today, anyway, yer know, about that, eh/ |
| 139 | P.W. | No, we've got a meeting with George and Brian at two thirty/ |

| 140 | Ray | Today? |
|-----|-----|--------|
| 141 | P.W. | today, |
| 142 | Ray | Aye. |
| 143 | P.W. | discussing these ramps/ |
| 144 | Ray | Yeah, |
| 145 | P.W. | well, my attitude now is gonna be, that I am not, I'm not going to sodding/ |
| 146 | Ray | I think George could bear thee out a lot of this yer know if you could talk him round, on these bases, |
| 147 | P.W. | Yeah, but George is apt, 'cos of his position, is sitting on a fence, and I don't blame him, |
| 148 | Ray | Yeah, yeah. |
| 149 | P.W. | he said, well/ |
| 150 | Ray | But he's a witness to what you've done, though, isn't he?/ |
| 151 | P.W. | Yes, but one thing that is missing out of here is that when we dug that hole, |
| 152 | Ray | Yeah. |
| 153 | P.W. | Brian went down it, George went down it, and George said to Brian, that stuff at the top is no bloody use. If Construction Co. have gone into this stuff then they've gone into the right stuff. |
| 154 | Ray | Yeah, this is it, this is what he approved and what he agreed/ |
| 155 | P.W. | Yeah, uhm/ |
| 156 | Ray | this is the sort of bottom we want – now, them's the exact words of him, of George, and Norman were standing around him/ |
| 157 | P.W. | But according to Brian, because the/ |
| 158 | Ray | Yeah/ |
| 159 | P.W. | ground level's like that, the clay should be like that, he doesn't allow for the fact that clay/ |
| 160 | Ray | Well, ask him a question, why they've gone right, so deep with that, if clay's so high up, why has that base gone down there, then, when it's in perfectly good clay, as you say? |
| 161 | P.W. | Uhm. |
| 162 | Ray | 'Cos that's why I said to Brian in that hole, I said, well if, if, if, stru . . . structural engineer thought this clay was good Brian, why's he gone right down here then?, we're down six foot, you could have knocked three foot of that off. Aye, and Brian made no comment – you know? – the reason why he's going down here Brian, he's going down for this sandy, stony clay, which is what we're on, and it |

|     |      | started just about there didn't it, when we were in' hole/ |
|-----|------|-----|
| 163 | P.W. | Yeah/ |
| 164 | Ray  | it were a bit, anywhere like . . . |
| 165 | P.W. | In view of the contour of the clay, the sandy clay in that hole, it just about proves that you can't have a level bed of it across the site. |
| 166 | Ray  | No, oh no. |
| 167 | P.W. | In fact, what I'm, I've got the machine-driver at the moment – the area that's going to be landscaped at the far end, |
| 168 | Ray  | Yeah. |
| 169 | P.W. | I'm getting him to dig me a base hole out there/ |
| 170 | Ray  | Aye, digging a trial hole/ |
| 171 | P.W. | and he's digging it the size and depth of a 'V' line base. |
| 172 | Ray  | Aye, I think you've plenty of ground to tread on Peter, I do, it's just a matter of, you know, convincing them beggars. And I think you've convin . . . , I think we've convinced 'em really, it's just that they won't damn well accept it, |
| 173 | P.W. | They won't accept it, no |
| 174 | Ray  | you know, I think you can prove incompetence all the way round on their part, and I said that to Brian this morning. |
| 175 | P.W. | All that they're, what they're doing, and I can't understand it, they seem to be going to great extremes in that letter, well, all they're doing, they're protecting Norman. |
| 176 | Ray  | Uhm. |
| 177 | P.W. | That letter is a cover for the inadequacies of their own Clerk o' Works. |
| 178 | Ray  | Yeah, yeah, . . . well they was given all the facilities, and all the chances to check them levels/ |
| 179 | P.W. | They were asked, they were asked/ |
| 180 | Ray  | they was asked to do when the first one came out, and Norman's exact words was, I'll check 'em now and again, I'll do one or two, which he never did . . . and that's what I said to Brian this morning. . . . |
| 181 | P.W. | Yer know, every time I think Tarmac have topped out I see another lift going in, |
| 182 | Ray  | Aye, yeah. |
| 183 | P.W. | 'Cos yesterday I looked at those column bars and they've turned out, into the slab, |
| 184 | Ray  | Yeas, as though they're finishing, |

185  P.W.  as though they're finishing, I don't know how they
            splice on the next uh,
186  Ray   yeah, . . . anyway I'll have a cup o' tea then Peter,
            and then I'll have t' go. . . .

(Ray leaves the scene to make a cup of tea in his office, and P.W. introduces a new topic with Ian, a rep. who had entered during the previous scene, but to which he had been a largely silent spectator. This concludes the scene.) Some fifteen minutes later after the rep. had gone, I asked the Project Manager – P.W., some questions about the previous scene. This forms Appendix 3, – 'Normal clay: reprise'.

# Appendix 3　Normal clay: reprise

P.W. the Project Manager had re-entered the office from having been
on the site with the rep., inspecting some materials. After having
bantered with Al, the Office Manager for a few minutes, there was a
lull in their talk; I asked him:

| 1 | S. | You been having bother with that agent again? |
|---|----|-----|
| 2 | P.W. | And how! |
| 3 | S. | What is it this time? |
| 4 | P.W. | Oh, arguments about a claim over the level to which we excavated the site. |
| 5 | S. | Have you taken out more than on the estimate, and they're claiming you didn't do it? |
| 6 | P.W. | We, we took out more than was on the drawings/ |
| 7 | S. | Yeah/ |
| 8 | P.W. | because we damn well had to. The ground conditions were such that we had to. |
| 9 | S. | It was a soft and/ |
| 10 | P.W. | Uhmm/ |
| 11 | S. | Yeah/ |
| 12 | P.W. | And they're claiming that, eh, they're not going to pay us extra, because we never notified them that we were taking out extra dig. |
| 13 | S. | And is it their job to be there to know that you're doing it? |
| 14 | P.W. | I am wrong, in so far as I did not say specifically 'I have gone down deeper', but what I did say to Clerk of Works on the very first base we dug, I said 'Right Norman, there it is, there's the formation level, I want you to approve the formation and agree the level with me, so that we can do it on every base in |

the future so that there's no argument at a later
stage, as to what level we went to'.

15 S. Uhmm

16 P.W. And he said, 'I won't bother to do it now, I'll check
one or two later, you know, as the job goes on,' and
he never checked one 'cos he can't use a ruddy
instrument, . . . that's my honest opinion.

17 S. So you're suffering for his inadequacies then,
really?

18 P.W. Yeah, that's the way I see it. Well, I'm, I'm, not
suffering, well/

19 S labouring under him, that's probably, the right
word/

20 P.W. either he goes, or I go.

21 S. Is there any way you can put pressure on the client?

22 P.W. No, not really. It just depends whether they want a
bolshie agent on the job/

23 S. Uhmm, and sometimes they do?/

24 P.W. No, well no, what I mean is, as I've already said, . . .
if they don't get him off my back I'm jacking, *or*,
any little favours they want done in future, I won't
do 'em. I've got a situation at the moment, where the
'eh, . . . the two big external ramps he's not quite
certain, the architect, whether his drawing is correct
or not, whether the two ramps might clash together,
would I mind setting it out on the ground, so that
he can see.

25 S. Uhmm,

26 P.W. All right, I mean, well there's no skin off my nose
really, in doing it, but I'm not doing it now, I will
do it, if he gives me a V.O. to cover it, and thereby,
it means he pays me extra, . . . for doing it.

27 S. Yeah.

28 P.W. By the same light he's, like all architects he draws in
two dimensions, he cannot visualize three dimensions,
. . . he would not agree last week at the meeting when
I told him that these ramps, geometrically must be a
spiral. Something which is circular on plan, and is
rising, like that, must be a spiral. He said, no it's
flat, I said, no it's a spiral. So I built a model, to
show him that you cannot bend plywood in two
directions, and, eh, we're having a meeting this
afternoon, him and the consulting engineer. Now,
not only am I right, but secondly, the bill of quantities, you get, various items on it, so much per . . .

of . . . a . . . description, soffit shuttering, so much
per square metre, ditto circular on plan, at an
enhanced rate. Now they've billed the soffit to those
ramps as circular on plan. Well it might be circular
on plan, but they're inclined, and the standard
method of measurement which is a standard book,
tells you that that's an extra item, so that they
haven't allowed for it in their bill of quantities,
which means now that I can submit what I call a
star rate, a new rate for doing this work. And
anything that's in the bill of quantities bears no
relationship to it whatsoever, so as far as he's
concerned he's going to be paying about fifteen quid
a square metre for that now, uh, I'll have him!

| | | |
|---|---|---|
| 29 | S. | And, if you get a situation like that then it gives you an opportunity to recover some of the variable costs elsewhere, you can put in a bigger figure than that?/ |
| 30 | P.W. | Yeah, all right then, say I reckon, say allowing for a bit of profit it's going to cost me eight quid a metre/ |
| 31 | S. | Yeah/ |
| 32 | P.W. | I'll say right, what the hell. I'll put ten quid in, |
| 33 | S. | Yeah, |
| 34 | P.W. | Plus, that by and large with a thing like that your, what I call, buggeration factor, |
| 35 | S. | Hmh, huh, what the, eh, stress, the strain? |
| 36 | P.W. | No, that, a, you never know, I mean, something like that, you get one job, and the radius and such might be such that you can use three quarter inch plywood, cut in strips, 'cos you gotta set each one, |
| 37 | S. | Uhm, |
| 38 | P.W. | this job might be, the radius might be too sharp, and I might find it doesn't work with three quarters, and so I've got to get some half-inch ply in, and because I'm using half-inch ply, I've got to use that many more bearers underneath it to stop it deflecting, you know, so you want something in for your buggeration factor. |
| 39 | S. | Uhm. |

# Appendix 4 Rod Steiger to Harold Wilson, and back to normal clay

The previous site-meeting has broken up temporarily, as a phone-call to B.S., the architect, has resulted in his having to leave the meeting, to attend to something somewhere else. During the course of the following dialogue, he re-appears back on the scene, and joins into the debate about 'normal clay'. The architect has just left the scene:

1   P.W.   Did you see television last night? – I watched the Al Capone,

2   G.E.   I didn't see that, unfortunately.

3   P.W.   which, oh, I bet the Labour Party are hopping mad, 'cos you see Al Capone film with Rod Steiger, and at ten o'clock they stopped it, and said, now a party political broadcast with the Right Honourable Harold Wilson,

4   G.E.   Yeah.

5   P.W.   and changing from Rod Steiger's face, the last thing you saw to Harold Wilson's,

6   G.E.   little fat face, yeah.

7   P.W.   and then back into the film again, huh huh.

8   G.E.   Oh dear, yer mean, it's not even a natural break, huh huh, sort of continuous, huh, aye. . . .

9   P.W.   Hey, here you are, read that letter, I'll, here y'are, where is it, where is it? . . . You're mentioned in here so,

10  G.E.   Am I?

11  P.W.   (reading from letter) they clearly state they eh. . . . When work commenced the first two or three bases were excavated, the formation at the bottom of the excavations was approved by the consulting engineer.

| 12 | G.E. | Is that you saying that, or? |
|---|---|---|
| 13 | P.W. | That's them, |
| 14 | G.E. | Yes. |
| 15 | P.W. | All right? – 'with the knowledge of the clerk' – which you did, which you did you came and looked and said if that's/ |
| 16 | G.E. | Aye/ |
| 17 | P.W. | the sort of formation you're digging, fine, |
| 18 | G.E. | Uhm. |
| 19 | P.W. | 'and the bases constructed. Thereafter work progressed on the excavations, the Clerk of Works being asked to approve the formation exposed. At no time, however, was his attention drawn to the fact that additional excavation had been carried out below the specified levels . . . uh, I've also been informed by consulting engineer that he was not made aware of the, eh, additional extractions,' |
| 20 | G.E. | No, no, nono, that's . . . quite true as well, |
| 21 | P.W. | Yeah, that's true, yeah . . . uhm . . . but that first bit. . . . 'Clerk of Works being ah, at no time was the additional extraction made explicit' – we asked him to take levels, that's the first point, and then it goes on – 'It would appear that a general instruction, general instruction, was given by your site-staff to the excavator driver to go down as far as he considered necessary, irrespective of the consulting engineer's drawings,' |
| 22 | G.E. | Just, just hang on, now then, he says – It would appear – is it right or is it not right? Did you tell him to do that? |
| 23 | P.W. | Course not! I don't turn a, a machine/ |
| 24 | G.E. | Well now, wh . . . where's he got that impression from? |
| 25 | P.W. | Norman, said that to Brian – It looks as though they've been tear-arsing around on site. |
| 26 | G.E. | Well, all right, y'know this/ |
| 27 | P.W. | It then goes on, ahblahblahblah. . . . 'My Clerk of Works was also not informed that your staff considered the basement-levels as shown on my drawings to be incorrect' – That is untrue, we said, all right, those levels, we'll take those levels as correct as the buildings were there. What we, or we said, we never found any basement bottom intact, to agree with that, they were just smashed to pieces. 'I therefore consider it unreasonable |

blahblahblahblahblah, investigation of the claimed
actual excavation levels reveals little or no consistency, thus leading one to assume that either the
satisfactory bearing strata varied from base to base'
– well it does, strata/

| | | |
|---|---|---|
| 28 | G.E. | You would expect it to vary. |
| 29 | P.W. | 'or as is more likely' – he's coming a bit harder now – 'the excavator driver carried out his work with wrong instructions and/or inadequate super-vision. My assistant inspected the excavation for the bases to column B.2 to B.5 inclusive and was satisfied that these bases were at the correct level, approximately two metres into stony clay', well you cannot argue it was two metres into stony clay, that clay's never stony, in façt the J.C.B. today, he's dug me another hole – you know where we get this paved area at the end of the building here? |
| 30 | G.E. | Hm, hm. |
| 31 | P.W. | He's dug me a base hole in line with 'B' line, and he's dug the same hole as a 'B' base, to the correct level, |
| 32 | G.E. | Uhm. |
| 33 | P.W. | as shown on your drawings, |
| 34 | G.E. | Yeah. |
| 35 | P.W. | and in fact I'd better go out there and have a look at it before it bloody well fills in with snow . . . adaadadah. . . . 'It is therefore unreasonable to assume that in view of this and the site-investigation report, clay was not encountered at anything other than the expected levels' – clay was encountered, but not the correct stuff. |
| 36 | G.E. | This is, you come back to this eh, y'know, couple of feet into this clay, the consultants said this and it would appear that they were near enough to being right, that the top, |
| 37 | P.W. | Uhm. |
| 38 | G.E. | layer of the ordinary clay, |
| 39 | P.W. | Uhm. |
| 40 | G.E. | was not adequate, for the needs. |
| 41 | P.W. | Uhm, the other thing is, Brian agrees with me, but he still writes that letter, that this bore-hole log is not worth the paper it's printed on, because there's no datum given, for the start of the bore, and I said, well how did you establish your figures?, and he said, Oh I interpolated from the original site survey. |

181

| 42 | G.E. | yes, the other thing is, even if he'd have got levels and whatever on there, these people do not take any responsibility. |
| 43 | P.W. | No. |
| 44 | G.E. | They offer that in good faith, |
| 45 | P.W. | Uhm. |
| 46 | G.E. | they do a certain exploration and it gives you the results, and what you interpret from that is your own responsibility. |
| 47 | P.W. | Yeah, but eh . . . they are wrong in fact to describe it all the way through as 'brown, sandy stony clay',/ it is not/ |
| 48 | G.E. | /It isn't/, it's not at the top surface, |
| 49 | P.W. | No. |
| 50 | G.E. | it's just ordinary clay, |
| 51 | P.W. | Yeah. |
| 52 | G.E. | muddy clay. |
| 53 | P.W. | Where their bore-holes were, they might have been lucky to hit the odd cobble, |
| 54 | G.E. | Uhm. |
| 55 | P.W. | and assume that eh, it's stony all the way through, but it isn't. |
| 56 | G.E. | They're only using that four-inch, tube, for this, and when they break it open, |
| 57 | P.W. | Uhm. |
| 58 | G.E. | you know, you can see whether it's clay or not. |
| 59 | P.W. | I mean Brian knows that when. . . . |
| 60 | G.E. | I suppose, as I'm asked, that, all that stony clay, I suppose was one strata, it just got more stony to the bottom. |
| 61 | P.W. | Uhm, uhm . . . if you relate, those bore-hole logs, I've done this meself, to the original/survey/ |
| 62 | G.E. | /Survey/, uhm. |
| 63 | P.W. | which was not presented, not the original survey by the Corporation, as I never saw one, only my own survey was done at the start of the job, naturally, the ground's falling that way, and across this, and, the clay, is thickest at that end of the site, |
| 64 | G.E. | Uhm. |
| 65 | P.W. | tapering, down this way, |
| 66 | G.E. | Yeah. |
| 67 | P.W. | and in fact you could see it, there on the base-holes, gradually going lower and lower down, it's following the sandstone, |
| 68 | G.E. | Yeah. |

| 69 | P.W. | ehm, that we'd dug, when we had, remember we had an argument about whether the clay was suitable for a sub-base out there, right at the start of the job/ |
|---|---|---|
| 70 | G.E. | Oh yes, I remember that. |
| 71 | T.M. | (the tea-man) How many sugars? |
| 72 | P.W. | Two. |
| 73 | G.E. | Two please. |
| 74 | P.W. | Just to satisfy Brian, and C. off the ring-road, some/ |
| 75 | G.E. | Let's have a look, let's have a look at the letter that they've sent. |
| 76 | P.W. | Yeah, somebody's just asked Ted, I got the drop, I got him to nose in, and dig a hole, about five feet deep, and again you saw it, clay, |
| 77 | G.E. | Uhm. |
| 78 | P.W. | then the odd boulder appearing, and then, the sandy stone, – which is a combination, literally, of the sandstone layer and the clay . . . and that base we've just eh, not the base we've concreted, the one next to it, |
| 79 | G.E. | This is, this is where they're going to win you know, |
| 80 | P.W. | What? |
| 81 | G.E. | that it's unreasonable of you to present a claim at this stage, now that everything's been back-filled, there would never have been a haggle, |
| 82 | P.W. | It was presented before we'd finished the ruddy bases. . . . I mean this, this argument's been going on now, they've known about this since way before Christmas. . . . No, my little crunch is going to come that when I, I joked about it this afternoon, I said as far as eh, the ramps are concerned, we go down to the level given on your drawings and stop there, an' I want everyone from the corporation to come and inspect the bottoms, |
| 83 | G.E. | Yeah, you'd be quite right to, demand it/ |
| 84 | P.W. | I will demand it and I will also, an' I'll say this in front of Brian/ |
| 85 | G.E. | and, in all fairness, if, if there's any doubt, or, if on the first few, I, I should come and see it, |
| 86 | P.W. | Yeah. |
| 87 | G.E. | Well, this is what Norman's here for, |
| 88 | P.W. | Yeah. |
| 89 | G.E. | to deci – and if he can't decide you've got to come back to me. |

| 90  | P.W. | And at that time, I will ask for Norman to take the levels, agree the levels, physically, on site. |
|-----|------|---|
| 91  | G.E. | Uhm . . . this is where it's slipped up actually. . . . |
| 92  | P.W. | But, I've said this all along, I was wrong, in not informing the Corporation myself, but at the same time I did ask the Corporation to check and agree levels. |
| 93  | G.E. | You'd think that, it all comes back to this, if you were asking for ten quid they'd give it to you rather than haggle with yer, |
| 94  | P.W. | Uhm. |
| 95  | G.E. | but because you're asking for, probably three thousand to eight thousand, or whatever the figure is, that's where you're coming unstuck. |
| 96  | P.W. | Well, there's two claims, mixed together, |
| 97  | G.E. | Yeah. |
| 98  | P.W. | there, there's the claim on the extra dig on the actual bases, there's also the fact that cellar walls were non-existent in accordance with our plan, |
| 99  | G.E. | Yeah. |
| 100 | P.W. | therefore we've got extra wide, to dig as well. . . . I can't even roll a decent cigarette now. . . . |
| 101 | G.E. | When I used to smoke I used to roll me own with me fingers. |
| 102 | P.W. | What, the Gary Cooper type? |
| 103 | G.E. | Ahhhh! |
| 104 | P.W. | I know what this is, I – do you know that for some reason or another, this town, you can't buy Job papers anywhere now, they've suddenly all sold out? |
| 105 | G.E. | So what have you got, Rizla? |
| 106 | P.W. | Yeah, don't like them at all. |
| 107 | G.E. | I used to use the green ones. |
| 108 | P.W. | Know the yel, yer know the yellow packet I use? |
| 109 | G.E. | Yeah. |
| 110 | P.W. | the Job, where yer have, where yer get two lots of paper in one packet, |
| 111 | G.E. | Huh huh. |
| 112 | P.W. | ehrr, I don't know, they seem to smoke better. . . . |
| 113 | G.E. | Yeah, it was ridiculous, when I was, so poor, I just didn't earn much money, I used to smoke, |
| 114 | P.W. | Huh. |
| 115 | G.E. | and when I could afford to smoke, I gave up. |
| 116 | P.W. | Well youn, young Peter there, I've got him on to rolling his own, since he came here, and he reckons it's marvellous, best thing I've done for him. |

| 117 | G.E. | Yeah, oh they're better than the other thing, I used to find those were very . . . I can't describe the taste now, they always used to be a richer taste. |
| 118 | P.W. | Yeah, these, these have taste to 'em, flavour, ehm/ |
| 119 | G.E. | Also a bit uhm, I don't know, they used to sort of make yer throat sore, and things/ |
| 120 | P.W. | I smoke, I smoke those convenience when I'm outside on the site uhm, |
| 121 | G.E. | Yeah |
| 122 | P.W. | when I'm driving, but, Peter was saying that it's the money saving, as far as he's concerned, that, he sort of, smokes a half ounce a day, |
| 123 | G.E. | Which costs you what, twenty p. a day? |
| 124 | P.W. | uh, eighteen p. |
| 125 | G.E. | Eighteen p., yeah. |
| 126 | P.W. | uhm, compared with uhm, he was spending about forty odd p. a day average on cigarettes. |
| 127 | G.E. | Yes. . . . |
| 128 | P.W. | Oh, someone's talking about me! |
| 129 | G.E. | So you've got your problems, eh, what's going to be the answer? |
| 130 | P.W. | On this, or generally? |
| 131 | G.E. | Well, this to start with. |
| 132 | P.W. | Eh, . . . well straight off, before we get into the, the nitty-gritty, of, the claim, we, Construction Co., or me, are writing a strong letter to the Corporation about the tone in which that letter was sent, the accusations of, incompetence, |
| 133 | G.E. | Uhm. |
| 134 | P.W. | I've also got Norman's Clerk of Works memoes, it refers to, not so much, he doesn't use the word incompetent, but he says it's about time you had a competent person, on site, which is/ |
| 135 | G.E. | Same thing/ |
| 136 | P.W. | same thing, |
| 137 | G.E. | Uhm. |
| 138 | P.W. | Uhm . . . cor . . . I need a hole in the back of my head . . . so having done that, as far as the claim is concerned . . . I'm getting eh, what's his name, young Ken/ |
| 139 | G.E. | Oh you said this, eh/ |
| 140 | P.W. | Well, I've got a rough one I did here. . . . |
| 141 | G.E. | Yes, but ehm, it's all going to come back to this, this, y'know, can you prove that you needed to go down? |

| | | |
|---|---|---|
| 142 | P.W. | Ehm. |
| 143 | G.E. | If you can prove that then you're away, how, how'll you prove it I don't know. |
| 144 | P.W. | Right, this is 'D' line, |
| 145 | G.E. | Uh hm. |
| 146 | P.W. | ignore the ground levels 'cos I don't, I don't quite know them, so those, those are the base, basement levels, |
| 147 | G.E. | Huh huh. |
| 148 | P.W. | and our bases, by and large, tie in, that we, what, that we proved the cellar bottom, that you get the odd one or two which apparently fall below, (Tea-man enters, bringing mugs of tea) |
| 149 | G.E. | Oh, great, thank you . . . it's all right, I've a bigger one than this at home. . . . |
| 150 | P.W. | If you take all the base-levels, you know we did a little, eh, wherever it is, |
| 151 | G.E. | That it? |
| 152 | P.W. | no, symbolic eh, bases, the one with all the bases . . . anyhow, we, we did a little sketch, a standard sketch of each base, uhm/ |
| 153 | G.E. | Half a sec, these are basement levels? |
| 154 | P.W. | Yeah. |
| 155 | G.E. | Then what the hell's that one doing stuck out there? |
| 156 | P.W. | Because of what we found. |
| 157 | G.E. | Oh. |
| 158 | P.W. | No, |
| 159 | G.E. | That's an odd one. |
| 160 | P.W. | no, this is a, forget it, it's a, an enlarged scale, I'll soon tell you what that is . . . that D.7 . . . D.7 was at ninety six, nine hundred, and the basement level was ninety eight, |
| 161 | G.E. | Oh, it's not that far/ |
| 162 | P.W. | no, ninety, no, |
| 163 | G.E. | Uh. |
| 164 | P.W. | Can't find a decent pen in this building now. |
| 165 | G.E. | I'll, I'll have to – oh, I've got a pencil. |
| 166 | P.W. | No, that's all right, I do have a drawer full. . . . ninety-eight o seven five, ninety/six nine hundred/ |
| 167 | G.E. | /six nine hundred/ |
| 168 | P.W. | ninety six nine hundred, five seven one, – one metre. |
| 169 | G.E. | It's near enough there, uhm, |
| 170 | P.W. | All right, but/ |

| 171 | G.E. | that's, that's as deep as you probably needed to have gone, theoretically. |
|-----|------|---|
| 172 | P.W. | Well, you don't know, what/ |
| 173 | G.E. | Well, you don't know, no. |
| 174 | P.W. | Now, D.7. occurs, there, |
| 175 | G.E. | Uhh. |
| 176 | P.W. | which is on the edge of that centre staircase . . . (takes out a set of technical drawing instruments) |
| 177 | G.E. | Them are rather grand aren't they? |
| 178 | P.W. | Bloody need 'em to settle these arguments now. . . . D.7. . . . D.7 lines up with. . . . Yeah, I'm not certain whether, that one's D.7, that one there, now notice that the cellar bottom, |
| 179 | G.E. | Yeah. |
| 180 | P.W. | there's no cellar bottom as such, it was just a hard muck level that we arrived at, now you can easily check that back from the existing ground level – that frame there, was the frame we made up for the excavator driver, |
| 181 | G.E. | Yeah, yeah. |
| 182 | P.W. | to see the size of a base to dig, so it's two, what is it, two six hundred metres that, so you can say that the depth of that hole there, |
| 183 | G.E. | Is two metres down. |
| 184 | P.W. | Two metres something, |
| 185 | G.E. | And a bit, yeah. |
| 186 | P.W. | to the cellar bottom, you can very soon verify that base detail from that photo. |
| 187 | G.E. | I don't think that the quibble's going to come, but, but, they're not going to say, you haven't dug down to those levels, they're probably quite happy to say, those levels – we're convinced they're right, |
| 188 | P.W. | Yeah, why did you do it. |
| 189 | G.E. | but did you need to do it, uhm. |
| 190 | P.W. | Uhm . . . here we are, D.1, 2, 3, 4, and 5, how'd they look? You see, there's the blinding |
| 191 | G.E. | Hmm, |
| 192 | P.W. | That pencil line round the shutter, is the bottom of your base |
| 193 | G.E. | Yeah, |
| 194 | P.W. | What we did, we put that in, filled it with hard core to that line, |
| 195 | G.E. | Yeah, |
| 196 | P.W. | drew it out, filled it with mass |
| 197 | G.E. | Yeah, |

| 198 | P.W. | and away we went. Now we're blinding, we're not such bloody fools that we're going to dig a hole a metre deep and fill it with blinding just for the hell of it |
|---|---|---|
| 199 | G.E. | Hmm, |
| 200 | P.W. | We dug, we wanted those bases in as quickly as possible, so we dig it out, we blind it, so as to get a move on with it. |
| 201 | G.E. | Yeah. |
| 202 | P.W. | We don't pour on any old kind of clay we dig up, it, it all comes down to what is clay, we couldn't have rooted out any higher on those bases, it was only puddle clay, we wanted that sandy, stony clay, (During 202 the architect, B.S. has re-appeared) whereas you say we can't differentiate between the two types of clay. |
| 203 | B.S. | Well, this, this has been my whole point all along, what is clay, what is stony clay, and what will basically take three tons? |
| 204 | G.E. | I mean, it's fair to say, I, I think their recommendation was the stony clay, eh, the soft clay overlying had obviously deteriorated, and certainly that stuff in there, I wouldn't have given it anything above about a ton and a half, |
| 205 | P.W. | No. |
| 206 | G.E. | at the very most. |
| 207 | B.S. | But, but you look at last paragraph in their report, before you actually get to the bore-hole areas. . . . |
| 208 | P.W. | If it. . . . ten ton. . . . |
| 209 | G.E. | No, that's the rock, right? |
| 210 | B.S. | Yeah. |
| 211 | P.W. | Now, what we want to look at, |
| 212 | G.E. | We want/ |
| 213 | P.W. | the low triaxal test result in attaining a depth of four feet in bore-hole two is probably the result of softening of the clay surface immediately below the fill material, |
| 214 | B.S. | Uhm. |
| 215 | G.E. | That's right, |
| 216 | B.S. | But you've/ |
| 217 | G.E. | and that, is that/ |
| 218 | B.S. | you've gone further, it says two tons, two feet in the clay is sufficient . . . somewhere. |
| 219 | G.E. | . . . specify a minimum depth of two feet into clay. . . . That's what they're saying isn't it?, |

| 220 | B.S. | Uhmm. |
|---|---|---|
| 221 | G.E. | the top layer is shot, it's not much use, |
| 222 | B.S. | Yeah. |
| 223 | G.E. | yer've just to get through that, which is that two feet, |
| 224 | P.W. | Uhmm, uhm. |
| 225 | G.E. | and, that's when it starts turning to more stony stuff, and you can see it as you went down/ |
| 226 | B.S. | Yeah, well, well, having said that, we, you know, we're coming down to it, we are, well . . . above the two feet in every condition, so my attitude is why? |
| 227 | P.W. | That we are/ |
| 228 | B.S. | Well, we're well, I looked, as I say in the letter, I looked at the bases at the far end of the grid-line, |
| 229 | P.W. | Uhm. |
| 230 | B.S. | the E, B, 1, 2, 3, 4, 5 – I think it was those, and those were, two metres, into clay. Now, presumably, and I think that you've accepted this, or Brian H. has accepted, (Brian H. is the consultant bore-hole engineer), that, that, these were taken down to the · specified levels, (Clerk of Works enters from site) |
| 231 | P.W. | Uhm. |
| 232 | B.S. | now, having said that, two feet – ehm, two metres, into clay were well below/ |
| 233 | G.E. | Well below what was recommended/ |
| 234 | P.W. | Yes, but/ |
| 235 | B.S. | and, and/ |
| 236 | P.W. | two metres into clay, but what sort of clay? |
| 237 | G.E. | Ah well, this, this, this, there's two/ |
| 238 | B.S. | Uhm, I take their report quite honestly, |
| 239 | G.E. | Uhm, uhm. |
| 240 | B.S. | and, and Norman's test, test metre readings have brought it out/ |
| 241 | N.T. | Yeah, two foot deep, I get a reading of four, four tons for down there/ |
| 242 | P.W. | You've taken theirs/ |
| 243 | N.T. | four tons per/ |
| 244 | P.W. | report, but that report, it's not a contractual document, it is not an instruction to us, the instruction to us is on that drawing, sandy, stony clay, a minimum of six hundred mills/ |
| 245 | N.T. | Yes but this report says that is sandy, stony clay, there's nothing on/ |
| 246 | B.S. | No, no, no, it doesn't differentiate/ |
| 247 | N.T. | only, no, it doesn't say there's any difference/ |

| 248 | B.S. | it says two feet into clay, |
|-----|------|------|
| 249 | N.T. | Yeah, yeah. |
| 250 | B.S. | and I asked specifically, ehm, you know, what was the difference between clay and what was the difference between sandy, stony clay, |
| 251 | P.W. | Uhm. |
| 252 | B.S. | this, this was all questionable and we were arguing all down the hole. |
| 253 | P.W. | This hole, that we went down the ladder, uhm, now you made another point, about the clay being at a sort of constant level across the site, |
| 254 | B.S. | I said I would expect it to be, yes. |
| 255 | P.W. | Yes, right, we went down that hole yesterday and we took one, two, three, four, five, six, seven, eight readings, admittedly it's just round the perimeter of one hole, |
| 256 | B.S. | Yeah. |
| 257 | P.W. | we got a variation of six hundred mill., up and down, up and down, all round the hole, from the line of the stony clay, which gave us an average depth, of ninety-eight one five o, that's for the top of it, I then deducted off my six hundred and ten mill., and gave me an average level of ninety-seven five forty, and if you look at this sheet of paper that I've drawn here, I drew a line across it, representing ninety-seven five forty, and I plotted in my bases in relation to it, the half that come underneath that line, all the one's in blue, are in basements, so they don't count, they would be below, anyhow, |
| 258 | B.S. | No, uhm. |
| 259 | P.W. | and, the others, like D.11, I've dotted, that's a debatable one, 'cos that came right on the edge of a ruddy cellar, yer know, in the full material, and if you, I've got Ken, at the moment, he's drawing me sections, of the site, on each grid-line, superim – eh, to an enlarged scale, superimposing the basements, the original formation level, our bases, and you'll find, and this is your other point, if we turn a machine-driver loose on that site, he's not going to dig this hole up, that one down, he'd have dug the whole bloody lot to a level, but as soon as you plot those in, in relation to those basements, you can see, that they all relate, to the bases, that we haven't gone tearing down a common level, |

| | | |
|---|---|---|
| 260 | N.T. | Can I get off this subject? I've asked for a cube out of these two bases, there, because eh, it, they wouldn't, eh, do a slump test on them, it'd collapse all together. |
| 261 | P.W. | Sorry? |
| 262 | N.T. | I've asked for a test cubes out of these two bases that you're just putting in now, because it wouldn't stand up for a slump-test, it'd just collapse . . . they were stood in t'wellington boots up, and' it were coming over'top of wellington boots. |
| 263 | G.E. | Have you got a cone? |
| 264 | N.T. | Oh I don't think that/ |
| 265 | P.W. | What is the slump test that we are allowed? What slump are we allowed? |
| 266 | N.T. | It int a matter of that, eh strength must have gone, if it's so sloppy, so I want a test-cube out of it to make sure. |
| 267 | P.W. | Aye, we'll take a test-cube, but what slump are we allowed? |
| 268 | G.E. | I'd have a guess, two, two and a half? Could be three.<br>(Construction Co.'s site quantity surveyor has followed Norman in) |
| 269 | Q.S. | Hang on, you can't take a slump at the moment because the concrete's been in about, half an hour, already. |
| 270 | N.T. | I want, I want a test-cube out of there, anyhow. |
| 271 | P.W. | Take, take a couple of cubes now. |
| 272 | G.E. | Y'mean, tek it actually out o' the base? |
| 273 | N.T. | Yes, I want it out of the base itself, yeah, not uhmmm, because it's clay an' all sorts, mixed in with it . . . clay an' water an' . . . |
| 274 | G.E. | What did it do? was it going in like soup? |
| 275 | N.T. | Well, it's either going in like soup, or else, it's water 'at were already int'err. . . . |
| 276 | P.W. | The bases were pumped, they were pumped out, Norman. |
| 277 | N.T. | Well, the next one isn't dry, the next one they're ready for concreting isn't dry, eh, Peter. Eh, you could see the clay-water, y'know, oozing, it's, well, it's still there if anybody wants to look at it. |
| 278 | P.W. | Where the hell do you have your slump-test in this mess? (Looking through the 'bill of works') |
| 279 | N.T. | I don't think it mentions it, t'be quite honest, Peter. |

| 280 | P.W. | No, I just want to see what it is, because in fact/ |
|---|---|---|
| 281 | G.E. | If, if it's in bases, you probably don't need much of a slump, |
| 282 | P.W. | No. |
| 283 | G.E. | yer may well have been limited to two inches about, |
| 284 | N.T. | It's a bit wide at two inches as far as I know, but 'em, |
| 285 | G.E. | yer, two inches/ |
| 286 | P.W. | We var, we vary the slump, we've had to vary it, there's so much steel, especially on the columns, we've increased the slump from two inch, to two and a half, to three, |
| 287 | N.T. | Yeah, well that'd collapse, you wouldn't get a slump on this, this is what I'm saying, it'd just collapse. |
| 288 | G.E. | Yeah, it'd just float the cone off? |
| 289 | N.T. | As soon as you lifted cone off, it'd just, zoom. |
| 290 | G.E. | I'd one, I couldn't hold the cone down on it. |
| 291 | N.T. | You wouldn't on this I don't think. |
| 292 | G.E. | An' that was on a slab. . . . |
| 293 | P.W. | I know why that has got a high slump on it, because this was, I rang, George up this morning, an' said, look I wanna do two bases, an' some columns today, it's cold, an' I can pour the concrete on etcetera., an' George said to me, |
| 294 | G.E. | Uhm. |
| 295 | P.W. | don't do the columns, just do the bases, so that mix has got a high slump on it because we were going to use it/ |
| 296 | N.T. | But it hasn't a slump on it, this is what I'm trying to say, huh huh, hasn't a slump on it at all, it's just puddled. . . . <br> (Exit of all concerned to the site, to inspect the pour.) |

# Notes

## 1 The problem of definition

1 Alphaville was a totalitarian fiction, like Huxley's (1950) *Brave New World*. Each day the 'bible' was changed by the police force of the State. The bible was what we should think of as a 'dictionary', but with one important exception. Each daily issue contained fewer words than the previous one, as 'illogical' words (such as 'conscience') were ruled out of meaning and out of use. In such a society the nihilistic implications of an arbitrary definition of power would merely throw into sharp relief the consequences of 'totalitarian' arbitrary definition. It may serve to obscure what might have been regarded as power, and still might be, albeit, its being concealed. Of course, the same problem is as evident in 'democratically plural' definition; the multiplicity of presumed meanings now serving to obscure 'being'.

## 2 Power, theorizing and reason

1 In my use of the notion of 'rationality' I acknowledge my reading of Rosen (1969) as helpful in formulating the subsequent discussion. However, it should also be quite apparent that I am arguing against his interpretation of Wittgenstein as a 'conventionalist' and 'nihilist'.

## 5 Social rules and the grammatical analogy

1 Cicourel (1968) has earlier referred to 'interpretive procedures' as 'background expectancies', and 'background assumptions', after Garfinkel's (1967) usage. Garfinkel refers to these as

the socially standardizing, 'seen but unnoticed', expected, background features of everyday scenes. The member of the society uses background expectancies as a scheme of interpretation. With their use actual appearances are for him recognizable and intelligible as the appearances of familiar events. Demonstratively he is responsive to this background while at the same time he is at a loss to tell us specifically of what the expectancies consist (Garfinkel, 1967, p. 37).

NOTES TO PAGES 74–121

2 This allusion is, of course, to the famous passage in Plato's *Republic*, 'The Simile of the Cave'.

## 7 'Rationality' in the organization

1 The concept of 'normal' has also been employed by sociologists. In particular, I would like to acknowledge Keddie's (1971) work; which I found very useful.

2 The Marxist theory of value has been subject to attack almost from its beginnings in *Capital*, where Marx (1930) developed it from strands of the classical thought of Smith and Ricardo. Perhaps the most famous criticisms were those made by Bohm-Bawerk (1966), launched from the marginal utility perspective developed in the 1870s by Jevons, Menger and Walras. In a sense, the criticisms and subsequent debate on the topic can be addressed in terms similar to those that I have used to discuss the grammar of the Community Power Debate.

The Marginalists start from a different conception of the problem of economics to that made by the Marxists. For the former, economics is a question of optimizing production and consumer satisfaction with given amounts of labour, technology, and resources, viewed under the pluralist-democratic notion of 'consumer sovereignty'. It is argued that consumers spend their money according to the additional utility they obtain from one marginal increment of the product, so that under conditions of 'pure competition', prices would have to be proportional to the marginal utility of the product. This conception of economics is oriented to resolving technical problems of investment, technology, production and labour quantities, in a given social situation, and abstracted from the everyday world of 'work'.

Marx was not interested in the technical efficiency of capital, but in a *political* rather than *technical* economics. His concern was with political economy, a world of real, actual working men inhabiting a social structure which they encounter as an alien thing, opaque to their understanding. Through penetrating this opacity, an opacity which was maintained by theoretic apologists for the regime, Marx affords us a ladder from the theoretic to the human relations of production which underly this everyday working life.

For a detailed Marxist account of the theory see Sweezy (1942); for a broad overview of both perspectives see Sherman (1972).

# Bibliography

ANSCOMBE, G. E. M. (1957), *Intention*, Oxford, Blackwell.
ARISTOTLE (1933), *Metaphysics, Book II*, Translated by H. Tredennick, London, Heinemann.
BACHRACH, P. and BARATZ, M. S. (1971), 'Two Faces of Power', in CASTLES, F. G., MURRAY, D. J., and POTTER, D. C. (eds), *Decisions, Organizations and Society*, Harmondsworth, Penguin, pp. 376–88. Originally published in *American Political Science Review*, vol. 56, 1962, pp. 947–52.
BACHRACH, P. and BARATZ, M. S. (1971), *Power and Poverty*, Oxford University Press.
BANFIELD, E. C. (1966), *Political Influence*, New York, Free Press.
BANTON, M. (1972), 'Authority', *New Society*, vol. 22, no. 523, 12 October, pp. 86–8.
BARTHES, R. (1967), *Writing Degree Zero*, translated by A. Lavers and C. Smith, London, Jonathan Cape.
BARTHES, R. (1970), 'Science versus Literature', in LANE, M. (ed.), *Structuralism: A Reader*, London, Jonathan Cape, pp. 410–16. Originally published in *The Times Literary Supplement*, 28 September 1967.
BITTNER, E. (1965), 'The Concept of Organization', *Social Research*, vol. 32, no. 3, pp. 239–55.
BLAU, P. (1964), *Exchange and Power in Social Life*, New York, John Wiley.
BLUM, A. F. (1971), 'Theorizing', in DOUGLAS, J. D. (ed.), *Understanding Everyday Life: Toward the Reconstruction of Sociological Knowledge*, London, Routledge & Kegan Paul, pp. 301–19
BLUM, A. F. (1974), *Theorizing*, London, Heinemann.
BLUM, A. F., FOSS, D., MCHUGH, P., and RAFFEL, S. (1974), *On the Beginning of Social Inquiry*, London, Routledge & Kegan Paul.
BLUM, A. F. and MCHUGH, P. (1971), 'The Social Ascription of Motive', *American Sociological Review*, vol. 35, no. 1, February, pp. 98–109.
BOHM-BAWERK, E. V. (1966), *Capital and Interest: A Critical History of Economic Theory* (3 volumes), translated by W. Smart, East Orange, N.J., Kelly.

BIBLIOGRAPHY

BRIDGMAN, P. W. (1927), *The Logic of Modern Physics*, London, Macmillan.

BURNHAM, J. (1941), *The Managerial Revolution*, New York, John Day.

CAVELL, S. (1962), 'The Claim to Rationality: Knowledge and the Basis of Morality', PhD thesis, Harvard University.

CAVELL, S. (1966), 'The Availability of Wittgenstein's Later Philosophy', in PICHTER, G. (ed.), *Wittgenstein: The Philosophical Investigations*, London, Macmillan, pp. 151–85. Originally published in *Philosophical Review*, vol. 71, pp. 67–93.

CAVELL, S. (1969), *Must We Mean What We Say*, New York, Scribner's.

CHILD, J. (1972), 'Organizational Structure, Environment and Performance: The Role of Strategic Choice', *Sociology*, vol. 6, no. 1, January, pp. 1–22.

CHOMSKY, N. (1968), *Language and Mind*, New York, Harcourt, Brace & World.

CICOUREL, A. (1968), *The Social Organization of Juvenile Justice*, New York, John Wiley.

CICOUREL, A. (1973), *Cognitive Sociology*, Harmondsworth, Penguin.

CLEGG, S. R. (1974), 'Power in Organization Theory: A Conceptual and Empirical Enquiry into Rules and Power in the Organization, employing Conversational Materials Collected on a Construction-site', PhD thesis, University of Bradford.

CROZIER, M. (1964), *The Bureaucratic Phenomenon*, London, Tavistock.

CYERT, R. M. and MARCH, J. G. (1963), *A Behavioural Theory of the Firm*, Englewood Cliffs, N. J., Prentice Hall.

DAHL, R. A. (1957), 'The Concept of Power', *Behavioural Science*, vol. 2, pp. 201–15.

DAHL, R. A. (1961), *Who Governs?* Yale University Press.

DAHL, R. A. (1967), *Pluralist Democracy in the United States: Conflict and Consent*, Chicago, Rand McNally.

DAHL, R. A. (1968), 'Power', *International Encyclopaedia of the Social Sciences*, London, Free Press and Macmillan.

D'ANTONIO, W. V., EHRLICH, H. J. and ERICKSON, E. C. (1962), 'Further Notes on the Study of Community Power', *American Sociological Review*, vol. 27, pp. 848–54.

DAWE, A. (1970), 'The Two Sociologies', *British Journal of Sociology*, vol. 21, no. 2, pp. 207–18.

DAWE, A. (1971), 'The Relevance of Values', in SAHAY, A. (ed.), *Max Weber and Modern Sociology*, London, Routledge & Kegan Paul.

DAWE, A. (1973), 'The Role of Experience in the Construction of Social Theory: An Essay in Reflexive Sociology', *Sociological Review*, vol. 21, no. 1, pp. 25–56.

DOUGLAS, J. D. (1971), *Understanding Everyday Life: Toward the Reconstruction of Sociological Knowledge*, London, Routledge & Kegan Paul.

DRUCKMAN, M. (ed.) (1971), *Community and Purpose in America: An Analysis of American Political Theory*, New York, McGraw-Hill.

EHRLICH, H. J. (1961), 'The Reputational Approach to the Study of Community Power', *American Sociological Review*, vol. 26, December, pp. 926–7.

EMMET, D. (1953), 'The Concept of Power', *Aristotelian Society Proceedings*, 54, pp. 1–26.

FOX, A. (1966), 'Industrial Sociology and Industrial Relations', Research Paper 3, *Royal Commission on Trade Unions and Employers Associations*, London, HMSO.

FREIDRICH, C. J. (1964), 'Authority', in GOULD, D. and KOULB, W. L. (eds), *A Dictionary of the Social Sciences*, London, Tavistock.

GALBRAITH, J. K. (1967), *The New Industrial State*, London, Hamilton.

GARFINKEL, H. (1956), 'Some Sociological Concepts and Methods for Psychiatrists', *Psychiatric Research Report*, vol. 6, October, pp. 181–95.

GARFINKEL, H. (1967), *Studies in Ethnomethodology*, Englewood Cliffs, N. J., Prentice-Hall.

GARFINKEL, H. and SACKS, H. (1970), 'On the Formal Structures of Practical Actions', in MCKINNEY, J. C. and TIRYAKIAN, E. A. (eds), *Theoretical Sociology: Perspectives and Developments*, New York, Appleton-Century-Crofts.

GITLIN, T. (1965), 'Local Pluralism as Theory and Ideology', *Studies on the Left*, Summer, pp. 21–45.

GOULDNER, A. (1955), *Patterns of Industrial Bureaucracy*, London, Routledge & Kegan Paul.

GOULDNER, A. (1959), 'Reciprocity and Autonomy in Functional Theory', in GROSS, L. (ed.), *Symposium on Sociological Theory*, London, Harper & Row.

GOULDNER, A. (1967), 'Reciprocity and Autonomy in Functional Theory', in DEMERATH, N. J. and PETERSON, R. A. (eds), *System, Change and Conflict*, New York, Free Press.

GOULDNER, A. (1971), *The Coming Crisis of Western Sociology*, London, Heinemann.

HAMPSHIRE, S. (1959), *Thought and Action*, London, Chatto & Windus.

HART, H. L. A. (1960), 'The Ascription of Responsibility and Rights', in FLEW, A. (ed.), *Logic and Language* (First Series), Oxford, Blackwell, pp. 145–66.

HEATH, S. (1972), *The Nouveau Roman: A Study in the Practice of Writing*, London, Elek.

HEIDEGGER, M. (1962), *Being and Time*, translated by J. Macquarie and E. Robinson, London, SCM Press.

HICKSON, D. J., HININGS, C. R., LEE, C. A., SCHNECK, R. E., and PENNINGS, J. M. (1971), 'A Strategic Contingencies Theory of Intra-Organizational Power', *Administrative Science Quarterly*, vol. 16, no. 2, pp. 216–29.

HIGGIN, G., JESSOP, N., BRYANT, D., LUCKMAN, J., and STRINGER, J. (1966), *Interdependence and Uncertainty: A Study of the Building Industry*, condensed and edited for publication by C. Crichton, London, Tavistock Publications.

HUNTER, F. (1953), *Community Power Structure*, Chapel Hill, University of North Carolina Press.

HUNTER, J. F. M. (1971), 'Wittgenstein on Meaning and Use', in KLEMKE, E. D. (ed.), *Essays on Wittgenstein*, London, University of Illinois Press, pp. 374–93.

197

HUXLEY, A. (1950), *Brave New World: A Novel*, London, Chatto & Windus.
JANIK, A. and TOULMIN, S. (1973), *Wittgenstein's Vienna*, London, Weidenfield & Nicolson.
KANT, I. (1964), *Critique of Pure Reason*, translated by N. K. Smith, London, Macmillan.
KAPLAN, A. (1964), 'Power in Perspective', in KAHN, R. L. and BOULDING, E. (eds), *Power and Conflict in Organizations*, London, Tavistock. pp. 11–32.
KARPIK, L. (1972), 'Les Politiques et les logiques d'action de la grande entreprise industrielle', *Sociologie du Travail*, no. 1, pp. 82–105.
KEDDIE, N. (1971), 'Classroom Knowledge', in YOUNG, M. F. D. (ed.), *Knowledge and Control: New Directions for the Sociology of Education*, London, Collier-Macmillan, pp. 133–60.
KUHN, T. S. (1962), 'The Structure of Scientific Revolutions' (1st edition), *International Encyclopaedia of Unified Science*, vol. 2, no. 2, London, University of Chicago Press.
KUHN, T. S. (1970a), 'The Structure of Scientific Revolutions' (2nd edition), *International Encyclopaedia of Unified Science*, vol. 2, no. 2, London, University of Chicago Press.
KUHN, T. S. (1970b), 'Reflections on my Critics', in LAKATOS, I. and MUSGRAVE, A. (eds), *Criticism and the Growth of Knowledge*, Cambridge University Press, pp. 231–77.
MCHUGH, P. (1968), *Defining the Situation*, Indianapolis, Bobbs-Merrill.
MCHUGH, P. (1971), 'On the Failure of Positivism', in DOUGLAS, J. D. (ed.), *Understanding Everyday Life: Toward the Reconstruction of Sociological Knowledge*, London, Routledge & Kegan Paul.
MACPHERSON, C. B. (1973), *Democratic Theory: Essays in Retrieval*, Oxford, Clarendon Press.
MARCH, J. G. and SIMON, H. A. (1958), *Organizations*, New York, John Wiley.
MARCUSE, H. (1971), 'Industrialization and Capitalism', translated by K. Morris, in STAMMER, O. (ed.), *Max Weber and Sociology Today*, Oxford, Blackwell, pp. 133–70.
MARSHALL, G. (1964), 'Sovereignty', in GOULD, D. and KOULB, W. L. (eds), *A Dictionary of the Social Sciences*, London, Tavistock.
MARSHALL, T. H. (1947), *Sociology at the Crossroads*, London, Longmans.
MARX, K. (1973), *Grundrisse: Introduction to the Critique of Political Economy*, translated and with a foreword by M. Nicolaus, Harmondsworth, Penguin.
MARX, K. (1930), *Capital*, (2 volumes), London, Everyman edition, Dent.
MARX, K. and ENGELS, F. (1965), *The German Ideology*, London, Lawrence & Wishart.
MAYER, J. P. (1956), *Max Weber and German Politics*, London, Faber & Faber.
MELDEN, A. I. (1961), *Free Action*, London, Routledge & Kegan Paul.
MERLEAU-PONTY, M. (1962), *The Phenomenology of Perception*, London, Routledge & Kegan Paul.
MERTON, R. K. (1968), *Social Theory and Social Structure*, New York, Free Press.

MILLS, C. W. (1957), *The Power Élite*, Oxford University Press.

NAGEL, J. H. (1968), 'Some Questions about the Concept of Power', *Behavioural Science*, vol. 13, no. 2, March, pp. 129–37.

PASSMORE, J. (1957), *A Hundred Years of Philosophy*, London, Duckworth.

PENNINGS, J., HICKSON, D. J., HININGS, C. R., LEE, C. A. and SCHNECK, R. E. (1969), 'Uncertainty and Power in Organizations: A Strategic Contingencies Model of Sub-Unit Functioning', *Mens en Maatscappij*, vol. 23 (November–December).

PERROW, C. (1970), *Organizational Analysis: A Sociological View*, London, Tavistock.

PETRIE, H. (1971), 'Science and Metaphysics: A Wittgenstein Interpretation', in KLEMKE, E. D. (ed.), *Essays on Wittgenstein*, London, University of Illinois Press.

PHILLIPS, D. L. (1972), 'Paradigms, Falsification and Sociology', *Acta Sociologica*, vol. 16, no. 1, pp. 13–30.

PHILLIPS, D. L. (1973), *Abandoning Method*, London, Jossey-Bass.

PITKIN, H. F. (1972), *Wittgenstein and Justice: On the Significance of Ludwig Wittgenstein for Social and Political Thought*, London, University of California Press.

PLATO (1965), *The Republic*, translated by H. D. P. Lee, Harmondsworth, Penguin.

POLANYI, M. (1969), *Knowing and Being*, ed. M. Greene, London, Routledge & Kegan Paul.

POLSBY, N. W. (1959), 'The Sociology of Community Power: A Reassessment', *Social Forces*, vol. 37, March, pp. 232–6.

POLSBY, N. W. (1963), *Community Power and Political Theory*, Yale University Press.

REX, J. (1971), 'Typology and Objectivity: a Comment on Weber's Four Sociological Methods', in SAHAY, A. (ed.), *Max Weber and Modern Sociology*, London, Routledge & Kegan Paul.

ROSEN, S. (1969), *Nihilism: A Philosophical Essay*, Yale University Press.

RUSSELL, B. (1967), *Power: A New Social Analysis*, London, Allen & Unwin.

RYLE, G. (1949), *The Concept of Mind*, London, Hutchinson.

SCHUTZ, A. (1953), 'The Problem of Rationality in the Social World', *Economica*, vol. 10, May.

SCHUTZ, A. (1962), *Collected Papers, Volume I, The Problem of Social Reality*, M. Natanson, The Hague, Martinus Nijhoff.

SCHUTZ, A. (1967), *The Phenomenology of the Social World*, translated by G. Walsh and F. Lehnert, Evanston, Ill., North-Western University Press.

SHERMAN, H. (1972), *Radical Political Economy: Capitalism and Socialism from a Marxist-Humanist Perspective*, New York, Basic Books.

SHIBBLES, W. (1967), *Wittgenstein, Language and Philosophy*, Dubuque, Iowa, Kendall/Hunt.

SHWAYDER, D. S. (1965), *The Stratification of Behaviour: A System of Definitions Propounded and Defended*, London, Routledge & Kegan Paul.

SILVERMAN, D. (1970), *The Theory of Organizations*, London, Heinemann.

SIMMEL, G. (1950), *The Sociology of Georg Simmel*, translated, edited and with an introduction by K. H. Woolf, London, Free Press–Collier-Macmillan.

SIMMEL, G. (1971), *On Individuality and Social Forms*, edited and with an introduction by D. N. Levine, University of Chicago Press.

SIMON, H. A. (1957), *Administrative Behaviour*, London, Macmillan.

SONTAG, S. (1967), *Against Interpretation, and Other Essays*, London, Eyre & Spottiswoode.

STRAUSS, A., SCHATZMAN, L., EHRLICH, D., BUCHER, R. and SABSHIN, M. (1963), 'The Hospital and its Negotiated Order', in FRIEDSON, E. (ed.), *The Hospital in Modern Society*, London, Collier-Macmillan.

STRAWSON, P. F. (1966), Review of Wittgenstein's *Philosophical Investigations*, in PITCHER, G. (ed.), *Wittgenstein: the Philosophical Investigations*. Originally published in *Mind*, vol. 63 (1954), pp. 70–99.

STROUD, B. (1971), 'Wittgenstein and Logical Necessity', in KLEMKE, E. D. (ed.), *Essays on Wittgenstein*, London, University of Illinois Press. Originally published in *Philosophical Review*, vol. 74 (1965), pp. 504–18.

SWEEZY, P. M. (1942), *The Theory of Capitalist Development: Principles of Marxian Political Economy*, London, Dobson.

THOMPSON, J. D. (1967), *Organization in Action*, New York, McGraw-Hill.

TUSMAN, J. (1960), *Obligation and the Body Politic*, Oxford University Press.

WALTON, J. (1966), 'Discipline, Method and Community Power: A Note on the Sociology of Knowledge', *American Sociological Review*, vol. 31, October, pp. 684–9.

WEBER, M. (1923), *General Economic History*, translated by F. H. Knight, London, Allen & Unwin.

WEBER, M. (1930), *The Protestant Ethic and the Spirit of Capitalism*, translated by T. Parsons, New York, Scribner.

WEBER, M. (1947), *The Theory of Social and Economic Organization*, translated by T. Parsons and A. M. Henderson, with an introduction by T. Parsons, New York, Free Press.

WEBER, M. (1948), *From Max Weber: Essays in Sociology*, translated, edited and with an introduction by H. H. Gerth and C. Wright Mills, London, Routledge & Kegan Paul.

WEBER, M. (1949), *The Methodology of the Social Sciences*, translated and edited by E. A. Shills and H. A. Finch, New York, Free Press.

WEBER, M. (1968), *Economy and Society: An Outline of Interpretive Sociology*, edited and with an introduction by G. Roth and C. Wittich, New York, Bedminster Press.

WEBER, M. (1972), 'Georg Simmel as Sociologist', translated with an introduction by D. N. Levine, *Social Research*, vol. 39, no. 1, pp. 155–63.

WEICK, F. D. (1969), *The Social Psychology of Organizing*, Massachusetts, Addison-Wesley.

WHITE, D. M. (1971), 'Power and Intention', *American Political Science Review*, vol. 65, September, pp. 749–59.

WIEDER, D. L. (1974), 'Telling the Code', in TURNER, R. (ed.), *Ethnomethodology*, Penguin.

WINCH, P. (1958), *The Idea of a Social Science and its Relation to Philosophy*, London, Routledge & Kegan Paul.

WITTGENSTEIN, L. (1956), *Remarks on the Foundations of Mathematics*, ed. by G. H. von Wright, R. Rhees and G. E. M. Anscombe, and translated by G. E. M. Anscombe, Oxford, Blackwell.

WITTGENSTEIN, L. (1961), *Tractatus Logico-Philosophicus*, translated by D. F. Pears and B. F. McGuinness, London, Routledge & Kegan Paul.

WITTGENSTEIN, L. (1966), *Lectures and Conversations on Aesthetics, Psychology and Religious Belief*, compiled from notes taken by R. Rhees, Y. Smythies and J. Taylor, and edited by C. Barret, Oxford, Blackwell.

WITTGENSTEIN, L. (1968), *Philosophical Investigations*, translated by G. E. M. Anscombe, Oxford, Blackwell.

WITTGENSTEIN, L. (1969a), *On Certainty*, edited by G. E. M. Anscombe and G. H. von Wright, translated by G. H. Paul and G. E. M. Anscombe, Oxford, Blackwell.

WITTGENSTEIN, L. (1969b), *The Blue and Brown Books: Preliminary Studies for the 'Philosophical Investigations'*, Oxford, Blackwell.

WITTGENSTEIN, L. (1970), Notes for lectures on 'Private Experience' and 'Sense Data', in MORRICK, H. (ed.), *Introduction to the Philosophy of Mind*, Glenview, Illinois, Scott Foresman.

WOLFINGER, R. E. (1971), 'Nondecisions and the Study of Local Politics', *American Political Science Review*, vol. 65, no. 4, December, pp. 1063–80.

WRONG, D. (1968), 'Some Problems in Defining Social Power', *American Journal of Sociology*, vol. 73, no. 6, pp. 673–81.

ZABEEH, F. (1971), 'On Language Games and Forms of Life', in KLEMKE, E. D. (ed.), *Essays on Wittgenstein*, London, University of Illinois Press, pp. 328–73.

ZIMMERMAN, D. (1971), 'Record-Keeping and the Intake Process in a Public Welfare Organization', in WHEELER, S. (ed.), *On Record: Files and Dossiers in American Life*, New York, Russell Sage Foundation.

# Index

# Routledge Social Science Series

Routledge & Kegan Paul   London and Boston

68–74 Carter Lane   London EC4V 5EL
9 Park Street   Boston   Mass 02108

# Contents

*Authors wishing to submit manuscripts for any series in
this catalogue should send them to the Social Science Editor,
Routledge & Kegan Paul Ltd, 68–74 Carter Lane,
London EC4V 5EL*

*●Books so marked are available in paperback
All books are in Metric Demy 8vo format (216 × 138mm approx.)*

# International Library of Sociology

*General Editor*　John Rex

## GENERAL SOCIOLOGY

**Barnsley, J. H.** The Social Reality of Ethics. *464 pp.*
**Belshaw, Cyril.** The Conditions of Social Performance. *An Exploratory Theory. 144 pp.*
**Brown, Robert.** Explanation in Social Science. *208 pp.*
● Rules and Laws in Sociology. *192 pp.*
**Bruford, W. H.** Chekhov and His Russia. *A Sociological Study. 244 pp.*
**Cain, Maureen E.** Society and the Policeman's Role. *326 pp.*
**Gibson, Quentin.** The Logic of Social Enquiry. *240 pp.*
**Glucksmann, M.** Structuralist Analysis in Contemporary Social Thought. *212 pp.*
**Gurvitch, Georges.** Sociology of Law. *Preface by Roscoe Pound. 264 pp.*
**Hodge, H. A.** Wilhelm Dilthey. *An Introduction. 184 pp.*
**Homans, George C.** Sentiments and Activities. *336 pp.*
**Johnson, Harry M.** Sociology: *a Systematic Introduction. Foreword by Robert K. Merton. 710 pp.*
**Mannheim, Karl.** Essays on Sociology and Social Psychology. *Edited by Paul Kecskemeti. With Editorial Note by Adolph Lowe. 344 pp.*
Systematic Sociology: *An Introduction to the Study of Society. Edited by J. S. Erös and Professor W. A. C. Stewart. 220 pp.*
**Martindale, Don.** The Nature and Types of Sociological Theory. *292 pp.*
●**Maus, Heinz.** A Short History of Sociology. *234 pp.*
**Mey, Harald.** Field-Theory. *A Study of its Application in the Social Sciences. 352 pp.*
**Myrdal, Gunnar.** Value in Social Theory: *A Collection of Essays on Methodology. Edited by Paul Streeten. 332 pp.*
**Ogburn, William F.,** and **Nimkoff, Meyer F.** A Handbook of Sociology. *Preface by Karl Mannheim. 656 pp. 46 figures. 35 tables.*
**Parsons, Talcott,** and **Smelser, Neil J.** Economy and Society: *A Study in the Integration of Economic and Social Theory. 362 pp.*
●**Rex, John.** Key Problems of Sociological Theory. *220 pp.*
Discovering Sociology. *278 pp.*
Sociology and the Demystification of the Modern World. *282 pp.*
●**Rex, John** (Ed.) Approaches to Sociology. *Contributions by Peter Abell, Frank Bechhofer, Basil Bernstein, Ronald Fletcher, David Frisby, Miriam Glucksmann, Peter Lassman, Herminio Martins, John Rex, Roland Robertson, John Westergaard and Jock Young. 302 pp.*
**Rigby, A.** Alternative Realities. *352 pp.*
**Roche, M.** Phenomenology, Language and the Social Sciences. *374 pp.*
**Sahay, A.** Sociological Analysis. *220 pp.*
**Urry, John.** Reference Groups and the Theory of Revolution. *244 pp.*
**Weinberg, E.** Development of Sociology in the Soviet Union. *173 pp.*

## FOREIGN CLASSICS OF SOCIOLOGY

●**Durkheim, Emile.** Suicide. *A Study in Sociology. Edited and with an Introduction by George Simpson. 404 pp.*
Professional Ethics and Civic Morals. *Translated by Cornelia Brookfield. 288 pp.*
●**Gerth, H. H.,** and **Mills, C. Wright.** From Max Weber: *Essays in Sociology. 502 pp.*
●**Tönnies, Ferdinand.** Community and Association. (*Gemeinschaft und Gesellschaft.) Translated and Supplemented by Charles P. Loomis. Foreword by Pitirim A. Sorokin. 334 pp.*

## SOCIAL STRUCTURE

**Andreski, Stanislav.** Military Organization and Society. *Foreword by Professor A. R. Radcliffe-Brown. 226 pp. 1 folder.*
**Coontz, Sydney H.** Population Theories and the Economic Interpretation. *202 pp.*
**Coser, Lewis.** The Functions of Social Conflict. *204 pp.*
**Dickie-Clark, H. F.** Marginal Situation: *A Sociological Study of a Coloured Group. 240 pp. 11 tables.*
**Glaser, Barney,** and **Strauss, Anselm L.** Status Passage. *A Formal Theory. 208 pp.*
**Glass, D. V.** (Ed.) Social Mobility in Britain. *Contributions by J. Berent, T. Bottomore, R. C. Chambers, J. Floud, D. V. Glass, J. R. Hall, H. T. Himmelweit, R. K. Kelsall, F. M. Martin, C. A. Moser, R. Mukherjee, and W. Ziegel. 420 pp.*
**Jones, Garth N.** Planned Organizational Change: *An Exploratory Study Using an Empirical Approach. 268 pp.*
**Kelsall, R. K.** Higher Civil Servants in Britain: *From 1870 to the Present Day. 268 pp. 31 tables.*
**König, René.** The Community. *232 pp. Illustrated.*
●**Lawton, Denis.** Social Class, Language and Education. *192 pp.*
**McLeish, John.** The Theory of Social Change: *Four Views Considered. 128 pp.*
**Marsh, David C.** The Changing Social Structure of England and Wales, 1871-1961. *288 pp.*
**Mouzelis, Nicos.** Organization and Bureaucracy. *An Analysis of Modern Theories. 240 pp.*
**Mulkay, M. J.** Functionalism, Exchange and Theoretical Strategy. *272 pp.*
**Ossowski, Stanislaw.** Class Structure in the Social Consciousness. *210 pp.*
**Podgórecki, Adam.** Law and Society. *About 300 pp.*

## SOCIOLOGY AND POLITICS

**Acton, T. A.** Gypsy Politics and Social Change. *316 pp.*
**Hechter, Michael.** Internal Colonialism. *The Celtic Fringe in British National Development, 1536-1966. About 350 pp.*
**Hertz, Frederick.** Nationality in History and Politics: *A Psychology and Sociology of National Sentiment and Nationalism. 432 pp.*

**Kornhauser, William.** The Politics of Mass Society. *272 pp. 20 tables.*
**Laidler, Harry W.** History of Socialism. *Social-Economic Movements: An Historical and Comparative Survey of Socialism, Communism, Co-operation, Utopianism; and other Systems of Reform and Reconstruction. 992 pp.*
**Lasswell, H. D.** Analysis of Political Behaviour. *324 pp.*
**Mannheim, Karl.** Freedom, Power and Democratic Planning. *Edited by Hans Gerth and Ernest K. Bramstedt. 424 pp.*
**Mansur, Fatma.** Process of Independence. *Foreword by A. H. Hanson. 208 pp.*
**Martin, David A.** Pacifism: *an Historical and Sociological Study. 262 pp.*
**Myrdal, Gunnar.** The Political Element in the Development of Economic Theory. *Translated from the German by Paul Streeten. 282 pp.*
**Wootton, Graham.** Workers, Unions and the State. *188 pp.*

## FOREIGN AFFAIRS: THEIR SOCIAL, POLITICAL AND ECONOMIC FOUNDATIONS

**Mayer, J. P.** Political Thought in France from the Revolution to the Fifth Republic. *164 pp.*

## CRIMINOLOGY

**Ancel, Marc.** Social Defence: *A Modern Approach to Criminal Problems. Foreword by Leon Radzinowicz. 240 pp.*
**Cain, Maureen E.** Society and the Policeman's Role. *326 pp.*
**Cloward, Richard A.,** and **Ohlin, Lloyd E.** Delinquency and Opportunity: *A Theory of Delinquent Gangs. 248 pp.*
**Downes, David M.** The Delinquent Solution. *A Study in Subcultural Theory. 296 pp.*
**Dunlop, A. B.,** and **McCabe, S.** Young Men in Detention Centres. *192 pp.*
**Friedlander, Kate.** The Psycho-Analytical Approach to Juvenile Delinquency: *Theory, Case Studies, Treatment. 320 pp.*
**Glueck, Sheldon,** and **Eleanor.** Family Environment and Delinquency. *With the statistical assistance of Rose W. Kneznek. 340 pp.*
**Lopez-Rey, Manuel.** Crime. *An Analytical Appraisal. 288 pp.*
**Mannheim, Hermann.** Comparative Criminology: *a Text Book. Two volumes. 442 pp. and 380 pp.*
**Morris, Terence.** The Criminal Area: *A Study in Social Ecology. Foreword by Hermann Mannheim. 232 pp. 25 tables. 4 maps.*
**Rock, Paul.** Making People Pay. *338 pp.*
●**Taylor, Ian, Walton, Paul,** and **Young, Jock.** The New Criminology. *For a Social Theory of Deviance. 325 pp.*

## SOCIAL PSYCHOLOGY

**Bagley, Christopher.** The Social Psychology of the Epileptic Child. *320 pp.*
**Barbu, Zevedei.** Problems of Historical Psychology. *248 pp.*
**Blackburn, Julian.** Psychology and the Social Pattern. *184 pp.*

●**Brittan, Arthur.** Meanings and Situations. *224 pp.*

**Carroll, J.** Break-Out from the Crystal Palace. *200 pp.*

●**Fleming, C. M.** Adolescence: Its Social Psychology. *With an Introduction to recent findings from the fields of Anthropology, Physiology, Medicine, Psychometrics and Sociometry. 288 pp.*

● The Social Psychology of Education: *An Introduction and Guide to Its Study. 136 pp.*

**Homans, George C.** The Human Group. *Foreword by Bernard DeVoto. Introduction by Robert K. Merton. 526 pp.*

● Social Behaviour: *its Elementary Forms. 416 pp.*

●**Klein, Josephine.** The Study of Groups. *226 pp. 31 figures. 5 tables.*

**Linton, Ralph.** The Cultural Background of Personality. *132 pp.*

●**Mayo, Elton.** The Social Problems of an Industrial Civilization. *With an appendix on the Political Problem. 180 pp.*

**Ottaway, A. K. C.** Learning Through Group Experience. *176 pp.*

**Ridder, J. C. de.** The Personality of the Urban African in South Africa. *A Thematic Apperception Test Study. 196 pp. 12 plates.*

●**Rose, Arnold M.** (Ed.) Human Behaviour and Social Processes: *an Interactionist Approach. Contributions by Arnold M. Rose, Ralph H. Turner, Anselm Strauss, Everett C. Hughes, E. Franklin Frazier, Howard S. Becker, et al. 696 pp.*

**Smelser, Neil J.** Theory of Collective Behaviour. *448 pp.*

**Stephenson, Geoffrey M.** The Development of Conscience. *128 pp.*

**Young, Kimball.** Handbook of Social Psychology. *658 pp. 16 figures. 10 tables.*


## SOCIOLOGY OF THE FAMILY

**Banks, J. A.** Prosperity and Parenthood: *A Study of Family Planning among The Victorian Middle Classes. 262 pp.*

**Bell, Colin R.** Middle Class Families: *Social and Geographical Mobility. 224 pp.*

**Burton, Lindy.** Vulnerable Children. *272 pp.*

**Gavron, Hannah.** The Captive Wife: *Conflicts of Household Mothers. 190 pp.*

**George, Victor,** and **Wilding, Paul.** Motherless Families. *220 pp.*

**Klein, Josephine.** Samples from English Cultures.
1. Three Preliminary Studies and Aspects of Adult Life in England. *447 pp.*
2. Child-Rearing Practices and Index. *247 pp.*

**Klein, Viola.** Britain's Married Women Workers. *180 pp.*
The Feminine Character. *History of an Ideology. 244 pp.*

**McWhinnie, Alexina M.** Adopted Children. *How They Grow Up. 304 pp.*

● **Myrdal, Alva,** and **Klein, Viola.** Women's Two Roles: *Home and Work. 238 pp. 27 tables.*

**Parsons, Talcott,** and **Bales, Robert F.** Family: Socialization and Interaction Process. *In collaboration with James Olds, Morris Zelditch and Philip E. Slater. 456 pp. 50 figures and tables.*

## SOCIAL SERVICES

**Bastide, Roger.** The Sociology of Mental Disorder. *Translated from the French by Jean McNeil. 260 pp.*

**Carlebach, Julius.** Caring For Children in Trouble. *266 pp.*

**Forder, R. A.** (Ed.) Penelope Hall's Social Services of England and Wales. *352 pp.*

**George, Victor.** Foster Care. *Theory and Practice. 234 pp.*
Social Security: *Beveridge and After. 258 pp.*

**George, V.,** and **Wilding, P.** Motherless Families. *248 pp.*

●**Goetschius, George W.** Working with Community Groups. *256 pp.*

**Goetschius, George W.,** and **Tash, Joan.** Working with Unattached Youth. *416 pp.*

**Hall, M. P.,** and **Howes, I. V.** The Church in Social Work. *A Study of Moral Welfare Work undertaken by the Church of England. 320 pp.*

**Heywood, Jean S.** Children in Care: *the Development of the Service for the Deprived Child. 264 pp.*

**Hoenig, J.,** and **Hamilton, Marian W.** The De-Segregation of the Mentally Ill. *284 pp.*

**Jones, Kathleen.** Mental Health and Social Policy, 1845-1959. *264 pp.*

**King, Roy D., Raynes, Norma V.,** and **Tizard, Jack.** Patterns of Residential Care. *356 pp.*

**Leigh, John.** Young People and Leisure. *256 pp.*

**Morris, Mary.** Voluntary Work and the Welfare State. *300 pp.*

**Morris, Pauline.** Put Away: *A Sociological Study of Institutions for the Mentally Retarded. 364 pp.*

**Nokes, P. L.** The Professional Task in Welfare Practice. *152 pp.*

**Timms, Noel.** Psychiatric Social Work in Great Britain (1939-1962). *280 pp.*

● Social Casework: *Principles and Practice. 256 pp.*

**Young, A. F.** Social Services in British Industry. *272 pp.*

**Young, A. F.,** and **Ashton, E. T.** British Social Work in the Nineteenth Century. *288 pp.*

## SOCIOLOGY OF EDUCATION

**Banks, Olive.** Parity and Prestige in English Secondary Education: a Study in Educational Sociology. *272 pp.*

**Bentwich, Joseph.** Education in Israel. *224 pp. 8 pp. plates.*

●**Blyth, W. A. L.** English Primary Education. *A Sociological Description.*
1. Schools. *232 pp.*
2. Background. *168 pp.*

**Collier, K. G.** The Social Purposes of Education: *Personal and Social Values in Education. 268 pp.*

**Dale, R. R.,** and **Griffith, S.** Down Stream: *Failure in the Grammar School.* *108 pp.*

**Dore, R. P.** Education in Tokugawa Japan. *356 pp. 9 pp. plates.*

**Evans, K. M.** Sociometry and Education. *158 pp.*

●**Ford, Julienne.** Social Class and the Comprehensive School. *192 pp.*

**Foster, P. J.** Education and Social Change in Ghana. *336 pp. 3 maps.*

**Fraser, W. R.** Education and Society in Modern France. *150 pp.*

**Grace, Gerald R.** Role Conflict and the Teacher. *About 200 pp.*

**Hans, Nicholas.** New Trends in Education in the Eighteenth Century. *278 pp. 19 tables.*

● Comparative Education: *A Study of Educational Factors and Traditions.* *360 pp.*

**Hargreaves, David.** Interpersonal Relations and Education. *432 pp.*

● Social Relations in a Secondary School. *240 pp.*

**Holmes, Brian.** Problems in Education. *A Comparative Approach. 336 pp.*

**King, Ronald.** Values and Involvement in a Grammar School. *164 pp.*

School Organization and Pupil Involvement. *A Study of Secondary Schools.*

●**Mannheim, Karl,** and **Stewart, W. A. C.** An Introduction to the Sociology of Education. *206 pp.*

**Morris, Raymond N.** The Sixth Form and College Entrance. *231 pp.*

●**Musgrove, F.** Youth and the Social Order. *176 pp.*

●**Ottaway, A. K. C.** Education and Society: An Introduction to the Sociology of Education. *With an Introduction by W. O. Lester Smith. 212 pp.*

**Peers, Robert.** Adult Education: *A Comparative Study. 398 pp.*

**Pritchard, D. G.** Education and the Handicapped: *1760 to 1960. 258 pp.*

**Richardson, Helen.** Adolescent Girls in Approved Schools. *308 pp.*

**Stratta, Erica.** The Education of Borstal Boys. *A Study of their Educational Experiences prior to, and during, Borstal Training. 256 pp.*

**Taylor, P. H., Reid, W. A.,** and **Holley, B. J.** The English Sixth Form. *A Case Study in Curriculum Research. 200 pp.*


## SOCIOLOGY OF CULTURE

**Eppel, E. M.,** and **M.** Adolescents and Morality: *A Study of some Moral Values and Dilemmas of Working Adolescents in the Context of a changing Climate of Opinion. Foreword by W. J. H. Sprott. 268 pp. 39 tables.*

●**Fromm, Erich.** The Fear of Freedom. *286 pp.*

● The Sane Society. *400 pp.*

**Mannheim, Karl.** Essays on the Sociology of Culture. *Edited by Ernst Mannheim in co-operation with Paul Kecskemeti. Editorial Note by Adolph Lowe. 280 pp.*

**Weber, Alfred.** Farewell to European History: *or The Conquest of Nihilism. Translated from the German by R. F. C. Hull. 224 pp.*

## SOCIOLOGY OF RELIGION

**Argyle, Michael** and **Beit-Hallahmi, Benjamin.** The Social Psychology of Religion. *About 256 pp.*
**Nelson, G. K.** Spiritualism and Society. *313 pp.*
**Stark, Werner.** The Sociology of Religion. *A Study of Christendom.*
Volume I. *Established Religion. 248 pp.*
Volume II. *Sectarian Religion. 368 pp.*
Volume III. *The Universal Church. 464 pp.*
Volume IV. *Types of Religious Man. 352 pp.*
Volume V. *Types of Religious Culture. 464 pp.*
**Turner, B. S.** Weber and Islam. *216 pp.*
**Watt, W. Montgomery.** Islam and the Integration of Society. *320 pp.*

## SOCIOLOGY OF ART AND LITERATURE

**Jarvie, Ian C.** Towards a Sociology of the Cinema. *A Comparative Essay on the Structure and Functioning of a Major Entertainment Industry. 405 pp.*
**Rust, Frances S.** Dance in Society. *An Analysis of the Relationships between the Social Dance and Society in England from the Middle Ages to the Present Day. 256 pp. 8 pp. of plates.*
**Schücking, L. L.** The Sociology of Literary Taste. *112 pp.*
**Wolff, Janet.** Hermeneutic Philosophy and the Sociology of Art. *About 200 pp.*

## SOCIOLOGY OF KNOWLEDGE

**Diesing, P.** Patterns of Discovery in the Social Sciences. *262 pp.*
●**Douglas, J. D.** (Ed.) Understanding Everyday Life. *370 pp.*
●**Hamilton, P.** Knowledge and Social Structure. *174 pp.*
**Jarvie, I. C.** Concepts and Society. *232 pp.*
**Mannheim, Karl.** Essays on the Sociology of Knowledge. *Edited by Paul Kecskemeti. Editorial Note by Adolph Lowe. 353 pp.*
**Remmling, Gunter W.** (Ed.) Towards the Sociology of Knowledge. *Origin and Development of a Sociological Thought Style. 463 pp.*
**Stark, Werner.** The Sociology of Knowledge: *An Essay in Aid of a Deeper Understanding of the History of Ideas. 384 pp.*

## URBAN SOCIOLOGY

**Ashworth, William.** The Genesis of Modern British Town Planning: *A Study in Economic and Social History of the Nineteenth and Twentieth Centuries. 288 pp.*
**Cullingworth, J. B.** Housing Needs and Planning Policy: *A Restatement of the Problems of Housing Need and 'Overspill' in England and Wales. 232 pp. 44 tables. 8 maps.*

**Dickinson, Robert E.** City and Region: *A Geographical Interpretation* *608 pp. 125 figures.*
    The West European City: *A Geographical Interpretation. 600 pp. 129 maps. 29 plates.*
● The City Region in Western Europe. *320 pp. Maps.*
**Humphreys, Alexander J.** New Dubliners: *Urbanization and the Irish Family. Foreword by George C. Homans. 304 pp.*
**Jackson, Brian.** Working Class Community: *Some General Notions raised by a Series of Studies in Northern England. 192 pp.*
**Jennings, Hilda.** Societies in the Making: *a Study of Development and Re-development within a County Borough. Foreword by D. A. Clark. 286 pp.*
●**Mann, P. H.** An Approach to Urban Sociology. *240 pp.*
**Morris, R. N.,** and **Mogey, J.** The Sociology of Housing. *Studies at Berinsfield. 232 pp. 4 pp. plates.*
**Rosser, C.,** and **Harris, C.** The Family and Social Change. *A Study of Family and Kinship in a South Wales Town. 352 pp. 8 maps.*

## RURAL SOCIOLOGY

**Chambers, R. J. H.** Settlement Schemes in Tropical Africa: *A Selective Study. 268 pp.*
**Haswell, M. R.** The Economics of Development in Village India. *120 pp.*
**Littlejohn, James.** Westrigg: *the Sociology of a Cheviot Parish. 172 pp. 5 figures.*
**Mayer, Adrian C.** Peasants in the Pacific. *A Study of Fiji Indian Rural Society. 248 pp. 20 plates.*
**Williams, W. M.** The Sociology of an English Village: *Gosforth. 272 pp. 12 figures. 13 tables.*

## SOCIOLOGY OF INDUSTRY AND DISTRIBUTION

**Anderson, Nels.** Work and Leisure. *280 pp.*
●**Blau, Peter M.,** and **Scott, W. Richard.** Formal Organizations: *a Comparative approach. Introduction and Additional Bibliography by J. H. Smith. 326 pp.*
**Eldridge, J. E. T.** Industrial Disputes. *Essays in the Sociology of Industrial Relations. 288 pp.*
**Hetzler, Stanley.** Applied Measures for Promoting Technological Growth. *352 pp.*
    Technological Growth and Social Change. *Achieving Modernization. 269 pp.*
**Hollowell, Peter G.** The Lorry Driver. *272 pp.*
**Jefferys, Margot,** *with the assistance of Winifred Moss.* Mobility in the Labour Market: *Employment Changes in Battersea and Dagenham. Preface by Barbara Wootton. 186 pp. 51 tables.*

**Millerson, Geoffrey.** The Qualifying Associations: *a Study in Professionalization. 320 pp.*
**Smelser, Neil J.** Social Change in the Industrial Revolution: *An Application of Theory to the Lancashire Cotton Industry, 1770-1840. 468 pp. 12 figures. 14 tables.*
**Williams, Gertrude.** Recruitment to Skilled Trades. *240 pp.*
**Young, A. F.** Industrial Injuries Insurance: *an Examination of British Policy. 192 pp.*

## DOCUMENTARY

**Schlesinger, Rudolf** (Ed.) Changing Attitudes in Soviet Russia.
2. The Nationalities Problem and Soviet Administration. *Selected Readings on the Development of Soviet Nationalities Policies. Introduced by the editor. Translated by W. W. Gottlieb. 324 pp.*

## ANTHROPOLOGY

**Ammar, Hamed.** Growing up in an Egyptian Village: *Silwa, Province of Aswan. 336 pp.*
**Brandel-Syrier, Mia.** Reeftown Elite. *A Study of Social Mobility in a Modern African Community on the Reef. 376 pp.*
**Crook, David,** and **Isabel.** Revolution in a Chinese Village: *Ten Mile Inn. 230 pp. 8 plates. 1 map.*
**Dickie-Clark, H. F.** The Marginal Situation. *A Sociological Study of a Coloured Group. 236 pp.*
**Dube, S. C.** Indian Village. *Foreword by Morris Edward Opler. 276 pp. 4 plates.*
India's Changing Villages: *Human Factors in Community Development. 260 pp. 8 plates. 1 map.*
**Firth, Raymond.** Malay Fishermen. *Their Peasant Economy. 420 pp. 17 pp. plates.*
**Firth, R., Hubert, J.,** and **Forge, A.** Families and their Relatives. *Kinship in a Middle-Class Sector of London: An Anthropological Study. 456 pp.*
**Gulliver, P. H.** Social Control in an African Society: a Study of the Arusha, Agricultural Masai of Northern Tanganyika. *320 pp. 8 plates. 10 figures.*
Family Herds. *288 pp.*
**Ishwaran, K.** Shivapur. *A South Indian Village. 216 pp.*
Tradition and Economy in Village India: *An Interactionist Approach. Foreword by Conrad Arensburg. 176 pp.*
**Jarvie, Ian C.** The Revolution in Anthropology. *268 pp.*
**Jarvie, Ian C.,** and **Agassi, Joseph.** Hong Kong. *A Society in Transition. 396 pp. Illustrated with plates and maps.*
**Little, Kenneth L.** Mende of Sierra Leone. *308 pp. and folder.*
Negroes in Britain. *With a New Introduction and Contemporary Study by Leonard Bloom. 320 pp.*

**Lowie, Robert H.** Social Organization. *494 pp.*
**Mayer, Adrian C.** Caste and Kinship in Central India: *A Village and its Region. 328 pp. 16 plates. 15 figures. 16 tables.*
   Peasants in the Pacific. *A Study of Fiji Indian Rural Society. 248 pp.*
**Smith, Raymond T.** The Negro Family in British Guiana: *Family Structure and Social Status in the Villages. With a Foreword by Meyer Fortes. 314 pp. 8 plates. 1 figure. 4 maps.*

### SOCIOLOGY AND PHILOSOPHY

**Barnsley, John H.** The Social Reality of Ethics. *A Comparative Analysis of Moral Codes. 448 pp.*
**Diesing, Paul.** Patterns of Discovery in the Social Sciences. *362 pp.*
●**Douglas, Jack D.** (Ed.) Understanding Everyday Life. *Toward the Reconstruction of Sociological Knowledge. Contributions by Alan F. Blum. Aaron W. Cicourel, Norman K. Denzin, Jack D. Douglas, John Heeren, Peter McHugh, Peter K. Manning, Melvin Power, Matthew Speier, Roy Turner, D. Lawrence Wieder, Thomas P. Wilson and Don H. Zimmerman. 370 pp.*
**Jarvie, Ian C.** Concepts and Society. *216 pp.*
**Pelz, Werner.** The Scope of Understanding in Sociology. *Towards a more radical reorientation in the social humanistic sciences. 283 pp.*
**Roche, Maurice.** Phenomenology, Language and the Social Sciences. *371 pp.*
**Sahay, Arun.** Sociological Analysis. *212 pp.*
**Sklair, Leslie.** The Sociology of Progress. *320 pp.*

# International Library of Anthropology

*General Editor* Adam Kuper

**Brown, Paula.** The Chimbu. *A Study of Change in the New Guinea Highlands. 151 pp.*
**Lloyd, P. C.** Power and Independence. *Urban Africans' Perception of Social Inequality. 264 pp.*
**Pettigrew, Joyce.** Robber Noblemen. *A Study of the Political System of the Sikh Jats. 284 pp.*
**Van Den Berghe, Pierre L.** Power and Privilege at an African University. *278 pp.*

# International Library of Social Policy

*General Editor* Kathleen Jones

**Bayley, M.** Mental Handicap and Community Care. *426 pp.*
**Butler, J. R.** Family Doctors and Public Policy. *208 pp.*
**Holman, Robert.** Trading in Children. *A Study of Private Fostering. 355 pp.*

**Jones, Kathleen.** History of the Mental Health Service. *428 pp.*

**Thomas, J. E.** The English Prison Officer since 1850: *A Study in Conflict.* *258 pp.*

**Woodward, J.** To Do the Sick No Harm. *A Study of the British Voluntary Hospital System to 1875. About 220 pp.*

# International Library of Welfare and Philosophy

*General Editors* Noel Timms and David Watson

● **Plant, Raymond.** Community and Ideology. *104 pp.*

# Primary Socialization, Language and Education

*General Editor* Basil Bernstein

**Bernstein, Basil.** Class, Codes and Control. *2 volumes.*
1. *Theoretical Studies Towards a Sociology of Language. 254 pp.*
2. *Applied Studies Towards a Sociology of Language. About 400 pp.*

**Brandis, W.,** and **Bernstein, B.** Selection and Control. *176 pp.*

**Brandis, Walter,** and **Henderson, Dorothy.** Social Class, Language and Communication. *288 pp.*

**Cook-Gumperz, Jenny.** Social Control and Socialization. *A Study of Class Differences in the Language of Maternal Control. 290 pp.*

● **Gahagan, D. M.,** and **G. A.** Talk Reform. *Exploration in Language for Infant School Children. 160 pp.*

**Robinson, W. P.,** and **Rackstraw, Susan D. A.** A Question of Answers. *2 volumes. 192 pp. and 180 pp.*

**Turner, Geoffrey J.,** and **Mohan, Bernard A.** A Linguistic Description and Computer Programme for Children's Speech. *208 pp.*

# Reports of the Institute of Community Studies

**Cartwright, Ann.** Human Relations and Hospital Care. *272 pp.*

● Parents and Family Planning Services. *306 pp.*

Patients and their Doctors. *A Study of General Practice. 304 pp.*

● **Jackson, Brian.** Streaming: *an Education System in Miniature. 168 pp.*

**Jackson, Brian,** and **Marsden, Dennis.** Education and the Working Class: *Some General Themes raised by a Study of 88 Working-class Children in a Northern Industrial City. 268 pp. 2 folders.*

**Marris, Peter.** The Experience of Higher Education. *232 pp. 27 tables.*

Loss and Change. *192 pp.*

Marris, Peter, and Rein, Martin. Dilemmas of Social Reform. *Poverty and Community Action in the United States. 256 pp.*

Marris, Peter, and Somerset, Anthony. African Businessmen. *A Study of Entrepreneurship and Development in Kenya. 256 pp.*

Mills, Richard. Young Outsiders: *a Study in Alternative Communities. 216 pp.*

Runciman, W. G. Relative Deprivation and Social Justice. *A Study of Attitudes to Social Inequality in Twentieth-Century England. 352 pp.*

Willmott, Peter. Adolescent Boys in East London. *230 pp.*

Willmott, Peter, and Young, Michael. Family and Class in a London Suburb. *202 pp. 47 tables.*

Young, Michael. Innovation and Research in Education. *192 pp.*

●Young, Michael, and McGeeney, Patrick. Learning Begins at Home. *A Study of a Junior School and its Parents. 128 pp.*

Young, Michael, and Willmott, Peter. Family and Kinship in East London. *Foreword by Richard M. Titmuss. 252 pp. 39 tables.*

The Symmetrical Family. *410 pp.*

# Reports of the Institute for Social Studies in Medical Care

Cartwright, Ann, Hockey, Lisbeth, and Anderson, John L. Life Before Death. *310 pp.*

Dunnell, Karen, and Cartwright, Ann. Medicine Takers, Prescribers and Hoarders. *190 pp.*

# Medicine, Illness and Society

*General Editor* W. M. Williams

Robinson, David. The Process of Becoming Ill. *142 pp.*

Stacey, Margaret, *et al.* Hospitals, Children and Their Families. *The Report of a Pilot Study. 202 pp.*

# Monographs in Social Theory

*General Editor* Arthur Brittan

●Barnes, B. Scientific Knowledge and Sociological Theory. *About 200 pp.*

Bauman, Zygmunt. Culture as Praxis. *204 pp.*

● Dixon, Keith. Sociological Theory. *Pretence and Possibility. 142 pp.*

●Smith, Anthony D. The Concept of Social Change. *A Critique of the Functionalist Theory of Social Change. 208 pp.*

# Routledge Social Science Journals

The British Journal of Sociology. *Edited by Terence P. Morris. Vol. 1, No. 1, March 1950 and Quarterly. Roy. 8vo. Back numbers available. An international journal with articles on all aspects of sociology.*

Economy and Society. *Vol. 1, No. 1. February 1972 and Quarterly. Metric Roy. 8vo. A journal for all social scientists covering sociology, philosophy, anthropology, economics and history. Back numbers available.*

Year Book of Social Policy in Britain, The. *Edited by Kathleen Jones. 1971. Published annually.*

Printed in Great Britain by Unwin Brothers Limited
The Gresham Press Old Woking Surrey
A member of the Staples Printing Group